CRITICAL ESSAYS
ON THE POETRY OF TENNYSON

THE AUTHOR

JOHN KILLHAM is British, and was educated at University College, London. He is at present a Lecturer in English at the University College of North Staffordshire, Keele.

CRITICAL ESSAYS
ON THE POETRY
OF
Tennyson

EDITED BY

John Killham

New York

BARNES & NOBLE, INC.

First published in the U.S.A. 1960

PR
5588
K48

© *John Killham* 1960

60-2070
10-5-4

Printed in Great Britain

CONTENTS

v

CONTENTS

vi

PREFACE

ALTHOUGH THE one hundred and fiftieth anniversary of Tennyson's birth fell on 6 August 1959, this collection of essays is not
intended to be a *Festschrift*. Nor do I think it necessary to defend
such a compilation as this from the common criticisms levelled
against multiple authorship, since there are certain advantages—
especially in literary criticism—in presenting various approaches
to the same topic. In fact the selection has been made as catholic
as possible.

Most of the essays have been reprinted from periodicals and
other works published here and in the United States and Canada.
Mr. G. M. Young's essay was originally delivered as a Warton
Lecture before the British Academy, reprinted in the *Proceedings of
the British Academy*, vol. XXV (1939). For permission to reprint it
I am indebted to the author, the Council of the British Academy,
and the Oxford University Press. The essays by Arthur J. Carr,
Mrs. Elizabeth Hillman Waterston, E. J. Chiasson, and F. E. L.
Priestley were published in the *University of Toronto Quarterly* (vol.
XIX, XX, XXIII), and my acknowledgements are due to them
and the editor. For permission to reprint H. M. McLuhan's essay
'Tennyson and Picturesque Poetry' I am obliged to the author and
the editors of *Essays in Criticism*, in vol. I of which it first appeared.
Robert G. Stange's first essay in this volume was originally
published in *Publications of the Modern Language Association of
America* (vol. LXVII), as was that of Lionel Stevenson (vol.
LXIII), and to them and to the Editorial Committee of that
periodical I am indebted for their permission to reprint them. Mr.
Stange's second essay was first published in *English Literary History*
vol. XXI, to him and the editor I also express thanks and acknowledgements. W. W. Robson's essay is reprinted by kind permission of the author and the editor of *The Listener*. The papers by

Graham Hough and Leo Spitzer were published in the former *Hopkins Review*, and to them and to the editor I am grateful for permission to reprint them. 'The Motivation of Tennyson's Weeper' is from *The Well-Wrought Urn*, copyright, 1947, by Cleanth Brooks, and is reprinted by permission of the author and Harcourt, Brace and Company, Inc. T. S. Eliot's '*In Memoriam*' is from *Essays Ancient and Modern*, 1936, and is reprinted by permission of the author, Faber and Faber Ltd., and Harcourt, Brace & Co. Inc.

The order of presentation of the essays and the views expressed in the Introduction are the entire responsibility of the editor.

JOHN KILLHAM

INTRODUCTION: TENNYSON,
A REVIEW OF
MODERN CRITICISM
John Killham

GENERALLY SPEAKING, the *avant-garde* critics in the period from the end of the first World War to the present time have concerned themselves very little with Tennyson's poetry. The number of critical essays has been small, and most critics have limited themselves to asides indicating various grounds for dissatisfaction. The reaction against Tennyson, being in large measure connected with the change in taste occurring in the last three decades of the nineteenth rather than with that of the twentieth century, was dying out soon after the first War. Yet there has been no attempt to express in modern terms what it is that Tennyson still means to us. Although he has a place in the anthologies, we cannot but admit that the reaction was over in another sense too; with a very few (but notable) exceptions, hardly anyone influential in forming taste reacted at all. The whole effort was going into settling a language in which to talk of the sudden advance into new literary territory. So successful has this been that the remarks which used to give satisfaction when uttered about Tennyson now seem vapid; while those which illumine our contemporary literature seem to throw only a fitful gleam upon Victorian poems we cannot but admire. It at first sight appears that there has been a radical break in our literary tradition; but language, the medium of literature, is by nature conservative, and it is most likely that our taste and critical standards have, in the heat of enthusiasm, become too narrow and too severe. The fact that the supposed discontinuity between our own age and the Victorian age and its aftermath now seems much less obvious than it did is a sign that a new perspective is emerging.

II

A word is perhaps due upon the various ways in which even the greatest of Tennyson's admirers of the last century began to see reasons for withholding the passionate admiration they once had had for his poetry. It was in the sixties of the last century that Walter Bagehot, Swinburne, and Hopkins all expressed various criticisms, particularly relating to *Enoch Arden* published in 1864, which have been subscribed to by innumerable critics ever since.[1] (Gosse, writing in 1910 at the height of the reaction, tells us, however, that *Enoch Arden* only momentarily loosened the octopus-grip of Tennyson's appeal to his generation.[2]) Bagehot thought that the 'ornate art' of *Enoch Arden* was adopted because the subject was inferior; and he gave his reason for thinking it inferior. Speaking of the representation of a man of a highly-developed moral character 'joined to an undeveloped intellectual nature, an undeveloped artistic nature, and a very limited religious nature', he gave it as his opinion that all men look in art for something more than mere morality, and that they need not be ashamed of doing so—'The soul of man . . . has many parts beside its moral part. . . . In Shakespeare, or Goethe, even in Newton or Archimedes, there is much that will not be cut down to the shape of the commandments.' Swinburne, long time a worshipper in the Tennyson fane, had a very few years later to defend *Poems and Ballads* in similar terms and took occasion to slight this side of Tennyson too. Hopkins, citing *Enoch Arden*, had written to W. M. Baillie in 1864 of his discovery that Tennyson did not always write under inspiration, and was capable of inserting lines which the reader

[1] See Walter Bagehot's essay 'Wordsworth, Tennyson, and Browning' (1864), reprinted in *English Critical Essays* (*Nineteenth Century*), ed. Edmund M. Jones (The World's Classics, 1916); and G. M. Hopkins's letter to W. M. Baillie dated 10 September 1864 in *Further Letters of Gerard Manley Hopkins*, ed. C. C. Abbott (1938), p. 68; and A. C. Swinburne's *Notes on Poems and Reviews*, 1866.

[2] 'A First Sight of Tennyson', *Portraits and Sketches* (1912), p. 129.

momentarily felt he might have been able to put in himself on Tennyson's behalf—'Parnassian' verse, he called it. Before long, as many parodists showed, people could say what Cowper said of Pope; that he

> Made poetry a mere mechanic art
> And every warbler has his tune by heart.

There is no doubt that *Enoch Arden* set the reaction off, and it is not difficult to see why the great majority of people were still set against the Tennyson of the Idyls after the first World War. We have only to recall D. H. Lawrence's words written in 1916 to see why the deliberate blurring of the facts in *Enoch Arden* which Bagehot so genially exposed ('People who sell fish about the country never are beautiful') was so disagreeable: 'The essence of poetry with us in this age of stark and unlovely realities is a stark directness, without a shadow of a lie, or a shadow of reflection anywhere.'[1] Now it is not true to say that, like Wordsworth, Tennyson fell off—say, after *Maud*—for he had the luxuriant *Enoch Arden* strain in him from the time when he was writing basketfuls of poems like 'The Gardener's Daughter' thirty years before *Enoch Arden* was published. By present-day standards, in other words, he always had this weak side. To say this may appear even more damaging than to say he went off, but this is not really the right view. The pattern of development in an artist's capabilities can take different forms, and the critic who superimposes upon Tennyson the pattern of Wordsworth's development (as traditionally received since Arnold, at any rate—it has been modified somewhat lately) can cause a reader to misjudge the nature of the later poet's powers. The remarkably clear rise-and-fall pattern in Wordsworth's work obviously does not fit Yeats: nor does it fit Tennyson. Tennyson is a poet whose sources of strength lay deep in his personality and came forth in a hundred streams, some piddling, some large but lazy, a few shining and pure. And they did so all his life.

The reaction started in the 1860's by *Enoch Arden* was much broadened towards the end of the century as a newer poetry got

---

[1] Letter of 11 January 1916, *The Letters of D. H. Lawrence*, ed. Aldous Huxley (1932), p. 308. Ezra Pound, too, wrote to like effect—there should be 'no Tennysonianness of speech'—in a letter written to Harriet Monroe in 1915, *The Letters of Ezra Pound 1907–41*, ed. D. D. Paige (1951), p. 91.

under way. W. B. Yeats led an assault upon his early favourite under the banner of Symbolism. In 1900, the year in which 'Victorianism had been defeated', he asked what change one should look for 'if people were to accept the theory that poetry moves us because of its symbolism'. He answered his own question with an eye on Tennyson: 'A return to the way of our fathers, a casting out of descriptions of nature for the sake of nature, of the moral law for the sake of the moral law, a casting out of all anecdotes and of that brooding over scientific opinion that so often extinguished the central flame in Tennyson, and of that vehemence that would make us do or not do certain things . . .'[1] This was a much more serious assault, for although Yeats's own remarks were not too shrewdly aimed, they formulated well enough the feeling that poetry should eschew moral earnestness for the sake of the 'purity' of poetry: '. . . although you can expound an opinion, or describe a thing when your words are not quite well chosen, you cannot give a body to something that moves beyond the senses, unless your words are as subtle, as complex, as full of mysterious life, as the body of a flower or of a woman'. (The symbolist aesthetic has an imaginative appeal of its own.) Despite the admiration of Poe, of Verlaine, Tennyson has a good deal of verse—much of *In Memoriam*, for example—which is *about* general human problems and social concerns, and does not conform to symbolist taste. But the work of many other poets does not either. The wide acceptance of a symbolist aesthetic in different guises has led to the endless discussion of how proper it is for a poet to introduce beliefs on moral and metaphysical matters into his works. It is perhaps sufficient to say here that no one could have been more aware of the issue than Tennyson: that some of his lyrics may certainly claim rather to 'be' than to 'mean', and that in any case some of his dramatic monologues offer a somewhat puzzling moral position for the reader to contemplate.

III

The coming of Tennyson's dread, ordeal by biography, was signalled by the publication of Lytton Strachey's *Eminent Victorians* in 1918. In two poems 'To ——, after reading a life and letters' (1848) and 'The Dead Prophet' (1885) he had censured the publica-

[1] 'The Symbolism of Poetry' (1900) in *Ideas of Good and Evil*, pp. 252–3.

tion of the details of authors' wholly personal relationships: (he had Lord Houghton's book on Keats and Froude's pieces on the Carlyles in mind):

> For now the poet cannot die
> Nor leave his music as of old,
> But round him ere he scarce be cold
> Begins the scandal and the cry:
>
> 'Proclaim the faults he would not show:
> Break lock and seal: betray the trust:
> Keep nothing sacred: 'tis but just
> The many-headed beast should know.'

(His own son Hallam, Lord Tennyson, printed from charred fragments of letters he had asked should be burnt—although Hallam's object in producing the valuable, muddled, and occasionally infuriating *Memoir* in two volumes was quite understandably to produce a work likely to bring his father fame.) It was in 1923 that two biographical studies of Tennyson appeared. One of them, Mr. Hugh I'Anson Fausset's *Tennyson: a Modern Portrait*, had the second of the two stanzas I have quoted above as its epigraph. Mr. Fausset's reaction against Tennyson was a new development, for it took Tennyson as representative of the 'establishment' of the day. Now we expect each generation (and especially each post-war generation) to be suspicious of its elders' motives. 'The best and bravest of my own contemporaries determined to have done with insincerity, to find ground under their feet, to let the uncertain remain the uncertain, but to learn how much and what we could honestly regard as true, and believe and live by it.' These are oft-uttered thoughts, and each age looks for the poet who can become the voice of this feeling. The youthful Froude, author of these words, found him in Alfred Tennyson. But for Mr. Fausset in 1923, Tennyson was a convenient symbol of a creed outworn: '[Tennyson's morality] satisfied for a time the selfish instincts of the favoured class to which he belonged, but it cannot bear the candid scrutiny of a generation which has reaped the bitter fruits of high-sounding egotism, and whose hopes have almost perished with their fears.' And again: 'The result of such high-mindedness was the catastrophe of savagery and folly which we have known, and the decimating of a generation young in hope and generosity, which had of itself willed no such thing.'[1] If words could have killed, Tennyson would have been stone dead after this. But in point of fact Tennyson is still very much alive, and younger readers are puzzled at the fuss over the reaction. But they are content to read him in selections. The four decades during which hardly a year passed without a complete edition of Tennyson's poetical works (or a part of one) issuing from English printing-houses ended just before the first War, and the age of Selections was already well under way in 1923. (It is a pity that critics will persist in solemnly condemning Tennyson for his bad things as if everyone reads the *Collected Works* from cover to cover.) It is this circumstance which made Sir Harold Nicolson's case, which also appeared in 1923, for reading Tennyson in selections so timely. Sir Harold, unlike Mr. Fausset, was bent upon saying a good word for Tennyson, to put in a caveat against the irreverencies, blithe or bitter, of the twenties. Moreover he showed himself aware of the forces which shaped the Victorian age, and was entirely able to explain to critics of this time (like Mr. Fausset) what was meant when we say that Tennyson was a Victorian poet, and how futile it is to blame an artist for the facts of history. But Sir Harold had the Strachey fashion to contend with, and understandably he was diffident about defending the Victorians as well as Tennyson— though he could see the tide turning well enough: 'We smile today at our Victorians, not confidently, as of old, but with a shade of hesitation: a note of perplexity, a note of anger sometimes, a note often of wistfulness has come to mingle with our laughter. For the tide is turning and the reaction is drawing to its close.' (The last note was struck by Mr. Alfred Noyes in his Lowell Lecture 'Tennyson and some Recent Critics', published the following year in *Some Aspects of Modern Poetry*.) He candidly revealed that he had 'worked out the several theses which could potentially be adopted ... by which Tennyson might be rendered almost palatable to modern readers'; for example, to write about him not as a Victorian at all but either as a late Georgian ('Much would be made of his youth and boyhood: of George III, of the Regency, of George IV, of press-gangs and crimping, of cock-fights and professional boxers, of Hessian boots and the smugglers' stories at Mable-thorpe') or, alternatively, 'to drape Tennyson in the fabric of the

---

[1] Pp. 299, 302. By 1942 Mr. Fausset had very much changed his views, as will be seen in the essay reprinted in his *Poets and Pundits* (1947).

middle eighties'. These certainly do avoid the temptation of emphasizing differences and resemblances between Tennyson and his
contemporaries which he considered mistaken and unremunera-
tive. Nevertheless, the thesis he did adopt (which has something
in common with some views in an admirable article published a
little earlier by Sir John Squire[1]), that there were really two
Tennysons—'the black, unhappy mystic of the Lincolnshire
wolds' and 'the prosperous Isle-of-Wight Victorian'—inevitably
compelled him to blame the age for encouraging the later Tennyson to appear when, 'had his lot fallen among other circumstances,
or in a less cloying age', he might have remained only a shadowy
possibility. What Sir Harold intended to be emphasized, however,
was that Tennyson's two sides showed a conflict 'between the remarkable depth and originality of his poetic temperament and the
shallowness and timidity of his practical intelligence'. (Tennyson's
'stupidity'—remarked by Matthew Arnold—is also frowned upon
by Mr. Auden.) Now it is clear that this remarkable thesis concerning the *two* Tennysons was erected to accommodate 'their'
poetry to what Sir Harold took to be the contemporary idea of
'what constitutes the highest poetry' ('. . . I think it may be said
without fear of contradiction that what the early twentieth century
primarily demands from poetry is a reality of emotional impulse');
for he found that despite many flinchings and evasions, Tennyson
could occasionally show us 'sudden panting moments when the
frightened soul of the man cries out to one like some wild animal
caught in the fens at night-time—moments when he lies moaning
in the half-light in an agony of fear'. The 'black, unhappy mystic'
was the Tennyson who wrote the 'pure' poetry that expressed
these agonized feelings: the 'prosperous Isle-of-Wight Victorian'
was made the culprit for 'applied poetry'; and Sir Harold com-
mented: 'It may be doubted, perhaps, whether the spirit of Poetry,
a spirit in its essence winged for some divine excess, could, in any
circumstances, find affinity with the spirit of compromise, whose
only purpose is the negation of excess'; the only way when reading
some poems wherein 'pure' and 'applied' poetry were mingled was
to avoid looking for Victorian applications, 'for of all poets,
Tennyson should be read very carelessly or not at all.'

   This, then, was the central critical position Sir Harold adopted,
and used as the basis for the selection of Tennyson's poetry which

---

[1] 'Tennyson', *The London Mercury*, ii. (1920), p. 443.

he felt had necessarily to be compiled if it was to find a modern audience. It does not strictly afford grounds for admitting to it 'Ulysses' and 'The Lady of Shalott' and the various complimentary poems which he generously praised as specimens of verse occupying an intermediate position between his two categories—and we may feel today that although his selection might be an acceptable one, the reasons for including certain poems would be different from his. But this is not to say that his book is without interest even for readers who do not subscribe to his exclusive taste, for part of his purpose was to treat the poet's life 'from our usual scavenger point of view', an expression which does him less than justice. When he lowered his bucket into the weedy pool of Hallam Tennyson's *Memoir* he seldom failed to bring up a delightful anecdote. He exposed his catch with the careful eye of a connoisseur in the unguarded follies of mankind, and decorated them with sprigs of fancy. The passage describing one of the poet's encounters with Mrs. Cameron in photographic mood—'and finally Tennyson would go home, rather wistfully perhaps, with the scent of sweet briar and chemicals in his nostrils—home to the red drawing room and to Mrs. Tennyson on the sofa'—is a little masterpiece in the best manner of the author of *Some People*. The Victorian monument is lowered from its pedestal, but gently, tenderly.

In Mr. C. H. O. Scaife's little book, *The Poetry of Alfred Tennyson —an Essay in Appreciation*, published in 1930, Sir Harold's desire for vivid *emotional* response to poetry was determinedly challenged. 'When we make a really wide survey of English poetry we find that a large proportion of the work of all the great poets has been, in the first place, of a kind which approximates more nearly to Mr. Nicolson's category of "applied" poetry than to poetry which is, in his sense, pure.' Moreover, Mr. Scaife protested that he was not convinced that the opinions of Tennyson's aunt or the poet's unwise investment in a scheme for mechanical wood-carving were relevant to a judgment upon the poetry. He went so far as to say that 'the less one knows of Tennyson's life, the more one is able to pick out that which is of value from the crude mass of his work'. (Incidentally, he offered a useful supplementation to D. G. James's later discussion of the differences between *The Prelude* and *In Memoriam*,[1] in terms of their 'philosophy' by claiming that the ex-

---

[1] 'Wordsworth and Tennyson', Warton Lecture on English Poetry, *Proceedings of the British Academy, 1950*, p. 113.

cellence of poetry is 'independent of materials, and is determined by the intensity with which thought or feeling is fused with language'.) It is well that this point was made, for despite Tennyson's own insistence that it was art, not personality, which should be the critic's concern, Henry James's not surprising discovery that Tennyson was himself not Tennysonian, and the modern reaction against the 'Life and Letters' approach to literature, writings on Tennyson's poetry still more than occasionally supply anecdotage, real or imaginary, in place of criticism, and of a sort to which Byron's comment is sufficiently apt:

> although truth exacts
> These aimiable descriptions from the scribes,
> As most essential to their hero's story,
> They do not much contribute to his glory.

Sir Harold's view was also challenged, again in 1930, by Humbert Wolfe. In a pamphlet (No. 3 of 'The Poets on the Poets') he deftly parodied the portrait of the 'wild' Tennyson ('the strange, dark boy, roaming the Somersby fens, a passionate lonely figure against those abrupt sky-lines') tamed by the 'radiant prig' Hallam, and went on, with true pamphleteer's fervour, to point out the greatness of *Maud* and to condemn the 'intellectual hostility' which underlay the depreciation of Tennyson as a mere mouthpiece for Victorianism.

But despite these able, and early, protests, Sir Harold's notion of the two Tennysons (one would object much less to the idea of twenty Tennysons) lives on, and appears in the most unexpected places.

IV

Having given some attention to the early book-length studies of 1923 and to the replies, I shall now turn to the influential criticism of about the same time, which, although not always directed at Tennyson specifically, is of material importance for understanding his present position. As Mr. Robert Fricker has shown,[1] the Victorian poets were seen in a common light. The critics writing

[1] 'Victorian Poetry in Modern English Criticism', *English Studies*, xxiv (1942), pp. 129–41.

in the *Criterion* and *London Mercury* after the first War, whose position can be termed neo-classical, sought in Victorian poetry, but seldom found, intelligibility, conciseness, dramatic distance, and respect for the traditional principles of poetic form. In the dry light of this approach—which can admirably illuminate a Marvell —the Victorians showed themselves as vague, self-preoccupied, concerned too much with sound and too little with sense, over-fond of decoration, and incompetent in the organization of their material. The great merit of this approach by way of form and expression is that it can avoid discussion of the poet's opinions and beliefs, though obviously the critics who adopt it are not on that account unaware of them.

Another mode of criticism which avoids direct discussion of beliefs is that which ultimately or directly derives from psychology. This also has been applied to Tennyson and the Victorians in the last few decades, and likewise had its origin in the twenties, as Mr. Fricker shows. Broadly speaking, two sorts of approach may be distinguished. The first is connected with normal psychology and has placed a premium upon complexity, which is taken under certain conditions as a hallmark of excellence: the second is related to depth psychology, and tends to cause the poem to be read with importance being attached to unconscious, as opposed to controlled, expressions of impulses in the poet's mind.

V

The first of these attitudes was prepared for by Professor I. A. Richards in *Principles of Literary Criticism* (1924). He regarded the arts as means whereby habitual narrowness of interests or bewilderment in face of contrary claims upon feeling and belief are replaced by 'an intricately wrought composure'. A good poem, in fact, can be seen to bring opposite mental impulses into equilibrium. He recognised, nevertheless, that poems which had earned considerable popularity hardly achieved it, and in fact communicated one impulse or emotion exclusively. He cited Tennyson's lyric 'Break, break, break' as a case in point, observing that it 'will not bear an ironical contemplation. . . . Irony in this sense consists in the bringing in of the opposite, the complementary impulses: that is why poetry which is exposed to it is not of the highest order, and why irony itself is so constantly a characteristic of poetry which is.'[1] He went on to suggest that there are 'two main ways in which impulses may be organised; by exclusion and by inclusion, by synthesis and by elimination'. Needless to say, it is the poetry which achieves synthesis of disparate experience which is esteemed. It is important to notice that this way of evaluating a work has little or no regard for the general validity of any beliefs it may seem to support, nor, despite the psychological theory behind it, any concern with the state of mind of the artist during composition. Every poem is a public possession, no longer the artist's, and criticism and analysis of the poem on the page start from the assumption that it is formulating in semi-dramatic terms a possible resolution of attitudes to be evaluated in the poem's own terms.

Professor Cleanth Brooks in *Modern Poetry and the Tradition* (1939) applied Richards's distinction between inclusive and exclusive poetry to a wide range of works, and stated that it was his belief that Victorian poetry as a whole was 'a poetry of sharp exclusions', and suggested that Tennyson's poem 'The Palace of Art' showed the sort of thing that he could write as a substitute for a genuine synthesis. This poem, he argued, first indulges the reader in all the luxury permitted by ivory-tower escapism, but finally, by way of an edifying moral, brings him to a sense of the immorality of this attitude. The two possible ways of living are confronted but not effectively wrought into any significant balance. But Brooks admitted that Tennyson had a stronger side, and in *The Well Wrought Urn* (1949) he demonstrated that in 'Tears, Idle Tears' ambiguity and paradox, the qualities in a poem which manifest the poet's awareness of the contrary impulses composing his experience, are present, even if in this poem Tennyson may only have blundered into exhibiting them.

The psychological basis upon which Brooks's detailed explication of this poem rests is shown by the comments he makes at various points. That the real occasion for tears in the poem occurs at such and such a point is, he finds, 'psychologically and dramatically right'. The sharpness and freshness of the images of the past account for 'the psychological problem with which the speaker wrestles in the poem'. Moreover the superiority of this poem over 'Break, break, break' consists in the fact that in the latter the poet, 'in avoiding the psychological exploration of the

---

[1] Second edn. (1926), pp. 249–50.

experience . . . risks losing dramatic force', though 'mere psychological analysis is, of course, not enough to insure dramatic force; and such analysis, moreover, carries its own risks'. It is not, then, psychological analysis *per se* which is valuable, but the successful communication (by way of a literary composition of a dramatic kind) of disparate and seemingly contradictory elements present in the poet's experience which the critic values. This is important, for it means that the critic should not be concerned with psychological analysis, but with the language-structure of the poem being read—metaphor, imagery, and the like.

It is interesting that the revival of interest in Donne's poetry which occurred during the latter part of the last century, culminating in Sir Herbert Grierson's edition of the poetry of his 'school' in 1921, caused Mr. Eliot, in his celebrated essay on the Metaphysical poets of that year[1] to suggest a distinction which has much in common with that of Professor Richards already discussed. He challenged Johnson's celebrated dictum on the Metaphysical poets by stating that 'a degree of heterogeneity of material compelled into unity by the operation of the poet's mind is omnipresent in poetry'. 'When a poet's mind is perfectly equipped for its work, it is constantly amalgamating disparate experience; the ordinary man's experience is chaotic, irregular, fragmentary. The latter falls in love, or reads Spinoza, and these two experiences have nothing to do with each other, or with the noise of the typewriter or the smell of cooking; in the mind of the poet these experiences are always forming new wholes.' He went on to advance, very tentatively, the theory that in the seventeenth century a dissociation of sensibility set in, a theory which has received its most recent challenge in Professor Kermode's brilliant study, *The Romantic Image*. According to this theory, the poets of the seventeenth century 'possessed a mechanism of sensibility, which could devour any kind of experience', and the difference he detected between passages from Lord Herbert and Tennyson (which he cited) is 'something which had happened to the mind of England between the time of Donne or Lord Herbert of Cherbury and the time of Tennyson and Browning; it is the difference between the intellectual poet and reflective poet. Tennyson and Browning are poets, and they think; but they do not feel their thought as immediately as the odour of a rose.' It is certainly most true that

---

[1] 'The Metaphysical Poets', *Selected Essays*, Third edn., p. 281.

Tennyson is a poet very different from Donne, and for the reasons Mr. Eliot gave, Donne has more in common with the poetry written in our own day. But Tennyson is not by any means a reflective poet exclusively. 'Ulysses' is a dramatic monologue of some complexity, but its manner of proceeding can never be understood by resort to the critical techniques applicable to Donne's poems.

VI

When we turn to the criticism, interpretative and evaluative, which has affiliations with the procedures of psychological analysis, we find ourselves no longer in a position to discuss the judgements reached in terms of principles which can be as easily defined and comprehended. The whole object of the critic is to get behind the poem to its author, to see it not as a public, but as a private, possession which does not so much express conscious thoughts and feelings as betray unconscious ones. Strictly speaking, studies on these lines should comply with a quasi-professional code. The analyst must not for instance pronounce moral judgements on the surmised mental states he is uncovering, though of course he must hold some ideas on health or normality. The great difficulty in work of this kind is that it is addressed to readers whose attitude is not equally professional, and who may indeed be highly prejudiced and censorious. Clearly, critics who use works of art for such a purpose must be on their guard.

A good example of care in this respect is to be seen in the introductory remarks of Professor W. D. Paden in his *Tennyson in Egypt: A Study of the Imagery in His Earlier Work* (1942). In this book Professor Paden acknowledged his debt to *The Road to Xanadu*, but observed that Lowes suggested as the motive for the poet's selecting the images he had traced to their source 'nothing except Coleridge's contemporary plans to write certain poems in which the selected imagery might directly or indirectly enter'. Paden felt that this explanation was sufficient in regard to Coleridge, who was a special case; but more often a poet's choice of imagery is governed by processes which have been made comprehensible by 'the science of psychiatry'. He described some of these processes, and stated:

I have suggested or implied in my discussion other psychiatric concepts that cannot be as simply stated in familiar terms; but no one of these, when it is fully expounded and understood within its technical context, is either more scandalous or more abnormal. I imply nothing discreditable about young Tennyson. The pattern of his mind, as I have come to see it, was not uncommon in kind, though it was unusual in depth and intensity of emotion.

I think it will be agreed that this passage reveals what is, or can be, dangerous about this approach; the reader unfamiliar with 'the science of psychiatry' *may* come to feel that the poetry reveals something abnormal about the poet's mind, that he is different from other men not merely in being a maker of poems. Professor Paden had to guard against this in advance, and the reader was not invited to reach any judgement of the quality of Tennyson's mind, only to consider a theory of composition based upon much interesting evidence.

The reading of poems from an analytic standpoint is different in kind altogether from that of Richards and Brooks. It is not concerned primarily with their structure, but what is presumed to be *unintentionally* revealed of the poet's state of mind. Naturally it is not verifiable, though some support may be derived from extra-literary data.

But this type of study is not quite the same as the investigation of poems which, though still dealing with the subject of mental operations, are of a dramatic cast, suggesting quite clearly that the speaker in the poem was *not* intended to be the poet himself. *Maud*, for instance, is obviously about a certain individual's mental condition over a certain length of time; the analyst critic, one would assume, would in this example have to establish that Tennyson was unconsciously identifying himself with the protagonist in face of his explicit statement to the contrary.[1] Professor Paden's remarks on *Maud* are of particular interest in this connection:

The poet drew his fullest picture of himself at this time in the monodrama of *Maud* (1855). The poem, which remained his favourite among his works for the rest of his life, may be read as a statement of Tennyson's solution—a partial solution—of the imaginative difficulties of his adolescence. . . . His youthful

---

[1] *Memoir*, i, p. 402.

troubles had lost immediacy, and he could see them in some perspective. But although a man can outgrow his youth, he cannot sever himself from it.[1]

This suggests unequivocally that the poet and the speaker in *Maud* are one, that the poet is not only the 'psychologist',[2] but also the patient, that he is not only describing but ministering to a mind diseased. Here, surely, Professor Paden goes perilously close to denying his earlier assertion that his book has no tendency to suggest that Tennyson's mind was, at some stage, 'abnormal'. After all, the poem was once given the sub-title, 'the Madness'.

By and large, there is something to be said for W. H. Auden's view that 'No other poetry is easier and less illuminating to psycho-analyse'. But whatever conclusion one reaches on this general issue, one can hardly fail to see how important it is not to give psychological explanations where simple literary or historical ones are available. A recent article called 'Tennyson and the Sinful Queen'[3] does this on a grand scale, and arrives at the fantastic conclusion that Tennyson derived from a boyhood reading of Milton 'the confused but indelible impression that at no time was a man in greater jeopardy than at the moment of sexual union with the woman of his choice'. The article is really a modern specimen of Stracheyan iconoclasm, and pursues the now old-fashioned sport of making the Victorians seem silly.

VII

The neo-classical (or perhaps humanist), the Richards–Brooks, and the analytic approaches to the Victorian poets (and Tennyson in particular) which I have so far discussed stem in some measure from attempts to accommodate modern thinking to modern poetry, and consequently do not face Victorian poetry on its own ground. Perhaps the central issue which Victorian poetry raises is the question of how far a poet like Tennyson may be said to have adjusted his private insights and feelings to the imperative demands of an age ardently seeking to make sense of events and

---

[1] p. 92.
[2] See Roy P. Basler, 'Tennyson's *Maud*', *Sex, Symbolism and Psychology in Literature* (1948), p. 73.
[3] *The Twentieth Century*, 158 (October 1955), p. 355.

ideas which undermined the relatively secure assumptions on which society had reposed for several centuries. The crisis which Professor Pinto takes as the end of the last great poetic era and the beginning of our own—which he puts at about 1880—'marks the end of the great period of human history which began with the Renaissance, and of which some of the chief aspects can be summed up in the words of humanism, individualism, capitalism and liberalism'.[1] It might be profitably argued that the crisis itself could be placed nearer 1830 with a lag of half a century in the appearance of the breach in the realm of purely literary history. Even the Prologue of *The Princess* (1847), which he cites as exemplifying a 'vision of an England with a happy contented population led by a beneficent class of enlightened squires and manufacturers', could be taken rather as evidence of the divide really separating 'the two nations' in a state of uneasy co-existence; while the poem itself, both in structure and thinking, shows clearly the fragmentation of an earlier artistic and social conformity.

Critics of Tennyson since the first World War have discussed the question of Tennyson's adjustment to the exigencies of his age with varying degrees of sympathy which, it might be argued, depend in turn upon their understanding of the social forces at work between 1830 and 1880. I have already mentioned Sir Harold Nicolson's expressed intention of neglecting this way of looking at Tennyson's poetry, but it was not in point of fact possible for him to avoid it. In the course of his book various opinions are expressed on the poet's 'compromise' with his age; these vary remarkably in sympathy. At one point Sir Harold dilates upon the unprecedented power of the forces shaping Victorian society; and we feel that he might be suggesting that Tennyson could hardly fail to show their mark in his work. But elsewhere he writes of Tennyson as one who sold his birthright. Inconsistency is not, however, the character of Mr. Paull F. Baum's study *Tennyson Sixty Years After* (Chapel Hill, 1948), a book giving the impression of having been written out of a sense of having a painful duty to perform. Indeed he says of his chapters on the 'domestic idylls' and 'the poet as interpreter of his age': 'Both are rather tedious because they cover a good deal of his inferior work, but they can-

[1] V. de S. Pinto, *Crisis in English Poetry 1880–1940* (1951), Introduction, p. 9.

not be scamped by the serious student because without them so much, alas so very much, of his lifelong devotion will be missed.' It is quite obvious that Mr. Baum does not subscribe to Dr. Johnson's doctrine that 'while an author is yet living, we estimate powers by his worst performance, and when he is dead, we rate them by his best'. The excellence of much of the poetry is taken for granted and the main weight of the discussion is directed towards pointing out faults. The critical test he claims generally to apply is the 'aesthetic rather than the moral'; and this leads him to praise the first parts of *The Princess* yet unexpectedly to handle *Maud* very roughly. Mr. Baum's approach is really much more traditional than he makes out: it combines the features of the biographical (his first chapter turns most embarrassingly upon Tennyson's deathbed, his funeral and obituaries) and the Arnoldian (Arnold is quoted approvingly for his general views on the inadequacy of poetry dealing with the problems of its own time). The whole book takes as its basic assumption that Tennyson pretended to be *sacer Victorianus vates*, and this Mr. Baum cannot forget, and clearly cannot forgive.

Yet Mr. E. D. H. Johnson is surely right in pointing out that the thing that strikes the unbiassed reader about nearly every eminent Victorian writer, including Tennyson, is that he was at odds with the prevailing *mores*, and that what perhaps makes him representative is 'that very quality of intransigeance as a result of which he repudiated his society and sought refuge from the spirit of the times in the better ordered realm of interior consciousness'. In his book *The Alien Vision of Victorian Poetry* (Princeton, 1952), he argues that until artists like Rossetti and Swinburne deliberately repudiated the mass-public, the Victorians were subjected to an almost intolerable tension between their urge fearlessly to express their insights and the awareness that the public would not be able to share them. He regards the notion that Tennyson, Browning, and Arnold 'compromised' as mistaken; rather they were among the last to seek a means whereby poetry could continue to function as a part of a popular culture; and the means they lighted upon was what he terms 'double awareness', an abililty to satisfy the broad demands of the social spirit prevailing (with which obviously they had a certain sympathy) while also incorporating insights of 'different and sometimes contradictory import'. Mr. Johnson's account of Tennyson's later work emphasizes that it

17

very often presents through dream, vision, and supernatural touches in otherwise straightforward narratives Tennyson's persistent awareness of the sterility and emotional inadequacy of life lived according to naturalistic beliefs. In the later dramatic monologues, not to speak of the *Idylls*, Tennyson is not offering trite moral lessons but, on the contrary, figuring the incompatibility between the ugly confusions, the moral and physical shortcomings of the world, and man's inner visions. For Tennyson, art was not an escape, but a preserve, a redoubt, doomed to fall, in which, like his own Tiresias, he could do no more than portray the vision (which still came upon him in glimpses) to a people who heard him but still went their own way.

VIII

Those critics like Baum and Johnson whose concern is with the poet's relationship with the time-spirit and the exigencies of a popular taste almost inevitably approach the dramatic monologues by way of a simple question: 'What did the poet *really* mean?' The question often assumes two things. First, that the mask of another identity assumed by the poet is a property affair, soon knocked aside by an informed critic as a charming artifice for concealing the poet's own features from the public at large: and secondly, that the monologue is rhetorical—that is, seeks to persuade this public at large to adopt a certain definable attitude to current living, an attitude which at a pinch could be summed up in a sentence or two. A corollary of these assumptions is often that the poet will 'compromise'—that is, promote some fashionable opinion, the object being, as commonly in rhetoric, to disarm the reader in order to capture him unawares.[1] Mr. Baum closely analyses 'Ulysses' wholly to point out the inconsistencies of the 'thought' (which somehow do not affect the impressiveness of the poem): he observes in *In Memoriam* 'his seeming helplessness be-

---

[1] See, e.g., E. D. H. Johnson's remark (op. cit., p. 31) concerning *Maud*: 'After this the third part of *Maud*, in which the hero vows himself to further purgation through a life of action in the Crimean War, seems hardly more than a sop to Victorian sentimentalism, though it is to be feared that its inclusion is one more indication of the poet's readiness to let his notion of the poet's public role usurp the place of artistic sensibility.'

fore simple logical processes'; he gives a summary of the plot of *Maud* and condemns Tennyson's 'interpretation' of the poem.

This seeking for the 'point' of the dramatic monologues, involving an examination of the true worth of their points of view from some non-dramatic standpoint, has been rendered questionable by Mr. Robert Langbaum's important study *The Poetry of Experience* (1957). Here it is suggested that a distinction must be made between two sorts of literature—that which deals in objectively verifiable meanings by exhibiting actions assessable because they can be related to a stable moral system, generally consented to; and that which is appropriate to an age without beliefs generally subscribed to, 'a literature which returns upon itself, making its own values only to dissolve them before the possibility of judgment, turning them into biographical phenomena, manifestations of a life which as life is self-justifying'. The sort of work which emerges in these latter circumstances turns not upon ethical absolutes but upon *character*,[1] and the dramatic monologue is seen as the modern genre from Tennyson's 'Ulysses' and Browning's *The Ring and the Book* to *The Waste Land* and Joyce's *Ulysses*. This is the poetry of experience as opposed to the poetry of meaning: and the criticism appropriate to the one is not appropriate to the other. Although Mr. Langbaum's book has more to say about Browning than about Tennyson (among the Victorians), his discussion of the significance of the dramatic monologue in post-Enlightenment literature is of great interest in showing the lines of a continuous tradition from the Romantic age to our own, and this is of great importance for understanding Tennyson. (His remarks incidentally bear an interesting resemblance to those of Sir Herbert Read

[1] It is not surprising that Mr. Langbaum quotes John Dewey's *Ethics*: 'When ends are genuinely incompatible, no common denominator can be found except by deciding what sort of character is most highly prized and shall be given supremacy.' He might have quoted Tennyson's early poem οἱ ῥέοντες in support of his case for seeing modern literature to be occupied with the 'life-flow' of character:

> There is no rest, no calm, no pause,
>   Nor good nor ill, nor light nor shade,
> Nor essence nor eternal laws:
>   For nothing is, but all is made.
> But if I dream that all these are,
>   They are to me for that I dream;
> For all things are as they seem to all,
>   And all things flow like a stream.

upon developments in painting in the nineteenth century and after.[1])

IX

The work of restoring equilibrium after the reaction not only against the Victorian poets but also against the Romantics must proceed in two ways. It is not sufficient to write literary history (as written it must be) as if nineteenth-century poetry was the culmination of literary art—as once it was written; nor is it adequate to attempt to re-write it wholly in terms appropriate to Metaphysical and symbolist poetry. The history of criticism shows clearly that the dominant aesthetic at any particular date is affected by the social and ideological situation, and that there is not so much development as adaptation. To dismiss an artist because of dislike of his inevitable conformity to his cultural 'context' is not, ultimately at any rate, particularly discriminating. The critic is serving one of his most valuable ends by expressing admiration where he feels it, even if this denies him space enough to condemn all he wants to condemn amongst the rest of the author's work. This—and the attempt at justification which accompanies it—is undoubtedly criticism's main task, whether addressing itself to new or traditional art.

The second way of restoring equilibrium, and one which also applies very particularly to Tennyson too, was so well put by Arnold in 1865 that I need only quote his words:

> Judging is often spoken of as the critic's one business, and so in some sense it is; but the judgement which almost insensibly forms itself in a fair and clear mind, along with fresh knowledge, and ever fresh knowledge, must be the critic's great concern for himself; and it is by communicating fresh knowledge, and letting his own judgement pass along with it,—but insensibly, and in the second place, not the first, as a sort of companion and clue, not as an abstract lawgiver,—that he will generally do most good to his readers.

[1] In the Introduction to *The History of Modern Painting from Baudelaire to Bonnard*, second ed. (Skira, Geneva, 1949); compare, for instance, the observations upon the dramatic monologue and Impressionist painting as modes of a quasi-scientific art of objective representation; cf. Langbaum, p. 96 and Read, p. xvii.

In the last resort, poems, plays, and novels succeed in proportion to their power to create in our minds a momentary flash, an imaginative spark across terminals placed by the artist to release the energy always waiting for release. The tapping of this potential may be contrived by an artist in a variety of ways; his mental circuits may be long or short, draw upon our fantasy or upon our experience, be it personal, temporal, or cultural. As time passes, and the brief life we each experience moves further and further away in character from that in which men moved even in the recent past, the charge 'held' in works of art may, in the absence of understanding, leak away, and we come sometimes to suspect that an artist was most of the time only trying to fob us off with a firecracker, a feeble substitute for the real thing. But all art is contrivance, and while even one of his creations elicits a response which irradiates and illumines, we should, in Wordsworth's wise words, 'give him so much credit for this one composition as may induce us to review what has displeased us with more care than we should otherwise have bestowed upon it'. And more particularly, of course, what has pleased us too.

I

*Tennyson in Temporal
Contexts—the Victorian
and the Modern*

THE AGE OF TENNYSON
G. M. Young

SOME THIRTY years ago, walking in Sussex, I fell into conversation with an innkeeper, very proud of his neighbourhood and of the great men who had honoured it by being born, or coming to live, there. Then, as he ended the list, he suddenly added, 'But there: not one of them could have written *Enoch Arden*. What a beautiful piece that is!'

The volumes of *Poems* (1842) established Tennyson in the regard of the critical public as the first, after Wordsworth, of living poets; a regard qualified, however, with certain misgivings as to his intellectual grasp, his power to bring under poetic control the turbulent manifold of contemporary life, misgivings which *The Princess* in 1847 certainly did not remove. *In Memoriam* was influential in extending his renown, but within a limited range: many of its earliest readers disliked it, many did not understand it, and those who admired it most were not always the best judges of its poetry. *Maud* in 1855 was a decided set-back: it puzzled, it irritated, it shocked. But with the first four *Idylls of the King* in 1859 the Laureate won the great educated public, and with *Enoch Arden* five years later, the people. Not in his own country only, for as his German biographer has written, 'with *Enoch Arden* Tennyson took the heart of the German people by storm': a fact well illustrating a truth of which we have constantly to remind ourselves, that our Victorian Age is only the local phase of a cultural period common to all Western Europe and North America. Indeed we need not limit our view to the West, because I am fairly sure that if the last canto of *Evgeny Onegin* in Professor Elton's translation fell anonymously into the hands of one of our younger reviewers, he would unhesitatingly characterize Tatiana's refusal to desert her elderly husband for the man whom she still loves, as a typical example of Victorian smugness, unless, indeed, complacency was the word that week in vogue.

For the rest of his life Tennyson was The Poet: and to the people poetry was the sort of thing that Tennyson wrote. There was, I well remember, a sixpenny encyclopaedia of great service to young schoolboys on the eve of examinations, which contained, with other useful matter, a list of the Hundred Greatest Men: 'to know their deeds is to know the history of civilization'; it began of course with Homer, and ended, not less of course, with Tennyson. Lord Morley once, wishing to affirm some idea of social stratification, divided the people of England into those who had a Tennyson at home and those who had not. When I cast my memory back to the bookshops in our more elegant suburbs, or at a seaside resort, the first picture I see is rows and shelves and boxes full of Tennyson; and just as John Stuart Mill used to fret himself with the thought that some day all melodious combinations of sound would be exhausted, and music come to an end, so I used to wonder, what more, when Tennyson had written

> Calm and deep peace on this high wold,
> And on these dews that drench the furze,
> And all the silvery gossamers
> That twinkle into green and gold:

> Calm and still light on yon great plain
> That sweeps with all its autumn bowers,
> And crowded farms and lessening towers,
> To mingle with the bounding main:

what more, I say, there was for poetry to do. And, let me add, this was not an inculcated sentiment: no one had told me to admire him: the star of Browning, the star of Meredith were blazing above a landscape all silver with the moonlight of Pater. I must conclude that Tennyson gave me what he gave to the earlier generation which placed him beside Virgil. I cannot conjure up again the enchantment, but I can indicate, I think, the field it covered, and the theme on which I wish to write is not the poetry of Tennyson by itself or the thought of Tennyson by itself, but the adjustment of both to the world in which he lived, an adjustment so perfect that, as Saintsbury once said, 'no age of poetry can be called the age of one man with such critical accuracy as the later Nineteenth Century is, with us, the Age of Tennyson'.

Take up the faded green Moxon volume with its list of Mr. Tennyson's other works, *Poems*, 16th edition, *The Princess*, 12th edition, *In Memoriam*, 15th edition, and imagine yourself to be one of its 60,000 purchasers: or better still, perhaps, sitting in the village schoolroom to hear it read by the vicar or the squire. What do you find? An abundance, a vast profusion of poetic learning, of ornate phrasing and verbal music—which you will recognize and admire, because it is the familiar accent of Tennyson, though in detail much of it may be above your head—applied to a tale of common life lived on the heroic level. Reading it again, I recalled the story of the French duchess who paid her social and charitable visits in the same attire, an old shawl and a diamond brooch, because, as she said, her rich friends only saw the diamonds and her poor friends only saw the shawl. Listen to the Laureate deploying all his magnificence of sound and imagery to bring before us the tropical island and the shipwrecked sailor waiting for a sail:

> No sail from day to day, but every day
> The sunrise broken into scarlet shafts
> Among the palms and ferns and precipices;
> The blaze upon the waters to the east;
> The blaze upon his island overhead;
> The blaze upon the waters to the west;
> Then the great stars that globed themselves in Heaven,
> The hollower-bellowing ocean, and again
> The scarlet shafts of sunrise—but no sail.

But listen also to what, if you are holding hands in the back row of the schoolroom, will touch you more nearly, the poet's tale of Enoch's ambition.

> Enoch set
> A purpose evermore before his eyes,
> To hoard all savings to the uttermost,
> To purchase his own boat, and make a home
> For Annie . . .

And all men look'd upon him favourably:
And ere he touch'd his one-and-twentieth May
He purchased his own boat, and made a home
For Annie, neat and nestlike, halfway up
The narrow street that clamber'd toward the mill.

When his child is born, then

In him woke,
With his first babe's first cry, the noble wish
To save all earnings to the uttermost,
And give his child a better bringing-up
Than his had been, or hers.

Accident and competition set him back. So he decides to stock a little shop for Annie, and ship himself on a China barque; meaning to trade and so

returning rich,
Become the master of a larger craft,
With fuller profits lead an easier life,
Have all his pretty young ones educated,
And pass his days in peace among his own.

He will in fact become a small employer; in 1867 Liberal speakers will challenge Bob Lowe to justify a law which excludes from the franchise our worthy neighbour Mr. Arden: while for the daughter there is evidently reserved the destiny of the young lady in the ballad:

And now she is the lawyer's wife
And dearly he does love her:
And she lives in a happy condition of life,
And well in the station above her.

To the simple-hearted reader or listener, in fact, Tennyson has done what the critic of 1842 demanded of him. He has brought the living world of shops and ships and going to sea and going to school, under poetic control. It is all there, and it is all poetry. We may object that it is not all there: that this living world is a highly selective composition, this poetry very largely a practised mannerism. I am not concerned to refute either objection, but I will ask you to consider for a little, not the ethical or artistic presumptions —if there be any such—by which poetry ought to be judged, but those which contemporaries actually applied.

'In metaphysical enquiries egoism is the truest modesty', and what little I understand of poetry regarded as an activity of the mind I learnt from a trifling incident in my own youth. The subject set for the Newdigate in my second or third year was King Charles at Oxford. I had no intention of competing, which was perhaps a pity, because the only copy which was submitted contained, I was afterwards told, the passage:

> The Queen from France with admirable tact
> Supplied the money which the Army lacked;
> Grateful the King accepts the proffered boon,
> And gives it to his troops who spend it soon.

But while I was thinking, in an idle and quite disinterested mood, how the theme could be treated, the notion—not the image—of Oxford, with its towers and lawns and trees lying like an island in the sea of civil strife, occurred to me, and with the notion came a line. I wrote it down, and the next line came at once, completing the couplet. In all, I wrote a simile ten lines long, as fast as if I was writing from dictation, and, as I wrote each word, not knowing in the least what the next would be. Then the spring failed as suddenly as it had started.

Guided by this experience of my own I have always supposed poetic experience to be a kind of compulsion which has its locus on the boundary between the apprehension of a theme and its rendering in metrical form; and there is this much truth, I believe, in Matthew Arnold's perilous doctrine of the Great Line, that such lines mark, as it were, the moments when the boundary disappears in a sudden intensity of poetic insight, so that apprehension and expression become a single act. Such moments are rare, and in the great bulk of every poet's work the two aspects, call them thought and form, are at least critically distinguishable. And corresponding to these two aspects of poetic activity there are, I think, two aspects of reception in the hearer or reader. He wishes to have certain things set before him because they interest him; and every age has its own set of interests. The later eighteenth century, for example, did not want to hear the things that Blake had to say, and so it hardly noticed that Blake was there. The early nineteenth century did most eagerly want something like *Childe Harold*, and having got it, went on to accept from Byron much which a less avid taste would have rejected. But the reader also desires to have these things set before him in a way which is poetically gratifying, and here also his pleasure and satisfaction are very largely conditioned for him by the aesthetic ambient of his time. All which things taken together produce what I have called adjustment; and, if I may ask you to admit one distinction more, within the aesthetic appeal and response itself two elements may be observed. In every work of art there is something which addresses the nerves, a thrill, beside those other things which reach the spirit. It is in virtue of this thrill, very often, that a writer makes his entry and secures his public—Swinburne is as good an example as one can recall—and I believe the curious anger, or detestation, so much beyond any reasonable ground of distaste, with which each age for a time regards the literature of the last, has its cause in this: that it perceives the appeal, but cannot answer it. Nothing is more exasperating to the nerves or the temper than a thrill which has begun to be a bore. You remember Mr. Pepys at *Midsummer Night's Dream*: 'Insipid: ridiculous: I shall never see it again!'

I am thinking now of those years between 1840 and 1860 when Tennyson was rising to the throne of poetry, and I ask what was the element in his art which was most stimulating to the nerves, and most satisfying to the taste of his contemporaries, and why. I call upon the memories of that young enthusiast, and without hesitation I answer; in the first instance his descriptive power. I need not tell again a tale which has been told so often, and, to relieve your anxieties at once, I may say I do not intend to mention Lady Winchelsea. But I must pause for a moment on a greater name, a more persistent influence. For about a century the repute and vogue of Thomson varied singularly little. 'From 1750 to 1850' one of his biographers wrote:

> Thomson was in England the poet, par excellence, not of the eclectic and literary few, but of the large and increasing culti-vated middle class. 'Thomson's "Seasons" looks best (I maintain it) a little torn and dogeared.'

He is quoting Lamb.

> When Coleridge found a dogeared copy of *The Seasons* in an inn, and remarked 'That is fame', Thomson's popularity seemed quite as assured as Milton's. As late as 1855 Robert Bell re-

marked that it seemed even on the increase. The date may be taken to mark the turning point in his fame, for since about 1850 he has been unmistakably eclipsed on his own ground, in the favour of the class to which he was once dear, by Tennyson.

For a generation or so before the birth of Tennyson English senses had been brought to a degree of fineness they had never possessed before. The practice of the poets counted for much, of Cowper and those others to whom in this context we need not deny their good old name of the Lake Poets. The new interest in landscape painting, the addiction to sketching in pencil or water-colour, are, as Hazlitt pointed out, influences not to be overlooked in studying the evolution of our literary tastes. I would add the habit of travel, especially of domestic travel imposed by the closure of the Continent and facilitated by the labours of Telford and Macadam. Finally, I would include an influence which I believe to be well worth the attention of some student of the literature of science: I mean the growing devotion to natural history in all its branches, the minute observation of form and colour in leaf and rock and feather and flower. High among those who formed the English aesthetic of the nineteenth century must always be placed the names of White and Gilpin and Bewick: after them of Lyell, and the contributors to the *Cabinet Encyclopaedia*.

This increasing fineness of observation demanded an increasing delicacy and exactitude of record, just as, in another sphere, the metrical practice of the great Romantic poets had created a demand for a richer and more various verbal music than had contented the Augustan ear. But as we go forward into the nineteenth century, this devotion to nature seems to become almost a nervous craving: possibly at the deepest level a biological necessity. The public of which I am speaking, Tennyson's public, was becoming, in spirit, suburban: a country-bred stock, entangled in a way of life which it had not learnt to control, was instinctively fighting for breath. And for sixty years its poet was there, flashing on it in phrases of faultless precision, pictures of the world from which it was exiled and in which it yearned to keep at least an imaginary footing.

The ground flame of the crocus breaks the mould.

That is Tennyson at twenty. It might be Tennyson at eighty.

Nothing in Tennyson's art is more admirable than the economy
and certainty of his touch when he is on this ground:

> On either side the river lie
> Long fields of barley and of rye
> That clothe the wold *and meet the sky*.

No wonder the *Quarterly*, whether Croker or his editor, stigmat-
ized that phrase, because, as everyone born in the eighteenth century would know, between the top of the wold and the bottom of
the sky there is in fact a considerable gap. I quote it as one of the
earliest and most convincing examples of Tennyson's mastery of
the illusionist style, where words have the value of things seen,
and the observation seems to go at once into poetry without any
pause for reflection, or mental arrangement of the particulars.
Think of the spring in *Balin and Balan*:

> the spring, that down
> From underneath a plume of lady-fern,
> Sang, and the sand danced at the bottom of it.

It does not matter whether you have ever seen that or not. If
you have not, you know now exactly what it looks like. If you
have, the words will keep it in your memory far more vividly than
any recollection of your own. Here, as Miss Sitwell has said of
Smart, 'the natural object is seen with such clarity that for the
moment nothing else exists', and in Smart's recently published
manuscript *Jubilate Agno* there is a sentence which I must quote because it seems to me exactly to describe the nature of the accomplishment which, after two generations of experiment, Tennyson
brought to perfection.

> My talent is to give an impression upon words by punching,
> that when the reader casts his eye upon them, he takes up the
> image from the mould which I have made.

Tennyson's imagery was studied by men of science, and never
once I think did they find his observation scientifically at fault.
That melancholy achievement was reserved for me. No one who
lives in downland and has ever seen a waning moon rising in a
windy sky, can fail to respond to the magical aptitude of the lines

> And high in heaven the streaming cloud,
> And on the downs a rising fire.

That fire is a stage illumination: that moon a property moon. I have it on the authority of the Astronomer Royal, and—

> Solem quis dicere falsum
> Audeat?

that on 10 October 1842, the day of Cecilia Tennyson's wedding here commemorated, the moon did not rise after supper. It rose before lunch.

I think it is true to say that Tennyson's accomplishment in this branch of his art served to constrict for a time the range of our poetry, and to narrow our critical judgement. After all, images of external nature are not the only things a poet has to provide: and in the later part of the century you may sometimes encounter a naïve habit of criticism, based on the popular notion, as I said, that poetry was what Tennyson wrote, which assessed the poets by the number of nature-touches, as they were known in the trade, to be found in their respective works. But I need not remind you that it has often been the fate of great poets—and a proof of their greatness: the fate of Chaucer and Virgil—to impede the progress of poesy by their very mastery, by the domination they exercised over their contemporaries and immediate successors.

I have placed this gift of Tennyson's in the forefront of his equipment, because it is here that we are most conscious—whether we can still feel it or not—of what I have called the thrill. The profusion of his natural imagery, domestic or exotic, is—or was once—as intoxicating as the liquid richness of his verse, and its ravishing surprises. We are not called upon to be intoxicated, but to understand those who were, and to follow them as they see their poet, the poet of 'Mariana' and 'The Lotos-Eaters', grow in stature as a philosophic and religious teacher. Here again, to begin with what is outward, his mastery of another mode, not less grateful to an age immersed in anxious moral speculation, is equally conspicuous, not to say obtrusive. I mean the gnomic, hortatory utterance, the ethical *sententia*. Few lines of Tennyson, for example, were more admired or more often quoted than these:

> Let knowledge grow from more to more,
> But more of reverence in us dwell;
> That mind and soul, according well,
> May make one music as before,

> But vaster.

Perhaps to our less robust and exuberant ethical sense, they are, if anything, too quotable, too suggestive of the birthday book, the calendar, or the chairman of the governors at a prize-giving. They seem, like so much of Tennyson's verse, to be designed for public performance. Indeed I knew a man who, until I convinced him otherwise, had gone through life believing that

> Heated hot with burning fears
> And dipt in baths of hissing tears,
> And battered with the shocks of doom
> To shape and use:

was the second verse of *Scots wha hae*. We must acknowledge that we have lost the taste for moral declamation, just as the nineteenth century lost the taste for social elegance. But it may come back. In any case I am not defending or assailing Tennyson's manner. I am speaking historically; I am trying to account for what I have called his adjustment. But may I in passing observe that the greatest body of reflective and ethical poetry in European literature actually was designed for public performance? I mean the choruses of the Athenian stage: and it is here, I have often thought, especially among the choruses of Sophocles, that we shall find the nearest analogy to such pieces as 'Of old sat Freedom on the heights', many of the lyrics which make up *In Memoriam*, or this, which the Attic Muse herself might not have disdained or disavowed:

> And when no mortal motion jars
>   The blackness round the tombing sod,
> Thro' silence and the trembling stars
>   Comes Faith from tracts no feet have trod,
>   And Virtue, like a household god
>
> Promising empire; such as those
>   Once heard at dead of night to greet
> Troy's wandering prince, so that he rose
>   With sacrifice, while all the fleet
>   Had rest by stony hills of Crete.

And this gnomic manner was not less pleasing to the ear of a romantic age, when it dissolved, as it often does, into a riddling, oracular style like this:

34

Pass not beneath this gateway, but abide
Without, among the cattle of the field.
For, an ye heard a music, like enow
They are building still, seeing the city is built
To music, therefore never built at all,
And therefore built for ever.

Now are those lines a genuine poetic experience, or merely the
application of poetic learning to a promising theme? Is Tennyson
expressing himself or exploiting himself? That is the doubt, already audible in the seventies, which grew and culminated in the
great revulsion from the Laureate and all his ways which is characteristic of the end of the last century and the beginning of this.
There is no need to deny that much of Tennyson's poetry is enveloped in an Alexandrian overgrowth of literary erudition, a
kind of Great Exhibitionism not unalluring to an age which loved
profusion, as much as it admired invention. He has passages which
Callimachus could have approved: others which Ovid might have
envied: and Mario Praz has actually called *Enoch Arden* a Hellenistic romance. I do not feel that judgement to be true, but if anyone chose to call the *Idylls*, where one can hardly say whether
the figures are ancients dressed like moderns, or moderns like
ancients, a Hellenistic epic, I am not sure I should greatly differ:
and the decorous eroticism which hangs over much—not all—of
that performance seems to me to have been finally and adequately
characterized by the American schoolboy who observed: 'There is
some pretty hot necking in Lord Tennyson, only they never quite
make it.'

But in the 'Northern Farmer', 'The Churchwarden', and 'The
Village Wife, or the Entail', we are far from Alexandria, we are
among the oak-woods of Acharnae: and you may think that the
spectacle of Tennyson unbending in dialect, and then resuming
his poise as Bard to write 'The Wreck' or 'The Children's Hos-
pital' indicates some weakness in the poetic fibre of the man, or
the poetic judgement of his age. If you do, I think you would be
right: and I wish to consider rather more closely what that weakness was.

I need not remark that the Christian religion and the elements
of propriety were not introduced into the United Kingdom by
Prince Albert of Saxe-Coburg-Gotha. At the beginning of the century, at least by 1805, the Germans had noticed and named as a

national characteristic, or Engländerei, that nervousness and reti-
cence in the sphere of passion which is popularly supposed to be a
Victorian characteristic, and which in passing I may recall, had
compelled Scott in 1824 to mar the catastrophe of *St. Ronan's Well*.
Those who believe in the economic interpretation of everything,
including poetry, may find it easier than I do to account for the
readiness with which the England of Chaucer and Fielding submitted itself and its literature to this new asceticism. Never I suppose was there a time when people were so willing to be shocked,
or when the habit of being shocked was so widespread and so
commendable that a man could assert his superior refinement best
by being shocked at something which no one else had noticed,
like the critic of *Enoch Arden*, for example, who censured Tennyson for failing to observe that bigamy was not a misfortune but a
criminal offence. Now it may be admitted that bigamy is rarer in
the upper than in the lower walks of society: and what I think was
in the back of the critic's mind was the notion that by taking Annie
to himself, without proof of Enoch's death, Philip was descending
from the station of a thoroughly respectable man.

I have always thought that the conception of respectability was
in its place and time of the greatest moral service to us. To be respectable is to emerge from the anonymous amorphous mass: to
be a personality: to live by a standard, actually, perhaps, the standard of the class just above that into which you had been born and
in which your fellows were content to live. If we stopped there,
we might think of respectability as the characteristic virtue of
competitive individualism practised under the eye of an approving
gentry. But we cannot stop there, because the respectable man is
not only bettering himself, he is bettering his family. Through the
family the most powerful of human instincts is harnessed to the
secular task of improving the race. So viewed, social progress is a
microcosmic section of the evolution of the world under the guidance of that Providence whose purpose, in the great words of
Malthus, is ever to bring a mind out of the clod, but a section
which has become conscious of itself and therefore capable of a
directed effort. As Pitt Rivers said to a concourse of archaeologists
shortly after the appearance of Darwin's *Descent of Man*, 'the
thought of our humble origin'—from what I have heard of Pitt
Rivers I think he must have said your humble origin—'may be an
incentive to industry and respectability'.

In other words respectability means the continual production and reproduction of distinguished varieties, and to laughter, as George Meredith taught us, the distinguished variety is peculiarly sensitive. In this way we may account for that vicious dichotomy, deep-seated in the Victorian mind, between the idea of comedy, and the idea of beauty, which is so observable, for example, in Dickens: beyond question one of the greatest of all comic writers —and yet, how unlovely is much of his satire, how tasteless his sentiment. Seeing that comedy, that wit and humour, are among the most powerful and penetrating instruments which the mind has to work with, we must, I think, acknowledge that this notion of the fenced, secluded area where laughter must not be heard, weakened and hampered the whole intelligence of the age: and in none of its great writers is the mischief more apparent than in Tennyson. Matthew Arnold said he lacked intellectual power. He said much the same of Shelley: and I am not sure that his intense, exclusive, humanism qualified him to judge the intellectual calibre of a poet, whose chief interests, apart from poetry, were scientific: I cannot recall any passage in Arnold's writing which suggests that he had ever given a thought to the ichthyosaurus. At all events, contemporaries, not less fitted than he to judge, did not observe the want, partly because they were under the same limitations themselves, but more because they found in Tennyson the most complete statement of the great philosophic issue of the age: if not an answer to its problems, at least an indication of the lines along which the answer was to be sought. What he did lack, and they did not require, was precisely that restraining touch of comedy to save him from becoming, as he can be at times, vapidly pontifical and almost embarrassingly silly.

This issue, the central problem round which the minds of thoughtful men were coming to revolve, can be very simply stated. What was the standing of personality, the finite human personality, in a world which every year was revealing itself more clearly as a process of perpetual flux?

> The hills are shadows and they flow
> From form to form, and nothing stands;
> They melt like mist, the solid lands,
> Like clouds they shape themselves and go.

We may perhaps forget, among our own more pressing concerns, how formidable an attack on human dignity and personal values, the ground of all Western philosophy and religion, was implicit in the new conceptions of geological and biological time. When once you have mastered the thesis that inconceivable ages have gone to make the race, and that after inconceivable ages to come the whole conscious episode may have been nothing more than a brief iridescence on a cooling cinder, what solid ground of conduct is left to you? And Tennyson had mastered the thesis; from his undergraduate days, when Darwin was on the high seas in the *Beagle*, he had meditated on the mystery of development and the succession of types.

Thus when he appeared as a philosophic poet with *In Memoriam* he was not only equipped for the great debate which was soon to open; he had anticipated it, had formulated at least a conceivable conclusion; and one based on personal experience: on the mystical, or almost mystical assurance, recorded at the close of *The Holy Grail*.

> Let visions of the night or of the day
> Come, as they will; and many a time they come,
> Until this earth he walks on seems not earth,
> This light that strikes his eyeball is not light,
> This air that smites his forehead is not air
> But vision—yea, his very hand and foot—
> In moments when he feels he cannot die,
> And knows himself no vision to himself,
> Nor the high God a vision, nor that One
> Who rose again.

That is no borrowed language, no such working up of many possibilities into one plausibility as Victorian theology was so largely engaged in. It is Tennyson's own voice: you hear it again in 'The Ancient Sage'.

> The first gray streak of earliest summer-dawn,
> The last long stripe of waning crimson gloom,
> As if the late and early were but one—
> A height, a broken grange, a grove, a flower
> Had murmurs 'Lost and gone and lost and gone!'
> A breath, a whisper—some divine farewell—
> Desolate sweetness—far and far away—
> What had he loved, what had he lost, the boy?
> I know not and I speak of what has been.
>   And more, my son! for more than once when I
> Sat all alone, revolving in myself

The word that is the symbol of myself,
The mortal limit of the self was loosed,
And past into the Nameless, as a cloud
Melts into Heaven. I touch'd my limbs, the limbs
Were strange not mine—and yet no shade of doubt
But utter clearness, and thro' loss of Self
The gain of such large life as match'd with ours
Were Sun to spark—unshadowable in words,
Themselves but shadows of a shadow-world.

It is Tennyson's own voice, telling of what he has known, and as such his age received it. *Perhibet testimonium de his, et scripsit haec: et scimus quia verum est testimonium ejus.*

But what in this vision of the world is the place of Christianity? Or, to put the question as Tennyson and his contemporaries felt it, when the traditional forms of faith have been subjected to the analysis of criticism and science, what will remain? The inerrancy of Scripture had gone, carrying with it both the cosmogony on which the scheme of redemption was founded, and the assurance of immortality. Was there anything left which might serve as a spiritual directive of progress? Now, from Tennyson's early grief over the loss of Hallam, there had emerged a belief in what I may call a hierarchy of types, each realizing possibilities only latent at a lower level, and indicating fresh possibilities to be realized at a higher. And here was a creed, or a supposition, reconcilable at once with the monistic or pantheistic trend which science was imposing on our thought, and on the other hand with historic Christianity, and the sublime claims which Christianity makes for personality, and on it. Granted that an initial act of faith is required, because, so far as we can see, progress may be morally downward as well as upward: granted also that the implied metaphysic will be in detail shadowy—a philosophy of Somehow, wavering between a hopeful doubt and a doubtful hope—yet it was open to any Christian to accept the hypothesis, in the assurance that the highest in this human hierarchy is a man, and that man Incarnate God. Thus the argument is rounded off, because, so conceived, personality is not an incident in evolution, but its consummation. Here then was a body of conviction, won from doubt, and even despair, which gave to thousands, in the season of their distress, the guidance and assurance for which they asked.

There is one passage in Tennyson and, as far as I can recall, one only, where he rises to the full poetic height of this argument, to a complete poetic apprehension of his own idea. I mean the close of *In Memoriam*.

> And rise, O moon, from yonder down,
> Till over down and over dale
> All night the shining vapour sail
> And pass the silent-lighted town,
>
> The white-faced halls, the glancing rills,
> And catch at every mountain head,
> And o'er the friths that branch and spread
> Their sleeping silver through the hills;
>
> And touch with shade the bridal doors,
> With tender gloom the roof, the wall;
> And breaking let the splendour fall
> To spangle all the happy shores
>
> By which they rest, and ocean sounds,
> And, star and system rolling past,
> A soul shall draw from out the vast
> And strike his being into bounds.

Con quanto di quel salmo è poscia scripto.

Here, or so it seems to me, Tennyson has done the utmost that can be asked of a poet, in one act embracing the whole range of his deepest personal thought, and rendering it in the loveliest and most natural imagery that poetry affords, the moonlit sea and the lovers sleeping by its shores.

1939

TENNYSON AS A MODERN POET
Arthur J. Carr

'MODERN FAME is nothing,' said Tennyson to William Allingham. 'I'd rather have an acre of land. I shall go down, down! I'm up now. Action and reaction.'

'Action and reaction' only partly account for Tennyson's fall. We cannot help feeling in the bard of Farringford and Aldworth, in the author of 'The May Queen', *Enoch Arden*, and 'The Promise of May', that depressing sense of an imagination 'more saved than spent', which made Henry James breathe, 'Oh, dear, oh, dear', upon discovering that Tennyson himself 'was not Tennysonian'.

Not until after the great dividing years of 1914–18 was it possible to view the dead laureate with some composure and to wish to retrieve at least the part of his work that was not official and 'Victorian'. For an age that demanded of poetry 'reality of emotional impulse,' Harold Nicolson boiled the essential Tennyson down to 'a morbid and unhappy mystic', 'afraid of death, and sex, and God'. A little later, T. S. Eliot boldly called him 'a great poet', because of his 'abundance, variety, and complete competence'. When W. H. Auden made up a selection of Tennyson's poetry very much as Nicolson had specified, he conceded that Tennyson 'had the finest ear, perhaps, of any English Poet'; then he added, 'he was undoubtedly the stupidest; there was little about melancholia that he didn't know; there was little else that he did'.

In the presence of such a figure it is no wonder that critics who are also poets grows nervous and exasperated. They see in Tennyson not an open but a covert capitulation, perhaps involuntary though not altogether unconscious. Yet he is our true precursor. He shows and hides, as if in embryo, a master theme of Joyce's *Ulysses*—the accentuated and moody self-consciousness and the sense of loss that mark Stephen Dedalus. He forecasts Yeats's interest in the private myth. He apprehended in advance of Aldous Huxley the uses of mysticism to castigate materialistic culture. And in *Maud*, at least, he prepared the way for the verse of Eliot's 'Preludes' and 'Prufrock'. At some crucial points Tennyson is a modern poet, and there are compelling reasons why we should try to comprehend him. Our uneasiness, our reluctance to acknowledge the relationship is understandable, and it explains how little we advance towards seeing what Tennyson's poetry is like.

Seeing what it is like, discerning the essentials without 'essentializing', as Kenneth Burke would ask, demands that criticism breathe a mixed atmosphere, neither wholly aesthetic nor wholly biographical. It is not a question of choosing to consult biography in order to chart the poem or of preferring to ignore the private reference. In Tennyson's poetry the private and public worlds are fused. In the presence of such poetry, criticism must act upon life as well as upon art. Tennyson's double nature does not divide itself between the poet and the man; his poetry has a double nature and reveals not only itself but the poet. This is the truth that Hallam Tennyson confessed in his preface to the *Memoir* of his father's life: '. . . but besides the letters of my father and of his friends there are his poems, and in them we must look for the innermost sanctuary of his being. For my own part, I feel strongly that no biographer could so truly give him as he gives himself in his own works'. Although we must look to the man to find the poet, we shall find the man in his poems.

The artistic and cultural crisis which underlies the swervings and sudden drops in his long career was clearly sketched for Tennyson while he was at Cambridge, from 1828 to 1831. It was the protean question that the members of the Apostles Club debated, and that some of them attempted to resolve in action. The ill-fated Torrijos expedition, vigorously recounted by Carlyle in his *Life of John Sterling*, was a point of focus. With a handful of exiled Spaniards around General Torrijos, a few of 'the young Cambridge democrats' joined in a pitifully brave and futile attempt to restore constitutional monarchy to Spain by simultaneous uprisings in the north and south. In the summer of 1830 Alfred Tennyson and Arthur Hallam carried messages through southern France to leaders of the northern conspiracy. At the same moment Torrijos and his compatriots were landing at Gibraltar with Tennyson's friends John Mitchell Kemble (later the editor of *Beowulf*) and Richard Chenevix Trench (later the Archbishop of Dublin).

Perhaps more lucidly than the other English youths, Trench saw it as a desperate venture of sensibility that charged the external political motives and the physical danger with symbolic drama concerning the role of the individual in society and the role of the artist in a disordered culture. To another of the Apostles, W. B. Donne, Trench wrote on the eve of his departure from England:

But the future, the future—who shall question that? What will one be? What will this age be? Must one end in a worldling; and our age, will it prove the decrepitude of the world? Are we not gathering up the knowledge of past generations because we are adding nothing ourselves? Do we not place the glory of our century in the understanding of past ages, because our individual energy is extinct, and we are ourselves nothing? After one or two revolutions in thought and opinion, all our boasted poetry, all, or nearly all, of Keats and Shelley and Wordsworth and Byron, will become unintelligible. When except in our times, did men seek to build up their poetry on their own individual experiences, instead of some objective foundations common to all men?[1]

The question of 'objective foundations' permeates Tennyson's career and binds his poetry to the crisis of the arts in our century. Tennyson took in the sickening fact that the continental areas of common values were breaking up. Myths, rituals, slogans, accustomed loyalties and animosities, the classic procedures of politics and warfare, the classic mysteries of philosophies, the groundwork of rational history and rational science, the themes and modes of art—all cemented by hallowed ethical and economic traditions—were coming loose fast. The sense of this fact is the

[1] M. Trench, *Richard Chenevix Trench, Archbishop; Letters and Memorials* (1888), i, 73.

atmosphere of his poetry and is present everywhere. It is evident in his exploitation of a multitude of traditional poetic forms, in the question of electing a tradition and in the desperate virtuosity of his style; in his private use of the public domain of myth and legend as he turns from the formal and familiar elements to the inward and particular. We may trace it in his anxiety to keep up with the thought of his day and to draw it—drag it, if necessary—into his poetry; in his quest for symbols; in his perplexity over the artist's involvement in affairs ('The Palace of Art' sprang from Trench's ultimatum, 'Tennyson, we cannot live in art'); and in his sad conviction that his work would fail.

Only a little altered in the fashion of their dress, these questions still pace our critical reviews and galleries of art. Tennyson's awareness of these issues, which the century since the publication of *In Memoriam* has tiresomely expounded, was never lucidly conceived. His ideas flow in the current of his melancholic sensibility. When that sensibility was fed, enormously, by such a loss as the death of Arthur Hallam, Tennyson's poetry swept the entire range of crisis.

The theme of loss appeared very early in Tennyson's poetry as the talisman of imaginative energy. Whenever this theme reappears, even after *In Memoriam*, it works its magic. This fact may explain why Tennyson often seems to force himself to remember the loss of Hallam, enclosing him in the figure of King Arthur in *Idylls of the King*, performing again the ritual of loss and recovery in 'Vastness', 'In the Valley of Cauteretz', 'Merlin and the Gleam', and 'Crossing the Bar', and implicitly in many other poems. When the private sensibility was not stirred, the awareness was wanting, and 'stupid' 'Alfred Lawn Tennyson', the Victorian, wrote masterly bathos.

Tennyson is the most 'occasional' of poets, but the occasions were not public, even when he made them so. His imagination rose only to its own promptings or to the lure of an event that suggested or reproduced the subjective drama of loss, defeat, and disappointment. Then manner and matter would unite, and even in the placid years he could write the 'Ode on the Death of the Duke of Wellington', of a man who reminded Tennyson of the statesman latent in Arthur Hallam, and *Idylls of the King*, which broods over the disintegration of an ideal society and the fall of a heroic lay-figure. Such a survival of imagination in spite of all that

44

was wasted taught Henry James to observe: 'As a didactic creation I do not greatly care for King Arthur; but as a fantastic one he is infinitely remunerative.' As Trench saw, there is a romantic entanglement of poet and poem. The concinnity of Tennyson's art rests on his 'individual experiences', rather than upon 'some objective foundations common to all men'.

II

The genetic view of Tennyson's poetry naturally swings towards his early work in search of the components of his sensibility. James Spedding had remarked in 1835 that his friend Tennyson was 'a man always discontented with the Present till it has become the Past, and then he yearns toward it and worships it, and not only worships it, but is discontented because it is past'. Many years later, Tennyson himself, speaking to Sir James Knowles about 'Tears, Idle Tears', said, 'It is what I have always felt even from a boy, and what as a boy I called the "passion of the past". And so it is with me now; it is the distance that charms me in the landscape, the picture and the past, and not the immediate to-day in which I move.'

Yet such moods of melancholy, sometimes mellow, sometimes acute, generate Tennyson's poetry. T. S. Eliot saw in Tennyson 'emotion so deeply suppressed, even from himself, as to tend rather towards the blackest melancholia than towards dramatic action'. It is a response to frustration not only felt but expressed, embodied in art and in the problems of art, in the search for theme and for symbols.

In the early poems the underlying theme of the 'divided will' is charged with the highest imaginative excitement, and most of the issues that were to be explored later are set forth. In what is possibly Tennyson's earliest poem, 'Armageddon',[1] the theme is a transcendent mystical revelation, like that which Tennyson said that he experienced repeatedly later in life. The poem approaches the instant of transcendental disclosure only through passages of ominous imagery and a sense of deep anxiety and awe. The hour is the typical Tennysonian twilight when sun and moon stand in

[1] Printed among the tantalizing oddments of *Unpublished Early Poems*, edited by the poet's grandson, Sir Charles Tennyson (1932). Rewritten, this poem became the basis for Tennyson's prize poem, *Timbuctoo*.

opposition. Then the poet enters the realm of the deeper consciousness and finds delight in himself:

> Yea! in that hour I could have fallen down
> Before my own strong soul and worshipp'd it.

Later, in 'The Mystic', in the crucial lyric 95 of *In Memoriam*, in *The Holy Grail*, and 'The Ancient Sage', Tennyson would have recourse to this theme. The ominous images and the sense of awe denote a dialectic clash between the attraction of the deepest subjective levels and the resistance and restraint of other sectors of reality.

Dream, memory, and desire come to represent in these early poems the modes of imaginative freedom that is restrained by forces not explicitly represented except as a category called 'conscience' or 'fear'. The dialectic is perfectly realized in the lyric 'In Deep and Solemn Dreams' (in *Unpublished Early Poems*), that forecasts the tonality and the problem of *In Memoriam*. The dreamer meets 'sunny faces of lost days . . . Forms which live but in the mind':

> And we speak as we have spoken
> Ere our love by death was broken.

But the wind of dawn shakes 'The large leaves of the sycamore' and breaks the 'sacred charm of tearless sleep':

> Dear lips, loved eyes, ye fade, ye fly,
> Even in my fear yet die,
> And the hollow dark I dread
> Closes round my friendless head.

Even in that strained and rhetorical poem 'Remorse' (in *Poems by Two Brothers*) there are sudden disclosures, though the cause of remorse is kept in mystery. The poet, cursed 'With too much conscience to have rest, Too little to be ever blest', recoils from himself:

> I would I'd been all-heartless! then
> I might have sinn'd like other men

and turns avidly towards the image of a final sleep in death, safe from 'the thrill of conscious fear'.

In 'Sense and Conscience' and 'Memory' (in *Unpublished Early*

Poems), Tennyson deals more objectively with the dialectic issues. The first of these is a fragment of an allegory suggesting the theme of *Idylls of the King*. 'Conscience' is laid asleep by 'Sense' in the midst of 'pleasurable flowers', often associated by Tennyson with erotic themes. He is visited by 'Delicious dreams' and 'witching fantasies', 'Lovely with bright black eyes', 'And lips which moved in silence.' But 'Memory' and 'Pain' arouse him:

> Rage seized upon him then
> And grasping with both palms his wondrous blade,
> Sheer through the summit of the tallest flowers
> He drave it. . . .
> The ivy from the stem
> Was torn, the vine made desolate; his feet
> Were crimson'd with its blood, from which flows joy
> And bitterness, first joy from bitterness,
> And then again great bitterness from joy.

No relief is obtained by laying waste the pleasurable flowers, whose blood is like his own; and he lives with Memory and Pain. To deny and stamp out Sense only leads to a repression of desire, and Conscience suffers all the more. Nor would Tennyson ever attempt again to reach an answer by annihilating one of the sources of his inspiration as well as of his pain.

The poem 'Memory'[1] almost succeeds in formulating the imaginative strife:

> Wherefore do I so remember
> That Hope is born of Memory
> Nightly in the house of dreams? . . .

[1] This poem parallels in several ways the lyric, 'O that 't were possible', which was the nucleus of *Maud*:

> Half the night I waste in sighs
> Half in dreams I sorrow after
> The delight of early skies;
> In a wakeful doze I sorrow
> For the hand, the lips, the eyes,
> For the meeting of the morrow,
> The delight of happy laughter,
> The delight of low replies.

Although the maddened lover is not Tennyson in any simple biographical sense, he wears the characteristic masks of Tennyson's personality. Tennyson does not fully disengage himself.

> Why at break of cheerful day
> Doth my spirit faint away
> Like a wanderer in the night?
> Why in visions of the night
> Am I shaken with delight
> Like a lark at dawn of day?

If memory becomes an avenue of desire, like dreams themselves, it must still turn and agonize around conscience and the wakeful forces of restraint. Hence the painful irony and paradox that Tennyson phrased distinctly.

As a recurrent poetic strategy, with its own dialectic equation, the interchanging play of memory and desire seems a mask of the personality. In his *Tennyson in Egypt* (1942), an excellent detailed study of erotic and symbolic elements in Tennyson's early verse, Professor W. D. Paden has called this strategy 'the mask of age'. In it the face of desire and anxiety appears as memory and regret. No doubt Tennyson was simply borrowing at first a Byronic attitude. The desirable future and the frustrations of the present come forth as the vanished past—recapturable in memory. The thirst of youth is presented as the dryness of age. The feelings of guilt inseparable from dream are costumed as remorse and self-reproach for what is gone and cannot be helped. The advantage of the strategy is that it marches towards some degree of objectivity: the imaginative forces are brought under partial control. Yet Tennyson's discovery of 'the magic cirque of memory' would be of only passing interest in his development did not the mask of age show forth again in poems of his best hours: in 'Ulysses', the hero about to embark on a voyage of desire towards reunion with 'the great Achilles, whom we knew'; in 'Tithonus', the immortal, aging lover trapped by senility in a heaven of erotic ease that he can taste only in memory; in 'Tears, Idle Tears'; in the 'mad scenes' of *Maud*; above all in the nature of *In Memoriam*.

If the strategy of the mask of age both conceals and connotes anxiety, it is also sufficient to bind together the elements of a divided sensibility. The war of sense and conscience is no simple opposition between frustration and desire. The dialectic plays in both the inner and the outer worlds at once. There are the arrows of conscience and the chains of obligation. There are the demands of duty and the commands of love. Consequently, the objects of sense pass swiftly into symbols of desire, and the laws of dreams are cast outwards over the objects of sense. In these terms Tennyson continues to explore the premises of romantic art, following Byron, then Keats and Coleridge, and even Shelley, in employing egocentric melancholy and the sensuous and supersensuous imagery of dream, and in debating the role of the artist in society. But he is not simply imitative. He accepts a tradition and goes beyond it to take what he can from whatever touches him in Western art.

Poems, Chiefly Lyrical (1830) and *Poems* (1833) display Tennyson's rapid and thorough engagement of his characteristic themes and, in particular, his concern with erotic motives to unfold the dialectic of sense and conscience. Fantasy beckons and repels. The gates of desire are defended by danger and wakeful fears. In 'Recollections of the Arabian Nights', the poet voyages through a sub-tropical paradise that opens only as he enters 'another night in night' and, in a dream within a dream, hears the Keatsian nightingale,

> Not he, but something which possess'd
> The darkness of the world, delight,
> Life, anguish, death, immortal love,
> Ceasing not, mingled, unrepressed . . .

'Entranced', he gazes on the 'amorous' Persian girl alone. The poem closes deep within the dream; there is no painful waking.

'A Dream of Fair Women' is a finer and more anxious poem. It begins with visions of

> Beauty and anguish walking hand in hand
> The downward slope to death.

Chaotic images of warfare, resembling the opening lines of 'Armageddon', culminate as the poet lifts his arm 'to hew down' a cavalier who is abducting a lady; then sleep and dream come upon him, and he is in the midst of an ominous and familiar forest, deadly still. It is just before dawn. The regressive stride into a deeper dream is made at once:

> The smell of violets, hidden in the green,
>   Pour'd back into my empty soul and frame
> The times when I remember to have been
>   Joyful and free from blame.

49

And from within me a clear undertone
    Thrill'd thro' mine ears in that unblissful clime,
'Pass freely thro'; the wood is all thine own
    Until the end of time.'

Yet the dangers and distress are not so easily exorcized. The interviews with Helen of Troy, Iphigeneia, Cleopatra, and other famous ladies are not lacking in overtones of awe, and the dream ends abruptly with the coming of dawn (as with 'In Deep and Solemn Dreams') and assumes the mask of age:

As when a soul laments, which hath been blest,
    Desiring what is mingled with past years,
In yearnings that can never be exprest
    By sighs or groans or tears. . . .

Significantly, the ladies of the dream are dead ladies. With remarkable persistence death becomes in all these poems the ambivalent counterpoise to love and desire. It embodies the hostility between sense and conscience and guards the thresholds of fantasy. Regression to a deeper level of consciousness must pass the danger of death; yet to reach the level of fantasy is to triumph over death. The symbol death has a double nature: frustration of desire is a kind of death; yet persistence of desire rouses the conscientious phantom of death. Nor are the deeper levels of dream free from phantoms. They haunt the idyllic museum of Western culture in 'The Palace of Art', and drive the Soul, for a while at least, into the world until she shall purge her 'guilt'. Only in those rare and brief disclosures of transcendental reality are the penalties of desire delayed, and even there the dark freedom of the mind is soon 'stricken through with doubt'.

Regression and withdrawal continue to mark Tennyson's later poetry. He sometimes falls back to a mental posture from which the return to erotic enjoyment and moral victory is facilitated. In *The Princess*, the Prince, 'Of temper amorous' and subject to sudden trances when aggression threatens, at first disguises his sex to enter the cloister of art and learning where Princess Ida keeps her college for young ladies. When the Prince, like the dreamer in 'A Dream of Fair Women', is striking a blow in battle to win the Princess, he is wounded, falls, and lies, embryo-like, 'silent in the muffled cage of life'. The Princess nurses him, assuming a role more maternal than erotic; then 'Leapt fiery Passion from the brinks of death', and without courtship the Prince wins his bride.

King Arthur, too, after renouncing Guinevere and being mortally wounded, recedes into the valley of Avilion, from which he will emerge in fresh power.

In such poems as 'Fatima' and 'Mariana' Tennyson attempted the delineation of erotic moods without recourse to dreams. But neither Fatima nor Mariana is a personality. They encase fevers of frustration and desire prolonged to the point of statuesque agony. There is no shadow of alleviation. Fatima is frozen at the point of hot desire, and in 'Mariana' the lines between inner and outer reality are obliterated and her house becomes a house of dreams, disappointment, and death.

One could make it a simple equation that the more complete is the damming up of desire, in the moods and situations of these poems, the more certain to rise is a Keatsian lushness of imagery and diction. This is the root of Tennyson's 'ornate' style in which, as Walter Bagehot noted, 'everything has about it an atmosphere of something else', suitable to subjects of 'half-belief' and to 'dubious themes'. Tennyson had learned to embody a problem in a mood and the mood in evocative, concrete, and disturbed imagery. To this ability he would soon add the use of myth and legend that made a hard and brilliant surface of traditional substance under which the private sensibility moved as if through water.

Tennyson had forged a poetic instrument out of the themes of loss and recovery through regression into dream and vision. Death and fear were established as the conventions that rule the dialectic of sense and conscience. This instrument became his means of apprehending the rational problems of his experience also, and lent them the deep sense of crisis that accorded well with the feelings of his class and of his age. The future of art, the nature of society, and the issues of science and religion, take the colours and disposition of his subjective strife. For this reason, the death of Hallam, a personal loss, became a magnet for larger issues. The subjective crisis and its non-rational modes encompass the crisis of Tennyson's culture.

These themes converge in 'The Palace of Art', where the Soul feels a conscientious despair that 'divided quite The kingdom of her thought'. But she does not, like Conscience, destroy the 'pleasurable flowers' of her paradise. Although she departs, she promises to return. If the issues of involvement and non-involvement were not to be settled easily, neither were they to be ignored. 'The

Lady of Shalott' sketches the predicament of a mind trying to free itself from a web of fantasy. When the Lady, moved by desire, looks away from the deep subjective mirror in which she read the shadows of the world, the mirror cracks from side to side. She accepts her destiny and dies as she drifts down to Camelot. It is the first poem in which Tennyson thoroughly controlled his legendary materials, so that the poem with its symbolic action becomes an image of the mind.

The liberating power of legend works also in 'The Lotos-Eaters'. Exactly because it is managed as an episode in the return of Ulysses to the responsibilities of Ithaca, Tennyson could follow very far the impulses to 'slothful ease' and vague erotic happiness. Yet in escaping so far, upon that island, the frustrations of conscience and the censures of the gods (who do not care), the poem risks the denial of transcendental reality, which was supported in Tennyson's experience by subjective revelations that lay deeper than fantasies of dream and vision. Because the poem is an episode of the wider legend, Tennyson does not have to make amends: the argument for responsibility was implied in the outer reaches of the story.

All these strands twine together in 'Œnone', the steadiest and most deftly woven of the poems that Tennyson wrote before the death of Arthur Hallam on 15 September 1833. Œnone's monologue combines day-dream and legend while elaborating the rigid erotic attitudes of 'Mariana' and 'Fatima'. Here Tennyson studies the issues of his poetry. They are expressed in the choice that Paris makes between the gifts proffered by the goddesses: power and fame, wisdom founded on self-restraint, and erotic bliss. Paris's lack of judgement in taking Aphrodite's bribe calls forth Œnone's prophecy of disaster to society through the sins of adultery (as in *Idylls of the King*). Although both the poet and the nymph applaud the ascetic principles of Pallas Athene, the secret of the poem lies in the symbol of Œnone herself, who combines the promise of erotic pleasure with wisdom that leads to power. In the warfare between Sense and Conscience, Tennyson achieves equilibrium, though not stability, for the symbol is genuinely ambivalent. The balance of powers is not guaranteed by any 'objective foundations common to all men'. That the basis of moral action has been defined is only the triumphant illusion of an art that looks neither far out nor in deep. It is the climate of the idyllic mood.

III

The idyllic mood was shattered, and the mask of age became the lineaments of reality. The strategy of memory and desire 'came true'. Word of Arthur Hallam's death in Vienna reached Tennyson at Somersby, Lincolnshire, on 1 October 1833. To Henry Alford, another member of the Apostles Club, it seemed 'a loud and terrible stroke from the reality of things upon the fairy building of our youth'. How much more so to Tennyson, who felt his personal grief re-echoing in every chamber of his being—so closely had he bound his rational doubts to fantasies of loss and death in the strife of Sense and Conscience.

The series of elegiac stanzas that would become *In Memoriam* was begun almost at once. The earliest to appear in J. M. Heath's *Commonplace Book* ('Fair ship, that from the Italian shore') bears the date 'Oct. 6 1833'. The substance of the poem is Tennyson's life, but the formal biographical structure is artificial. Sections written early are set down in the midst of later ones, and the three Christmases and the other anniversaries are formal devices. There is no evidence for supposing that Tennyson actually toiled three years in the cycle of moods through which the poem runs. Nor is the theme of the poem seriously philosophical, as Tennyson was at pains to point out. The 'brief lays, of Sorrow born' reflect only the 'random influences' of controversy.

The theme of *In Memoriam* is loss and the subjective crisis it provokes. For this reason, the poem recapitulates much of Tennyson's previous development: the moods of frustration and longing, the strategy of the mask of age, the issues of sceptical doubt, the question of the poet's involvement in the world of affairs, and the issues of social disorder and social inertia encountered in the political songs. Tennyson was fully aware that his private grief for Arthur Hallam involved his 'passion of the past' and worked its way through all his being:

> Likewise the imaginative woe,
>   That loved to handle spiritual strife,
>   Diffused the shock thro' all my life,
> But in the present broke the blow.

The melancholic temperament upon which Tennyson had boldly erected the structure of his art was now baptized in the experience of real grief. Freud theorized 'that melancholia is in some way related to an unconscious loss of love-object, in contradistinction to mourning, in which there is nothing unconscious about the loss'.[1] Freud's insight would reveal the nature of Tennyson's fixed response to 'the picture and the past', that he idealized in 'Tears, Idle Tears' and stated more explicitly, long afterwards, in 'The Ancient Sage'.

> . . . for oft
> On me, when boy, there came what then I call'd,
> Who knew no books and no philosophies,
> In my boy-phrase, 'The Passion of the Past.'
> The first gray streak of earliest summer-dawn,
> The last long stripe of waning crimson gloom,
> As if the late and early were but one—
> A height, a broken grange, a grove, a flower
> Had murmurs, 'Lost and gone, and lost and gone!'
> A breath, a whisper—some divine farewell—
> Desolate sweetness—far and far away—
> What had he loved, what had he lost, the boy?
> I know not, and I speak of what has been.

This passage leads at once to a description of such a mystical trance as takes the centre of 'Armageddon'. If there is a definitive Tennysonian theme, this is it—a reiterated and dreamlike sense of loss that becomes idyllic self-assurance.

If we suppose such a loss or alienation, Arthur Hallam's role in Tennyson's development would be to clarify the motive in Tennyson's remarkably dependent nature that rendered his mind sluggish in freeing itself from supporting ideas and habits and that made him lean heavily upon his friends, his wife, and his son. It is a supposition that lets us see in Arthur, the symbolic figure of *In Memoriam* and of the *Idylls of the King*, the means by which Tennyson gained some conscious control over his divided nature. The conscious loss of Arthur Hallam enables Tennyson to confront the demon of his temperament. If we are to see in Arthur Hallam a possible surrogate for Tennyson's father,[2] we may better under-

---

[1] *Collected Papers* (1925), iv, p. 155.

[2] Dr. George Clayton Tennyson died in March 1831. Paden thinks it probable that the death of Dr. Tennyson rather than that of Hallam is the personal theme of 'Morte d'Arthur', because it deals with 'the end, not the beginning, of an epoch'. Certainly Hallam's death felt to Tennyson like the end of an

stand what the friendship meant to Tennyson and why the loss of
Hallam seemed more than the death of a friend. Hallam's death
would re-enact the father's death and would arouse again the sense
of guilt that springs from the repression of aggressive impulses,
'the blindfold sense of wrong' that Tennyson finds alien to his
love for Hallam and that yet marks the anniversary of his death 'as
with some hideous crime'. Later, the imaginative reunion with
Hallam might also touch some thrilling overtones of reconciliation with the father. To the degree that the unconscious elements
of melancholia are not entirely resolved in conscious grief, *In
Memoriam* would remain somewhat asymmetrical and strange:

> But there is more than I can see,
> And what I see I leave unsaid,
> Nor speak it, knowing Death has made
> His darkness beautiful with thee.

Because the death of Arthur Hallam is both a real and a symbolic loss that radiates from the centre of Tennyson's art, the tone
of amatory affection which suffuses *In Memoriam* cannot be read as
simple evidence of an erotic relationship in fact between Tennyson
and his friend. It is enough that the loss of Hallam touches Tennyson at every nerve and that the demand for reunion is expressed
with an energy that will not forgo the connotations of physical
bereavement. Hallam himself had emphasized the intimate connection between intense spiritual devotion and erotic expression in his
'Remarks on Professor Rossetti's "Disquisizione sullo spirito
antipapale" ': 'What is the distinguishing character of Hebrew
literature, which separates it by so broad a line of demarcation
from that of every ancient people? Undoubtedly, the sentiment of

---

epoch. But it is not necessary to make a simple choice between the father and
the friend.

Freud's hypothesis would also intimate why *In Memoriam* opens with what
may be a covert allusion to the grave of Tennyson's father (section 2) and
ends not simply with a marriage-song but with the rebirth of a being like
Hallam. And it would clarify the otherwise clouded theme of section 102,
in which 'Two spirits of a diverse love Contend for loving masterdom' as
Tennyson is on the point of leaving the Somersby home. In the face of his
father's ambiguous comment, Hallam Tennyson plainly identified the two
spirits as Alfred's father and Arthur Hallam (*Memoir*, i, p. 72).

To see the function of melancholic sensibility in Tennyson's poetry does
not require, however, that we disentangle the subtle skein of biography, interesting though it is to try.

erotic devotion that pervades it.' Whatever we may choose to call the bond between Tennyson and Hallam, the crisis of *In Memoriam* would not have been induced by the rupture of feelings less complex and profound.

The stages and the achievement of *In Memoriam* are in some respects more clearly visible in those other poems that the death of Hallam almost immediately called forth. 'The Two Voices' (at first called 'Thoughts of a Suicide') bears in the *Poems* of 1842 the significant date '1833'. In J. M. Heath's *Commonplace Book* 'Ulysses' is dated 'Oct: 20 1833', and 'Tithonus', which Tennyson called a 'pendant' to 'Ulysses', was drafted at about the same time, although not published until 1860. 'Morte d'Arthur' was in hand before the end of 1833. Considered together, these poems strongly suggest that Tennyson rapidly passed through the stages projected across a longer scheme of time in *In Memoriam*.

The theme of all these poems that cluster together is loss, frustration, and the need to explore,

> How much of act at human hands
> The sense of human will demands
> By which we dare to live or die.

'The Two Voices', a diffuse debate between Self and Soul, turns on the question of whether life can be endured. The affirmative not easily gained, rests upon 'the heat of inward evidence', like that cry of 'I have felt', in section 124 of *In Memoriam*. The poet then passes into the vernal woods that symbolize his reborn existence. Characteristically, the impulse towards 'suicide' is more fully objectified in the imaginative sympathy that Tennyson shows for the legend of Tithonus. The poem 'Tithonus' is an elaborate and beautiful ritual for release from frustration. If love is withheld, death is desired. Tithonus, caught in the web of memory and desire, appeals for a release no less idyllic than the erotic vision of Aurora that motivates his plea.

'There is more about myself in "Ulysses",' said Tennyson. 'It was more written with the feeling of his loss upon me than many poems in "In Memoriam".' As in 'The Lotos-Eaters', the Ithaca of responsibilities is renounced, this time explicitly, in favour of a voyage into ever-widening 'experience'. But this is not mere experience and it is not true that 'the margin fades, Forever and forever when I move'. Ulysses moves towards a possible reunion, as in the dream-voyage described in *In Memoriam*, section 103, to-wards the Happy Isles and a meeting with 'the great Achilles, whom we knew'. In small compass, Tennyson forecasts the dual answer of *In Memoriam*: life and nature are a continuum extending uninterruptedly towards a spiritual climax; yet at some point the 'lower' material world passes over into the 'higher' spiritual world. The continuum belongs to the world of nature and history; in the subjective vision of reunion with Hallam the poet crosses the bar between two separate spheres.

'Morte d'Arthur' unites the themes of all these poems in Sir Bedivere who must 'go forth companionless', and in the death of King Arthur. Defeated in the material world, he voyages without abrupt transition to the happy island-valley of Avilion. A vision of his return and a dream of reunion with him close the lines which frame the epic fragment.

The theme of reunion is the personal core of *In Memoriam*. It develops in a series of fairly distinct approaches that culminate in the trance-vision in section 95 and the dream of the future in sec-tion 103. In these two lyrics Tennyson contrives to knit the past to the present and the present to the future. The stages of ap-proach to reunion are most clearly defined in sections 41–7, which discuss death as a barrier to reunion, sections 60–5, which suggest that friendship may cross the barrier, and the series of dreams, sections 67–71. These advance painfully, through imagery recall-ing the ominous preludes of 'Armageddon' and 'A Dream of Fair Women', to a sleep, akin 'To death and trance And madness', in which there is 'forged at last'

> A night-long Present of the Past
> In which we went thro' summer France.

After a pause quickened only by the lyrics of spring (83 and 86), the forward movement begins again with vivid recollections of Hallam's presence at Cambridge and at Somersby (87 and 89).

Sections 90–5 achieve reunion with Hallam in the present. The ritual preparation is fastidious. It begins (90) with a passionate invocation—'Ah dear, but come thou back to me'—that is quali-fied (91) by a rejection of mere dreams of the past—'Come: not in watches of the night.' Sections 92 and 93 refuse to invoke a stage-phantom, 'a wind Of memory murmuring the past'. Tenny-son thus invites the return of a mystical disclosure, and section 94

E   57

is symbolic lustration. Then, in the moonlight on the lawn of
Somersby (95), in the midst of images from memory,

> The dead man touch'd me from the past,
> And all at once it seem'd at last
> The living soul was flash'd on mine . . .

>   . . . at length my trance
> Was cancell'd, stricken thro' with doubt.

In 'the doubtful dusk' of dawn, the breeze that had trembled in
'In Deep and Solemn Dreams' shakes sycamore and elms, and dies
away at the talismanic hour when

> East and West, without a breath,
> Mixt their dim lights, like life and death. . . .

The lyrics concerning Tennyson's departure from Somersby
are crowned by the dream (103) that blends many elements of
Tennyson's poetry and merges the present in the future. The Hall
with a river flowing past recalls 'The Lady of Shalott' and 'The
Palace of Art'. The 'summons from the sea' and the poet's voyage
with maidens down the river towards the sea have affinities with
'Ulysses', 'Morte d'Arthur', 'Locksley Hall', and 'Crossing the
Bar'. The magic of the dream increases,

> Until the forward-creeping tides
>   Began to foam, and we to draw
>   From deep to deep, to where we saw
> A great ship lift her shining sides.

> The man we loved was there on deck,
>   But thrice as large as man he bent
>   To greet us. Up the side I went,
> And fell in silence on his neck . . .

Although the reunion with Hallam's spirit is imperfect and
consequently demands renewal (for example, in section 122), Hallam becomes the symbolic thread that knits Tennyson's world of
experience together again. Section 103 is followed at once by the
'third Christmas' lyrics (104, 105) that renounce the observance of
'an ancient form Thro' which the spirit breathes no more'. The
New Year song (section 106) celebrates instead 'the Christ that is
to be'; and section 107 ('It is the day when he was born') estab-

lishes the observance of Hallam's nativity. The remaining lyrics of *In Memoriam* are the apotheosis of Hallam as 'herald of a higher race' who redeems from doubt and pain the intellectual difficulties that had joined in the train of personal grief.

If the nature of Tennyson's subjective crisis had made him unusually sensitive to the moral implications of the revolution that was occurring in art, in society, in science, and in history, the loss of Hallam had quickened that awareness. He perceived the approach of Darwinian materialism and the rising class struggle as outward manifestations of that loss of values which he had suffered in his own life. Unsanctified by tradition and lacking 'objective foundations' in common morality, the scientific view of nature and the liberal position in politics resolve the conflict between good and evil into a mere struggle for existence and cast the artist to the mercy of his impressions:

> This round of green, this orb of flame,
> Fantastic beauty; such as lurks
> In some wild Poet, when he works
> Without a conscience or an aim.

The full weight of modern knowledge, 'Submitting all things to desire', seemed cast into the balance on the side of sense. In the dialectic of his poetry, Tennyson had rendered himself fully responsive to the attractions of materialism and of a monistic ontology, most visibly in 'The Lotos-Eaters', to which he could not commit himself. If art, nature, and history are empty of a higher will,

> 'Twere best at once to sink to peace,
> Like birds the charming serpent draws,
> To drop head-foremost in the jaws
> Of vacant darkness and to cease.

But when he finds darkness 'made beautiful' by reunion with Hallam, that friend becomes the 'higher hand' that frees knowledge from the bonds of sense.

Yet, as 'Ulysses' showed, Tennyson's answer to the intellectual difficulties that he faced is paradoxical. He tries to accept the materialist–monistic continuum of nature and of history as a scale upon which evil is merely historical process. Ends justify the means, and evil is redeemed in the evolutionary faith,

That all, as in some piece of art,
Is toil coöperant to an end.

At some point the material cosmos is to sail smoothly and imperceptibly across into the realm of spirit. The presence of spiritual
and 'higher' values renders the materialist continuum tolerable,
yet at times unendurable. A thoroughly material progress was not
the answer to Tennyson's needs, and he spurns a purely evolutionary faith in 'the greater ape', whose scheme of values gave no
room to the qualities that endeared Arthur Hallam to his friend.
The 'far-off divine event' could not happen in the Malthusian
world of Huxley and Darwin.

The material world must be, at length, defeated; the great result
of time must be negated. The Battle in the West and the defeat of
Arthur herald his departure into the happy island of Avilion. The
way to transcendental values lies through loss, death, and defeat.
No accumulation of material advances can leap the transcendental
barrier. Tennyson is tossed between the wealthy attractions of
materialistic monism and the dualistic demands of his subjective
strife and system of values. The world of nature can be sanctified
only by another and a higher. At least once, he got the paradox
fully stated:

Dear friend, far off, my lost desire,
    So far, so near in woe and weal;
    O loved the most, when most I feel
There is a lower and a higher;

Known and unknown; human, divine;
    Sweet human hand and lips and eye;
    Dear heavenly friend that canst not die,
Mine, mine, for ever, ever mine;

Strange friend, past, present, and to be;
    Loved deeplier, darklier understood;
    Behold, I dream a dream of good,
And mingle all the world with thee.

The irredeemable flaw of Tennyson's poetry is that he habitually weakens and dulls his perception of this paradox. Because he
could sometimes make the transcendental leap in his own experience, he is bemused into regarding it as an objective truth common to all men. Thus he inclines to further in his art the idyllic

mood rather than the tragic perspectives that a genuine dualism might have afforded. Nevertheless, the tragic view develops, almost surreptitiously, in the themes of defeat and disaster that dominate *Idylls of the King* and even the plays. Without the constant support of any traditional systems of value, Tennyson contrived to face, and in part to comprehend, the problem of tragedy in modern art. No English poet explored more widely the range of possibilities that had closed.

IV

Tennyson is a modern poet, also, in his attempt to provide the personal themes of *In Memoriam* with a formal structure responsive to both private instinct and the elegiac traditions. His attempt embodies in practical form the question of the artist's involvement or non-involvement in the life of his culture. Tennyson withholds himself from the objective form of the pastoral elegy and at the same time he draws upon its inherent strength. *In Memoriam* was undertaken 'for his own relief and private satisfaction', and was anonymously published. Yet it is, of course, an enormously ambitious work, and imbedded in its discursive and informal manner are many of the traditional elegiac conventions. It opens with a formal invocation to a higher power and closes with an epithalamium. It describes the funeral procession (the voyage of the ship returning Hallam's body to England) and the mourning of nature, which is a kind of death. The poet himself represents the mourners. In accordance with the sophisticated tradition of the elegy, Tennyson launches forth on sober and noble themes, both personal and general, concerning the meaning of history, the nature of nature, and his personal destiny as man and as poet. The poem draws to a close with a lengthy apotheosis that dismisses the mood of grief, settles the perplexities, and issues upon a higher plane.

The presence of these traditional elements helps Tennyson in playing out the ritual of his private grief and in giving it objective form. Under the personal theme lie the ancient elegiac conventions, and through them the poem observes a simple, pastoral ritual of the cycle of the year: the death and reawakening of nature. This 'natural piety' underlies the comparatively superficial time-scheme of three years and is organically related to the theme of loss and reunion. It is adumbrated rather than announced. The death of nature is symbolized by the autumn and winter imagery dominating the allusions to nature in the poem as far as section 83, by the mournful observances of Christ's nativity (sections 28–30, 78), and by the commemoration (section 72) of the 'disastrous day' of Hallam's death. Section 83, a sudden invocation of spring, initiates the series of springtime poems (sections 86, 88, 89, 115, 116) that light the way towards reunion with Hallam and his apotheosis. As the statesman that he might have become, Hallam symbolizes that 'life in civic action warm' that may turn society from its wavering course. He also represents that wisdom of a 'higher hand' that must control the results of scientific and practical 'Knowledge'. Hallam's efficacy as a symbol that 'touches into leaf' the issues that had been filled with pain and death depends on the subjective experiences which revivified Tennyson's universe of values. The experience of loss itself became endeared as the prelude to reunion:

> That out of distance might ensue
> Desire of nearness doubly sweet,
> And unto meeting, when we meet,
> Delight a hundredfold accrue . . .

The cycle of nature is completed, and into the future is projected the passion of the past. The marriage-song that finishes the poem can welcome again the imagery of living nature and the conception of a child whose birth is the rebirth of Hallam and of Tennyson.

Beyond this achievement Tennyson could not or did not go. In his individual experience he had not found the objective foundations that he required. This he sometimes recognized and sometimes forgot. When he forgot, he became facile, sentimental, and mechanical, though there are few poems in which the pulse of uncertainty does not stir at all. The history of his career after 1850—indeed, almost from 1833 onwards—is basically a recapitulation of his earlier developments. Even *Idylls of the King*, defaced in parts by his delusions of certainty, was a project which he had begun to conceive before the death of Hallam. It is a poem, on the warfare of Sense and Soul, that is wrenched from its idyllic oversimplifications into a study of erotic and mystical motives and the disintegration of an ideal society. The defect and the nature of the poem are manifest in its strange hero, who does not himself embody the conflicting values but shares them with Lancelot.

Because he did not really advance towards 'solutions', and because he reached in *In Memoriam* the clearest apprehension of his own nature that he was capable of, Tennyson's later poetry does not break from the pattern of his past. This is why he could revise his early work, as he did for the *Poems* of 1842, with as much grace and tact as if he were still in the midst of writing it for the first time; he had not moved beyond it. With thorough integrity he could publish in his later books some poems written long before and could introduce passages of this early work into poems written a half-century later. The persistence of his motives brings his later poetry back to the inescapable themes: in 'The Ancient Sage' he returns to the debate of 'The Two Voices', in 'Lucretius' to the fierce and open warfare between erotic and conscientious impulses, in 'Demeter and Persephone' to the ritual of the death and reawakening of nature, in 'Crossing the Bar' to the dream-voyages of 'Morte d'Arthur' and *In Memoriam*, and in his last book to 'The Death of Œnone'. Force of habit sometimes dulled, sometimes strengthened, his artistry.

The Tennysonian theme is frustration, and his poetry offers an analysis of its symptoms rather than the cure. What is overcome through the elaborate strategies of dream and vision is not the frustration but the disappointment that follows it. It is a poetry of illusions, some painful, some happy, none of them wearing the ultimate authority of reality. The recurrent pattern is a transition through death, loss, or dream towards ideal moods that dissolve the edges of thought and appetite. Under such illusions, Tennyson sometimes mistakes the sense of relief for the signs of truth. But because the sources of his poetry lay, finally, beyond his control, he could not get free of what is genuine as well as painful.

What saved him, at last, was that he felt his predicament even if he did not thoroughly comprehend it. He saw the crisis of art and society as a war of values, a matter of conscience. He does not theorize about it nor arrive at systematic principles. Yet in viewing the function and origin of conscience, he offers a more complex and subtler insight than T. H. Huxley, who supposed conscience to be merely a social monitor, the inner voice of social obligations. For Tennyson, it is more primitive and more powerful, arising in partly unconscious levels of the mind and presenting to the reason and the will an ambiguous scene of unreconciled motives and values. In Tennyson's anatomy of conscience, our human action upon nature and society meets a crisis of the divided will, which cannot be healed until it frees itself from fantasy and despair. That freedom Tennyson could not really win. His failure accurately represents the continuing crisis of our culture.

Walt Whitman, who liked Tennyson, discerned that 'his very doubts, swervings, doublings upon himself, have been typical of our age'. The price that Tennyson pays for being a 'representative' poet is great. He suffers our disease and our confusion. He triumphs not as a master but as a victim. It is a vicarious role, and upon him we heap our detested sins. If the circumstances of his breeding, his generation, and his temperament had made him a convert to Catholicism, socialism, or theosophy, he might have written more interestingly to us. He might have been admired to the extent that he escaped the general malaise. But he kept to the mid-stream of his culture. As a result, he works out remorselessly the fatal consequences of the romantic tradition, bankrupts its style by his lavish expenditures, and reduces its intellectual ambitions to the accidents of individual perceptions and personal blindness. After him the deluge, the spreading chaos of 'modern art'. He is one of its makers.

There is no Tennyson tragedy. The themes of frustration can scarcely amount to that, and the tragic order of values is lacking. Besides, the victim himself, though not our father, turns out to be a well-remembered uncle, and no hero. Yet there was in him, as Hawthorne instantly perceived, 'the something not to be meddled with', as he moved with the shuffling gait of a man whose injury cannot be healed and who makes of it, by force of will, the secret of his strength.

1950

II

Tennyson In Artistic Contexts

TENNYSON AND PICTURESQUE
POETRY

H. M. McLuhan

IN HIS *Autobiographies* W. B. Yeats mentions that a great advantage
which he enjoyed over his fellows of the Cheshire Cheese was his
acquaintance with Arthur Hallam's review of Tennyson's poems
(*The Englishman's Magazine*, 1831). Hallam's essay is worth close
study. It is a manifesto as decisive in the issues it raises as Wordsworth's Preface to *Lyrical Ballads* or Mr. Eliot's 'Tradition and the
Individual Talent'. In 1895 Yeats found it invaluable as a key to
the French symbolists who were puzzling his friends. Had it been
understood in 1831 the energies of the Pre-Raphaelites might have
found more direct channels to what in English poetry did not
occur until the advent of Joyce, Pound, and Eliot.

Hallam's essay suggests that from his meeting with Tennyson
at Trinity in 1829 until his death in 1833 his intense aesthetic interests were of the greatest importance to Tennyson's development as a poet. Until 1842 Tennyson seems to have retained Hallam's insights exclusively. Thereafter he began to admit rhetoric
and reflection into his verse, wonderfully purging this admixture
from the great 'Rizpah' of 1880 and from several subsequent
poems.

Hallam's aesthetic theory was the result of studying Dante
through the poetry of Keats. But the extraordinary precision and

elaboration of English impressionist criticism and speculation, which had persisted from the 1780s, was still there to sharpen perception and judgement in 1830. The main effort of speculation had been directed towards landscape painting, for reasons which will be mentioned later on. All the Romantic poets were nurtured in this speculation; but Hallam's essay draws into a sharp focus some of the neglected implications for poetry:

> Whenever the mind of the artist suffers itself to be occupied, during its periods of creation, by any other predominant motive than the desire of beauty, the result is false in art.

Of course, he goes on, there may be states of mind in which thought and reflection are themselves unified by intellectual emotion:

> But though possible, it is hardly probable: for a man whose reveries take a reasoning turn, and who is accustomed to measure his ideas by their logical relations rather than the congruity of the sentiments to which they refer, will be apt to mistake the pleasure he has in knowing a thing to be true, for the pleasure he would have in knowing it to be beautiful, and so will pile his thoughts in a rhetorical battery, that they may convince, instead of letting them flow in a natural course of contemplation, that they may enrapture. It would not be difficult to show, by reference to the most admired poems of Wordsworth, that he is frequently chargeable with this error; and that much has been said by him which is good as philosophy, powerful as rhetoric, but false as poetry.

This passage arrives at once at the twentieth-century controversy over poetry and beliefs. It implies the Symbolist and Imagist doctrine that the place of ideas in poetry is not that of logical enunciation but of immediate sensation or experience. Rhetoric must go, said the symbolists. Ideas as ideas must go. They may return as part of a landscape that is ordered by other means. They may enter into a unified experience as one kind of fact. They may contribute to an aesthetic emotion, not as a system of demonstration but as part of a total order which is to be contemplated.

So Hallam pronounces in favour of the Cockney School over 'the Lakers':

We shall not hesitate to express our conviction, that the cock-ney school (as it was termed in derision from a cursory view of its accidental circumstances) contained more genuine inspira-tion, and adhered more steadily to that portion of truth which it embraced, than any *form* of art that has existed in this country since Milton ... Shelley and Keats were indeed of opposite genius; the one was vast, impetuous, and sublime, the other ... does not generalize or allegorize nature; his imagination works with few symbols, and reposes willingly on what is freely given ... They are both poets of sensation rather than reflection ... Rich and clear were their perceptions of visible forms; full and deep their <u>feelings of music</u>. So vivid was the delight attending the simple exertions of eye and ear, that it became mingled more and more with their trains of active thought, and tended to absorb their whole being into the energy of sense. Other poets seek for images to illustrate their conceptions; these men had no need to seek; they lived in a world of images; for the most important and extensive portion of their life consisted in those emotions which are immediately conversant with sensa-tion ... Hence they are not descriptive, they are picturesque.

The force of this last antithesis depends on knowledge of the aesthetic developments of the eighteenth century, which are sum-marized in Christopher Hussey's classic *The Picturesque* (1927). 'The picturesque view of nature,' says Hussey, 'led towards the abstract appreciation of colour and light that in painting marks the work of Turner and Constable.' At the end of the epoch of picturesque experiment and exploration there is Cézanne in paint-ing, and Rimbaud in poetry. That is, the impressionists began with sensation, discovered 'abstraction', and achieved, finally, a meta-physical art. The picturesque begins with work like Thomson's *Seasons*, in the search for significant art-emotion amidst natural scenes; and it achieved plenary realization in Rimbaud's meta-physical landscapes—*Les Illuminations*. The early Romantics sought aesthetic emotion in natural scenes; the later Romantics confidently evoked art-emotion from art-situations. The early Romantics ransacked nature, as the Pre-Raphaelites did literature and history, for situations which would provide moments of in-tense perception. The Symbolists went to work more methodic-ally. As A. N. Whitehead showed, the great discovery of the nineteenth century was not this or that fact about nature, but the discovery of the technique of invention, so that modern science can now discover whatever it needs to discover. And Rimbaud and Mallarmé, following the lead of Edgar Poe's aesthetic, made the same advance in poetic technique that Whitehead pointed out in the physical sciences. The new method is to work backwards from the particular effect to the objective correlative or poetic means of evoking that precise effect, just as the chemist begins with the end-product and then seeks the formula which will produce it. Mr. Eliot states this discovery, which has guided his own poetic activity since 1910 or so, in his essay on *Hamlet*:

> The only way of expressing emotion in the form of art is by finding an 'objective correlative'; in other words, a set of objects, a situation, a chain of events which shall be the formula of that *particular* emotion; such that when the external facts, which must terminate in sensory experience, are given, the emotion is immediately evoked.

Mr. Eliot is saying *à propos* of 'sensory experience' exactly what Hallam was saying about Shelley and Keats: 'They are both poets of sensation rather than reflection.' Clearly Hallam is setting them above Wordsworth in tendency rather than achievement. And the tendency which he approves in them is precisely what we have more recently come to consider as the 'unification of sensibility'. Hallam refused to accept the magnificent rhetoric of Wordsworth as a substitute for such an integral poetry. That such integrity was possible he was sure, because of the poetry of Keats especially. We have the achievement of Joyce, Yeats, Pound, and Eliot to assure us not only that Hallam was entirely right but that Keats had not gone far enough.

What must have been the effect of Tennyson's five years of such conversation and study with Hallam? The volumes of 1830 and 1833 try to surpass Keats in richness of texture and sensuous impact. And 'Mariana' is there to prove that the most sophisticated symbolist poetry could be written fifty years before the Symbolists. On a dependent and uncertain temper such as Tennyson's the effect of the death of the vigorous and clear-headed Hallam was not merely that of personal loss. It was more nearly the loss of his poetic insight and his critical judgement.

Hallam's essay goes on to define the kind of poetry which his age demanded, and which Tennyson was later to provide in such abundance:

> Since then this demand on the reader for activity, when he wants to peruse his author in a luxurious passiveness, is the very thing that moves his bile, it is obvious that those writers will be always most popular who require the least degree of exertion. Hence, whatever is mixed up with art, and appears under its semblance, is always more favourably regarded than art free and unalloyed. Hence, half the fashionable poems in the world are mere rhetoric and half the remainder are, perhaps, not liked by the generality for their substantial merits. Hence, likewise, of the really pure compositions, those are most universally agreeable which take for their primary subject the usual passions of the heart, and deal with them in a simple state, without applying the transforming powers of high imagination. Love, friendship, ambition, religion, etc., are matters of daily experience even amongst unimaginative tempers. The forces of association, therefore, are ready to work in these directions, and little effort of will is necessary to follow the artist. For the same reason, such subjects often excite a partial power of composition, which is no sign of a truly poetic organization. We are very far from wishing to depreciate this class of poems, whose influence is so extensive, and communicates so refined a pleasure. We contend only that the facility with which its impressions are communicated is no proof of its elevation as a form of art, but rather the contrary.

Hallam is insisting, just as much later Mallarmé, Eliot, and Valéry were to insist, that in 'pure poetry', the poetry of suggestion rather than statement, or poetry in which the statements are themselves suggestions and in which the poetic form is the mode of the creative process itself, the reader is co-creator with the poet; since the *effect* depends on the reader's precision of response, and the poet is himself only another reader of his own poetry. So that Harold Nicolson showed himself unaware of this class of poetry, which is often present in Tennyson, when he remarked that 'of all poets, Tennyson should be read very carelessly nor not at all'.

When Hallam finally turns to introduce Tennyson, he makes claims which the modern critic is now prepared to accept with little modification:

Mr. Tennyson belongs decidedly to the class we have already described as Poets of Sensation . . . We have remarked five distinctive excellences of his own manner. First, his luxuriance of imagination, and at the same time, his control over it. Secondly, his power of embodying himself in ideal characters or rather moods of character, with such extreme accuracy of adjustment, that the circumstances of the narration seem to have a natural correspondence with the predominant feeling, and, as it were, to be evolved from it by assimilative force. Thirdly, his vivid, picturesque delineation of objects, and the peculiar skill with which he holds all of them *fused*, to borrow a metaphor from science, in a medium of strong emotion. Fourthly, the variety of his lyrical measures, and exquisite modulation of harmonious words and cadences to the swell and fall of the feelings expressed. Fifthly, the elevated habits of thought, implied in these compositions, and imparting a mellow soberness of tone, more impressive to our minds, than if the author had drawn up a set of opinions in verse, and sought to instruct the understanding rather than to communicate the love of beauty to the heart.

The fact that Tennyson is in great measure a landscape poet led Hallam to define him in 1831 by the then technical term 'picturesque'. In 1897 Francis Palgrave, another intimate acquaintance, published *Landscape in Poetry from Homer to Tennyson*. It is a poor book, lacking in technical and critical insights, but it makes plain the kind of traditional perspective in which Tennyson set his craftsman's interest in the problem of landscape.

From the first of Thomson's *Seasons* (1726) to the *Lyrical Ballads* of Wordsworth and Coleridge (1798) English landscape art in paint, poetry, and prose had undergone a very great technical development, which was also a growth of awareness at once psychological and naturalistic. Scientific observation and psychological experience met in landscape. Shelley, Keats, and Tennyson, as well as Ruskin and the Pre-Raphaelites, were not only quite conscious of these eighteenth-century discoveries, but set themselves the task of further advance along the same lines. It might be suggested that landscape offered several attractive advantages to the poets of the mid-eighteenth century. It meant for one thing an extension of the Baroque interest in *la peinture de la pensée*, which the study of Seneca had suggested to Montaigne and Bacon and

Browne—an interest which reached a maximal development, so far as the technique of direct statement permitted, in Pascal, Racine, and Alexander Pope.

But landscape offered a broader and less exacting course for those who were preoccupied with the new psychological interests on one hand and with means of evading the new insistence on non-metaphorical and mathematical statement as the mode of poetry, on the other hand. With Blake there are many moments when the new landscape interests and techniques are fused with the wit and paradox of Pope. But his success passed unnoticed until it had been reduplicated by the Symbolists. Wordsworth, Shelley, Keats, and Tennyson typically use landscape without the precision and wit provided by apposition of situation without copula. They achieve an exclusive rather than an inclusive consciousness.

Looking back over the landscape developments of a century and more, Ruskin in introducing the Pre-Raphaelites in 1851 summed up what was a commonplace to Wordsworth in 1798 and also to Tennyson in 1830:

> The sudden and universal Naturalism, or inclination to copy ordinary natural objects, which manifested itself among the painters of Europe, at the moment when the invention of printing superseded their legendary labours, was no false instinct. It was misunderstood and misapplied, but it came at the right time, and has maintained itself through all kinds of abuse; presenting in the recent schools of landscape, perhaps only the first fruits of its power. That instinct was urging every painter in Europe at the same moment to his true duty—*the faithful representation of all objects of historical interest, or of natural beauty existent at the period*; representation such as might at once aid the advance of sciences, and keep faithful record of every monument of past ages which was likely to be swept away in the approaching eras of revolutionary change.

This amalgam of moral duty, aesthetic experience, scientific discovery, and political revolution was first effected in the age of Leibniz, Locke, and Newton; and we are still engaged today in contemplating its unpredictable derivatives. For the moment, and in the arts, the terminus appears as the fascinating landscapes of *Finnegans Wake* and *Four Quartets*. So that, if we take our bearings with reference to this new work, it will be easier to assess the intentions and achievement of Tennyson, whose work falls just midway between that of James Thomson and Mr. Eliot. The huge tapestries of the *Wake* are not merely visual but auditory, talking and moving pictures; not just spatial in their unity, but effecting a simultaneous presence of all modes of human consciousness, primitive and sophisticated. Rocks, rivers, trees, animals, persons, and places utter with classical dramatic decorum the kind of being that is theirs. The poet in effacing himself utterly has become a universal Aeolian Harp reverberating the various degrees of knowledge and existence in such a hymn of life as only the stars of Pythagoras were ever conceived to have sung. To this concert there came all the arts and sciences, trivial and quadrivial, ancient and modern, in an orchestrated harmony that had first been envisaged by Joyce's master Stéphane Mallarmé.

Flaubert and Baudelaire had presided over the great city landscape of *Ulysses*. And Mr. Eliot's *The Waste Land* in 1922 was a new technical modulation of *Ulysses*, the latter of which had begun to appear in 1917. The *Quartets* owe a great deal to the *Wake*, as does *The Cocktail Party*. There is in all these works a vision of the community of men and creatures which is not so much ethical as metaphysical. And it had been, in poetry, due to the technical innovations of Baudelaire, Laforgue, and Rimbaud that it was possible to render this vision immediately in verse without the extraneous aids of rhetoric or logical reflection and statement. The principal innovation was that of *le paysage intérieur* or the psychological landscape. This landscape, by means of discontinuity, which was first developed in picturesque painting, effected the apposition of widely diverse objects as a means of establishing what Mr. Eliot has called 'an objective correlative' for a state of mind. The openings of 'Prufrock', 'Gerontion', and *The Waste Land* illustrate Mr. Eliot's growth in the adaptation of this technique, as he passed from the influence of Laforgue to that of Rimbaud, from personal to impersonal manipulation of experience. Whereas in external landscape diverse things lie side by side, so in psychological landscape the juxtaposition of various things and experiences becomes a precise musical means of orchestrating that which could never be rendered by systematic discourse. Landscape is the means of presenting, without the copula of logical enunciation, experiences which are united in existence but not in conceptual thought. Syntax becomes music, as in Tennyson's 'Mariana'.

In the landscapes of the *Quartets* as in those of the *Wake* everything speaks. There is no single or personal speaker of the *Quartets*, not even the Tiresias of 'Gerontion' and *The Waste Land*. It is the places and things which utter themselves. And this is also a stage of technique and experience achieved by Pound in his *Cantos*, and by St. Jean Perse, just as it had earlier been reached by Mallarmé in *Un Coup de Dés*. Browning was groping for it in *The Ring and the Book*. One might say that as the effect of Laforgue had been to open Mr. Eliot's mind to the effects of Donne and the Metaphysicals, so the effect of Rimbaud was to make him more fully aware of the means by which Dante achieved a zoning of states of mind through symbolic landscape.

Facing this unrivalled sophistication and self-awareness of metaphysical landscape in modern poetry, it is easier to observe what the eighteenth century was striving for as well as what effects Wordsworth, Coleridge, and their successors were interested in obtaining. Hitherto the eighteenth century has been examined in retrospect from Wordsworth and Coleridge rather than from Keats and Tennyson. The Lake poets have often been supposed to have exhausted its potencies and to have settled its problems. Such, however, was not the view of Arthur Hallam and Alfred Tennyson. But looked at now across the work of Cézanne and Rimbaud it takes on a different and more impressive character than has usually been allowed it aesthetically. And today we are far from having explored the speculations of Burke and Blake, or even of Knight and Price. What is put forward here as a suggested view of the eighteenth-century attitude to landscape has primarily relevance to what became Tennyson's idea of the function of landscape in poetry. For Tennyson, while accepting much of Wordsworth, certainly differed from him in important respects.

It is plain, for example, that Tennyson did not agree with the author of *The Prelude* in expecting an automatic amelioration of the human condition from the workings of external landscape on passive childhood, youth, and age. Tennyson could see very little valuable truth in Wordsworth's programme for the recovery of a terrestrial paradise. He had many reasons for thinking it what Wordsworth incredulously queried in the preface to *The Excursion*:

> A history only of departed things,
> Or a mere fiction of what never was?

Then Wordsworth takes up the great eighteenth-century theme:

> For the discerning intellect of Man,
> When wedded to this goodly universe
> In love and holy passion, shall find these
> [i.e. 'Paradise and groves']
> A simple produce of the common day,
> I, long before the blissful hour arrives,
> Would chant, in lonely peace, the spousal verse
> Of this great consummation:—and, by words
> Which speak of nothing more than what we are,
> Would I arouse the sensual from their sleep
> Of Death, and win the vacant and the vain
> To noble raptures; while my voice proclaims
> How exquisitely the individual Mind
>   ... to the external World
> Is fitted:—and how exquisitely, too—
> Theme this but little heard of among men—
> The external World is fitted to the Mind;

the notion of this pre-established harmony between the individual mind and the external world is the key to the eighteenth-century passion for landscape. Wordsworth naturally underrates the degree to which this 'theme' was rehearsed among men from 1730 onwards, if only because anybody tends to be least aware of the decades immediately before his own time. They are taken for granted, as known. For by then the civilized world had much recovered from the dismay felt by Pascal and his contemporaries at the vision of an infinity of worlds, and had begun to speculate on the possible psychological nexus between man and a geometrically perfect universe. They turned from reflection on man's wretched insignificance to the thought of his sublimity of comprehension, by a simple reversal of the telescope.

Swift spotted the human vanity in the workings of this psychological mechanism and spoofed it at once in *Gulliver's Travels*, but without disturbing the course towards which things were shaping. For it was to be in the main a century of simple psychological mechanisms which were not to break down until Malthus and Darwin had shifted attention to the biological level. It was Leibniz who, as Professor Lovejoy suggests, translated the cosmological

76

and mathematical views of his time into psychological terms. The hierarchy of creatures in his monadology 'is defined primarily in psychological rather than morphological terms; it is by the levels of consciousness which severally characterize them, the degrees of adequacy and clarity with which they "mirror" or represent the rest of the universe, that the monads are differentiated'.

As soon as Newton had added to this view the proof that the universe which we (or rocks, trees, flowers) mirror is a marvel of automatic precision, the road is clear to Wordsworth's therapeutic idea of the educational power of the external world. For it was not enough to know that the mind of man is exquisitely fitted to the external world. It was also necessary to be sure that the external world was exquisitely harmonious with itself. It naturally follows for the early Wordsworth and Coleridge that the best mirrors of the radiant universe of life are those simple, spontaneous natures who have received the least admixture of social artifice and corruption. For it is the necessary operation of traditional society to implant within our natures 'a universe of death'. It has been not uncommon to accept not only this phrase from *The Prelude* but Wordsworth's poetic as expressive of a revulsion from the Newtonian world of science. Professor Willey, for example, says that Wordsworth's 'more positive beliefs, those by which he appears in reaction against the scientific tradition, were built up by him out of his own poetic experiences . . . to animize the "real" world, the "universe of death" that the "mechanical" system of philosophy had produced, but to do so without either using an exploded mythology or fabricating a new one, this was the special task and mission of Wordsworth'.

But neither Wordsworth nor Tennyson rejected science as presenting a 'universe of death'. For if they had done so there would have been no predominance of landscape in their aesthetics, and, most pertinently, there would have been none of Tennyson's celebrated 'accuracy' of observation and description, which, of course, can be matched in the painters and in poets like Barnes and Hopkins. Rather, in their view, science and poetry were near twins, of which poetry was a little the elder. And *The Prelude* passage (Book xiv) not only locates the 'universe of death' as a product of divided aims, selfish passions, mean cares and low pursuits, but goes on to contrast it with that which moves with light and life informed,

Actual, divine, and true.

It is the objective world observed by science and mirrored by simple, loving souls which Wordsworth sets over against the toy-shop of vanities that is the soul of man, sensual and dark, under the régime of social custom and private egotism.

The study and discipline of the passions had from the time of Aristotle's *Rhetoric* been a branch of that art. It was the business of the orator to enlist the passions for political ends; and the function of literature was to enlarge, purge, and order the passions for the exercise and solace of the good life. Dr. Johnson was simply expressing this view when he said of Richardson that 'he teaches the passions to move at the command of virtue'. It is important for a grasp of the meaning of landscape in the eighteenth century to see that traditional politics and literature were, in contemporary opinion, being supplanted by science. Men took readily to the notion that the disordered passions of the human heart might be restored to their pristine integrity by the automatic and unconscious operation of landscape on the passive mind—especially when a Newton had guaranteed the exquisite mathematical order of the external world.

The first published essay of Edmund Burke was his ironical *Vindication of Natural Society* (1756), which ridicules the deistic doctrines of Bolingbroke while appearing to utter them. Burke built no political hopes on the new idea that a true social harmony would be born of the direct operation of external nature on the passions of men. Nor could he accept the deistic verdict on human history as an artificial pageant of blood and butcheries perpetrated by 'a few, mad, designing, or ambitious priests'. But he was too intelligent a man of his time not to have made psychology the ground of his inquiry into the origin of our ideas of *The Sublime and The Beautiful*. For that age was committed by its science to the testing of art and external nature as a school of the affections, with landscape art, in particular, cast in the role of teacher of men. The artifice and guile of traditional oratory, art, and politics were to be supplanted by the practice of the contemplation and recollection of the external creation which speaks directly to the human heart.

That Burke's treatise had the greatest effect on the later eighteenth century is admitted by historians. Its influence on Coleridge and Poe, and through them on Baudelaire and the Symbolists, still deserves to be traced very carefully. For its speculations on the nature and effect of landscape art serve to unify the development of poetry from James Thomson to the present. It is in this treatise that are to be found the definitions of 'state of mind' in art, of 'emotions of the mind', of aesthetic emotion, objective correlative, and of the relation between beauty and melancholy as used later by Coleridge, Poe, and Baudelaire. Burke arrived by a single stride at the position that the cognitive process was also the creative process. And it is that awareness in Cézanne and Mallarmé, as later in Joyce and Eliot, which produced the doctrine and practice of 'significant form' in modern art. That this same notion of form was apprehended by Arthur Hallam is plain in the passage already quoted from him concerning Tennyson's *fusion* of objects in the medium of a predominant emotion. Hallam could have had this from Coleridge, but he knew Burke directly.

From the dream of universal social therapy and regeneration which Wordsworth and Coleridge had at first accepted as a necessary consequence of submission of the heart to the pure messages of the external world, Coleridge awakened with his 'Dejection: An Ode' in 1802. The Aeolian lute in his window, type of the poet and the faithful medium of the voices of the external world, now tells him not of the enchantment of a prospective Elysium, but of torture, Devil's yule, and

> of the rushing of an host in rout,
> With groans of trampled men . . .

If Shelley perhaps persisted in the cosmic optimism, Keats did not. He knew the beauty of the natural order, and the beauty of art, but also the human

> Weariness, the fever, and the fret
> Here, where men sit and hear each other groan . . .

There had been not only the wreck of the French Revolution, but the vision of the 'hungry generations' in the doctrine of Malthus and the first fruits of the industrial towns to digest by this time. There had come the end of the notion of the external universe as a great clock which could order the inner passions of those who fed their minds on landscape in a wise passiveness. Nature was soon to be officially accepted as 'red in tooth and claw', and the age of private enterprise to get under way. Biological automatism was ready to take over educational and political theory after a century of psychological automatism. Byron, however, was the appointed spokesman of disenchantment with the Newtonian sleep, which had sealed the spirits of the landscape idolators, when he proclaimed himself 'a link reluctant in a fleshly chain'. He was not in the least charmed by the great deist doctrine that 'I live not in myself but I become portion of that around me'. And he gave a cue and a credo to the new race of aristocratic dandies from Lytton to Disraeli, Poe, Baudelaire, and Wilde. They took up again the burden of individual consciousness which had been systematically relinquished in the first landscape era. And it is this which links them to the Augustans. The young Tennyson was a bohemian devotee of Byron. The young Arnold was a dandified gentleman, whose muse deserted him with his dandyism. It is hard to see how there could have been any nutriment for the development of Wordsworth's poetic sensibility along his first lines in a milieu that had suddenly abandoned Newton and cosmic automatism. Faced with an equally dramatic reversal of milieu, W. B. Yeats remade himself as a poet. Wordsworth instead settled down to edit his own work.

It was in this milieu that Tennyson was shaped as a poet. His predecessors, expecting to be made whole, had immersed themselves in a cosmic landscape bath certified by Newton. His contemporaries had begun to suspect that the bath was poisoned. His successors, such as Hardy, were sure it was.

When the eighteenth century plunged into the cosmic landscape it was consciously and scientifically seeking to reunite itself with primal energies from which it felt remote. The dim past, the age-old face of the earth, the primitive, the child-like, the pastoral were alike landscapes in which the sophisticated sought to merge themselves. But this merging was also, for civilized men, an act of symbolic suicide, a wilful extinction of personality. So that there is over the eighteenth century both the light of natural reason and a cloud of intense melancholy, which led the French to call eighteenth-century England the 'land of spleen and suicide'. (Karl Polanyi's *The Great Transformation* traces the effect of the Newtonian and deist doctrines of cosmic harmony on the idea of a self-regulating market in land, labour, and capital. Quite unaware of the artistic parallels, Polanyi's work is yet of the greatest interest for aesthetics.) Similar ambivalence attends nineteenth-century England, but for opposite reasons. It was the re-awaking of the individual ego after the self-forgetful plunge into landscape that produced both the social optimism and the personal melancholy which Tennyson reflects. To have awakened in the lap of a trusted Nature that now seemed diseased and malignant brought on a new suicidal gloom which the century never resolved or dissipated. If this were just a question of the 'history of ideas' there would be little excuse for pursuing it in connection with Tennyson. But the interest in landscape had, from the time of Claude and Poussin in the seventeenth century, been closely associated with the new science. So that when landscape was no longer supported by Newtonian physics for Coleridge and Keats, it was reinforced by botany, biology, and geology for Tennyson, Ruskin, and the Pre-Raphaelites. Science remained as an important prop for interests which were primarily aesthetic. But unlike the later Hopkins and Cézanne, Tennyson and the Pre-Raphaelites were unable to achieve the intensity of contemplation which led to the metaphysical break-through of that later art. They remained picturesque. That is, they devoted themselves to the means of prolonging the moment of aesthetic emotion or of arrested experience, and failed to accept such moments as the thread through the labyrinth of cognition. They substituted immediate feeling and emotion for the process of retracing.

Tennyson began, and, for the most part, remained at the very interesting Constable level. Hopkins, pursuing 'inscape', as Joyce did 'epiphanies', broke through to the life which restored body and solidity to art in an existential vision that is truly metaphysical:

> It is the forged feature finds me; it is the rehearsal
> Of own, of abrupt self there so thrusts on, so throngs the ear.

But, thoroughly trained in the picturesque school, Tennyson never fails to compose his larger pictures with the utmost care for the texture and placing of objects (and words as objects), light and shade. So that the enjoyment of his best poetry calls for the most patient and alert attention. The derision which was once shed indiscriminately on his 'accuracy' and his flag-waving reflects a recent period when, for various reasons, it was thought that art could be taken at the gallop. We are not likely to repeat that mistake. But Tennyson now deserves to be re-read and revalued with the aid of recovered reading ability. And it will be the Tennyson of the precise ear and eye who will provide the most unexpected and persistent enjoyment.

The gallery of pictures which is 'The Palace of Art' is a re-creation of the 'worlds' discovered by painters like Wilson, Turner, Danby, and Martin. They are not just descriptions of scenes or paintings but immediate impressionistic evocations of situations in which it is the state of mind of the protagonist that is central, situations which as in Maturin's tales, present 'those struggles of passion when the soul trembles on the verge of the unlawful and the unhallowed'. So that each brief vista is an objective correlative for a moment of concentrated awareness:

> One seem'd all dark and red—a tract of sand,
> And some one pacing there alone,
> Who paced for ever in a glimmering land
> Lit with a low large moon.

Tennyson is here practising the art of compression which Mr. Eliot carried even further in such effects as

> Madame de Tornquist, in the dark room
> Shifting the candles, Fraulein von Kulp
> Who turned in the hall, one hand on the door.

This concentration, which requires the utmost precision of eye, of phrase, and rhythm, Tennyson never ceased to exercise. 'Mariana' is a triumph of the sustaining of such concentration; and 'Œnone' is only less successful because of the admixture of the narrative flash-back which Tennyson could never handle. But in 'The Voyage of Maeldune' (1881) he solved the problem by only appearing to narrate. It is because of his habitual definition of a moment of awareness in terms of objective landscape that Tennyson found his strength in the short poem such as the sections of *In Memoriam* tend to be. And his longer poems are always risky expansions of these moments, as is plain in the *Idylls of the King*. But the short tale in verse, of which Crabbe was the master Tennyson admired, never ceased to tempt him.

It is in this matter of the landscape or episode which defines and concentrates an intense experience, that Tennyson both inspired and surpassed Rossetti, Morris, and the Pre-Raphaelites. Browning, too, was, in a more dramatic mode, concerned with rendering the intense 'immortal moment' which unified a lifetime of awareness. And Proust, the student and admirer of Ruskin, also lavished his art on the expansion of the 'immortal moment'. Staying close to the lyric mode in which he was so great a technician, Tennyson impresses many today as more successful because less tempted merely to decorate and comment on an experience which commonly eludes us in Browning and the Pre-Raphaelites when they fail to 'force the moment to its crisis'. At his frequent best he never departs from the critical insights that Hallam arrived at concerning rhetoric, Wordsworth, and the slackening effect of intellectual comment.

But the best of Wordsworth is also landscape in the picturesque mode, and 'The Solitary Reaper' is not unrelated in theme and technique to 'La Figlia che Piange'. Modern criticism with its tools ready for the anatomy of verbal wit and dramatic ambiguities will have to go to school to the painters again before it can do justice to the variety and skill of conscious landscape art in prose and poetry after Thomson. Modern verbal criticism finds itself equally mute before Dante's visual art and that of Spenser. Spenser was, inevitably, a master of the picturesque poets from Thomson to Tennyson. Music would appear to be a resource of the poet seeking visual and plastic effects with words—much more so than in the case of the kinæsthetic and dialectical verbal drama of a Donne or Hopkins. For subtleties and ambivalence of mood are managed less by tropes than impressionistic devices. 'She was a phantom of delight' is, for example, a triptych of condensed impressions which rival a cinematic rapidity and nuance. And so it is with the best of the Romantics. Looked at with the camera eye 'The Ancient Mariner' or 'Resolution and Independence' seem to be immediately contemporary with ourselves. The Romantics had nothing to learn from cinema. It is rather cinema that can learn from them.

If anybody ever had and consciously cultivated a movie-camera eye it was Tennyson. But if one asks what it was of landscape art that the Romantics and the Victorians did not achieve, it must be replied, *le paysage intérieur*, which had to wait for Baudelaire, Laforgue, and Rimbaud. It was this discovery that gave the later poets and painters alike, the power to be much more subjective and also more objective than the Romantics. For all their skill in discovering and manipulating external-nature situations by which to render states of mind, the Romantics remained tied to the object when they wished only to present it as a point from which to leap to another kind of vision. So they repeatedly bog down in reflection just at the moment when they are ready to soar. They could not discover the technique of flight. It would be interesting to inquire how far the cessation of the poetic activity of Wordsworth and Coleridge was connected with this technical frustration. By means of the interior landscape, however, Baudelaire could not only range across the entire spectrum of the inner life, he could transform the sordidness and evil of an industrial metropolis into a flower. With this technique he was able to accept the city as his central 'myth', and see it as the enlarged shape of a man, just as Flaubert did in *The Sentimental Education*, Joyce in *Ulysses*, and Mr. Eliot in *The Waste Land*. (It is noteworthy that the English novel also preceded English poetry in the management of the city as 'myth'. Dickens was the first to make London a character or a person. And James and Conrad in their different modes preceded Joyce and Eliot in assimilating the urban to the stuff of poesy.) Moreover, the technique of inner landscape not only permits the use of any and every kind of experience and object, it insures a much higher degree of control over the effect; because the arrangement of the landscape is the formula of the emotion and can be repeatedly adjusted until the formula and the effect are in precise accord. Whereas the romantic poet and painter were much more dependent on the caprices of external nature, sketching, as Ruskin says of Turner, 'the almost instantaneous record of an *effect* of colour or atmosphere taken strictly from Nature . . .', the romantic and picturesque artists had to take advantage of accidents. After Baudelaire there is no need for such accidents. The picturesque artists saw the wider range of experience that could be managed by discontinuity and planned irregularity, but they kept to the picture-like single perspective. The interior landscape, however, moves naturally towards the principle of multiple perspectives, as in the first two lines of *The Waste Land*, where the Christian Chaucer, Sir James Frazer, and Jessie Weston are simultaneously present. This is 'cubist perspective' which renders, at once, a diversity of views with the spectator always in the centre of the picture, whereas in picturesque art the spectator is always outside. The cubist perspective of interior landscape typically permits an immediacy, a variety, and solidity of experience denied to the picturesque and to Tennyson.

But the Romantics and Victorians, lacking this comprehensive and elastic technique, were compelled to remain 'nature' poets whether they liked it or not. They were certainly conscious of having new 'art-emotions', but they were unable to achieve art-conditions for them, and so continued to use external nature as a vehicle for art-emotions. It was the science of their time that taught them to like nature, just as it is the science of our time that has freed us from their particular kind of bondage to external nature. For it is, perhaps, a mistake to regard nature as the subject-matter of the Romantics. They wanted not just to see it but to see through it; and failing that they made it an objective correlative for states of mind that are independent of it.

1951

TENNYSON AND THE ROMANTIC EPIC

H. M. McLuhan

In 1884, in an essay on 'The Art of Fiction', Henry James made a distinction between the attitudes of the producer and of the consumer of art and literature which has even more relevance today:

> The novel and the romance, the novel of incident and that of character—these clumsy separations appear to me to have been made by critics and readers for their own convenience, and to help them out of their occasional queer predicaments, but to have little reality or interest for the producer, from whose point of view it is of course that we are attempting to consider the art of fiction.

As critics and historians have sought for convenient ways of packaging the increasing bulk of poems, plays, and novels, they have devised many categories of storage-space. As these categories have multiplied, an even more elaborate system of reference has been found necessary. But all of these strategies are remote from the point of view of the writers themselves. It is quite natural that Poe and James and Pound and Eliot should have been the first to strive for the producer-outlook in letters, just because America has in all matters of art and letters been excessively passive and appreciative. I would like to suggest an explanation for this situation which is not likely to occur to anyone who is not native to North America.

For a century and more the American child has found his untaught delight, from earliest years, in the poetry of technology, and more especially in the poetry of powered objects in motion. Pound tells of the joy he and his young friends found in looking through illustrated hardware catalogues. It is not the verbal universe that provides the first or basic poetry for North Americans, so that when our children go to school they are told that art and poetry belong to the verbal universe which they have not yet experienced. To make a bridge from the technological to the verbal universe was the task undertaken by Edgar Poe. For Baudelaire, Rimbaud, Mallarmé, and Valéry, Poe succeeded in uniting these seemingly antithetic realms and in swinging critical discussion from connoisseurship and consumer-satisfaction round to the point of view of the artist and producer. But my point is that Poe had no choice. He had, as an American, either to bridge these two worlds or else to remain shut off from the verbal universe. And so he made a technological bridge over into the poetic world. At the same time he invented two new forms, the symbolist poem and the detective story, both of which make the reader co-creator in an eminent degree. And here it was that he was joined by the French tradition. It was this astonishing switch from consumer to producer roles for the reader, a switch first pointed out by Poe, that excited Baudelaire, Mallarmé, and Valéry about Poe. James, Pound, and Eliot in their own ways followed the Poe strategy, as did the French. The reader must assume the poet's role. The poem is to be a do-it-yourself kit rather than a fully-processed consumer-commodity.

No more stark reversal than this could be imagined in the first industrial heyday when England and America were filling up with consumer-goods. The efforts of Tennyson, Arnold, and Browning to stem the tide of consumer-passivity now look rather half-hearted compared with the symbolist strategy. And the Victorian novel in particular looks like a large and tasteless meringue for collective nibblers.

If the North American has tended to be isolated from the verbal universe by the poetry of his technology, the European has been able to approach technology only by means of fanciful verbal systems. Our 'new criticism' is not nearly as amusing to Europeans as their metaphysics of 'le jazz hot' or of the skyscraper as 'hot jazz in stone' is to us. Le Corbusier and Siegfried Giedion have lavished as much verbal analysis on our technology as the American 'new critics' have on poetry. Presumably technology as a direct poetic experience is as inaccessible to Europeans as the European arts have been to us. A European seems to find his earliest positive experience in language itself.

It was a sure instinct which led Tennyson to devote himself to Theocritus and the idyll or little epic,[1] for the conditions which had brought about the cultivation of the romantic or little epic in the Hellenic world were largely paralleled in England in the nineteenth century. As J. W. Mackail shows in his *Lectures on Greek Poetry*, 'the diffused poetical life of the sixth century B.C. had flooded in upon Athens and concentrated there. Now it ebbed outwards. But the world into which it passed out was immensely enlarged, and had lost its responsiveness to the poetical instinct. Life was on a larger scale, but at a lower tension and feebler vitality. . . . Greece in the old sense ceased to exist: the Hellenic life was absorbed and diluted in the quasi-Hellenized world of the Graeco-Macedonian empires.'

Mackail also points to the multiplication of books and readers both as index and cause of the decline of the productive impulse: 'Already in the fifth century, collections of the poems of the earlier lyrists were habitually made to be read or sung: the old wine was preferred to the new.' When the scale of things became too great the centre of poetry was lost:

> Poetry seemed a thing done with, an art of the past. It had ceased to be a living function and interpretation of life. Those who felt within them the instinct for imaginative creation did not quite know what they would be at . . . They were over-shadowed by their own classics. The great poets reared a menacing and seemingly insurmountable barrier between them and poetry. . . . 'Homer is enough for everybody'—the remarkable phrase used by Theocritus, expresses not only the cynical doctrine of the outer world, but the deep-seated belief of scholars and the despondent conclusion of poets.

In Tennyson's day accessibility to the literature and the folklore of the entire world had at once obliterated the earlier channels

[1] 'What we need,' wrote Ezra Pound in *The Spirit of Romance*, 'is a literary scholarship which will weigh Theocritus and Yeats in one balance.'

of tradition and had revealed new sources of inspiration within the native tradition. In a more limited way the same dual situation had arisen in Alexandria and had been exploited by the Romans to a degree first recognized by Tennyson and then consolidated by 'outsiders' like Yeats and Joyce, Pound and Eliot. Theocritus and the Alexandrians, though hampered by erudition and excessive literary production, had been driven back to the roots of ritual and myth as the basis for art. Homer's revolution had been to substitute art for ritual in the drive towards defining the individual and the state. As ritual receded and the state enlarged far beyond the city walls, art in Alexandria returned to ritual. And such would seem to have been the development from Tennyson to Eliot. In a world of universal suffrage, assured of order by the police, primitivism seems to be an inevitable reaction.

In the world of Theocritus nationality had almost ceased to exist. Politics had become the business of huge bureaucracies. In the fourteenth idyll of Theocritus a despairing young man deserted by his girl is urged to enlist in Egypt. 'The tone and spirit of the scene,' says Mackail, 'are quite mid-Victorian; one seems to hear a young provincial Englishman of the fifties being advised to emigrate to Australia . . . Tennyson himself had very nearly done the same thing.' Mackail continues:

> Such was the world of Theocritus: immense, well-policed, monotonous; penetrated through and through by commercialism; pleasant for the well-to-do, and not unbearable for the poor . . . the great towns provided endless shows, public doles and pageants; the seat of a widespread if superficial culture among the professional classes . . . full of distinguished men of science, fuller still of clever and facile artists . . . that was the environment; that was the life with which poetry had, somehow or other, to get itself into relation.

The urge to get poetry into relation with life is naturally explicit in a literary world, since the very medium of writing demands a radical translation of the external scene. The translation of the written word back into the three-dimensional world, when done in silence and solitude by a private reader, intensifies the sense of separation between literature and life. But the Alexandrians, with their analytic sense of the centrality of myth and ritual, had the same hypertrophic sensitivity as the Victorians and ourselves to the need for a new bond between the arts and every-day concerns. Mackail's words (1910) concerning Theocritus as key figure must have provided keen stimulus to Mr. Eliot and others at a crucial time:

> The return to nature took with him as with his contem-poraries two forms. First, it was a sustained attempt to translate the old motives, the traditional subjects, of poetry into modern terms, to re-create or re-envisage them in the surroundings of modern art, modern surroundings, a modern attitude towards life. Secondly, it was an attempt which they all to some degree shared, but which Theocritus pursued with more skill and felicity than the rest, to bring the common things of life, its occupations, studies, amusements, the middle-class range of thought and sentiment and emotion, within the sphere of poetry ... Poetry had to find new patterns, had to attach itself as it could to a life that lay, swarming and monotonous, flat amid immense horizons, in the endless aimless afternoon. Poetry had to do this or die.

The strategy of pastoral in poetry pursued by Theocritus and his contemporaries is not unlike that of primitive myth and ritual as incorporated in the art of our century. In his essay on Theocritus, Rapin noted 'for as much as the Golden Age is to be preferred be-fore the Heroic, so much the Pastorals must excel Heroic Poems'. And in pastoral there is not only neatness, elegance, sweetness, but higher meaning than meets the eye. In the same way Porphyry had in 'The Cave of the Nymphs' assigned a higher theological level of meaning to minor epic than to major epic.

The Elizabethans came to the Alexandrian pastoral and roman-tic epic through the mediation of Catullus, Virgil, Dante, and Chaucer, for whom the Hellenic idyll and epyllion had been the basis and the fabric of their art. It was not until the nineteenth cen-tury that Greek studies got to the point of separating the Greek achievement from the Roman assimilation. Roman *humanitas* and urbanity had been viewed by the romantics with the same eye as Rousseau had turned upon megalopolis. In the age of Tennyson, Browning, and Arnold, scholarship had handed to the poets a Greek poetry that was guaranteed primitive and purged of the Roman components so prized in the Renaissance. *Urbanitas*, ele-gance and wit, incorporated by Ben Jonson and the Cavalier tradition, was by-passed for what was hoped to be a primaeval communion with the springs of Being. (Unfortunately for the Victorians, the same methods of scholarship applied to the elucidation of pre-literate societies was soon to provide a degree and breadth of primitivism which made Greek primitivism of small account. While the poet sat for his portrait by G. F. Watts in 1892, Hallam Tennyson read to his father the first volumes of *The Golden Bough*.) The long line of anthropological studies of the classical world which succeeded *The Golden Bough* has transformed our idea of their arts and our own.

The three phases of epic traced by G. R. Levy in his *Sword from the Rock* (1953) move from the cosmic, aetiological myth of the little epic, to the heroic epic and the emergence of the human individual. These correspond to the ages of gods, heroes, and men, and are as necessary to an understanding of art in pagan Greece and Rome as in the twentieth century. Alexandrian idyll and epyllion or little epic were as concerned with the gods as our own time is with the art, ritual, and motivations of pre-literate societies. The esoteric meaning of idyll and little epic relates to the drama of cosmic powers which today we discuss as 'myth'; hence idyll and little epic are often referred to as aetiological poems; that is, they are concerned with ultimate or final causes, whereas Homer and the dramatists were concerned with proximate moral causes.

The Frankforts and others in *Before Philosophy* point out that 'the ancients like the modern savage saw man always as part of society, and society as embedded in nature and dependent upon cosmic forces'. One result was that 'natural phenomena were regularly conceived in terms of human experience and that human experience was conceived in terms of cosmic events . . . for modern scientific man the phenomenal world is primarily an "It"; for ancient and also for primitive man it is a "Thou" '. This 'Thou' reveals itself in unpredictable and capricious ways like a poet's muse. It is felt as a presence or an 'epiphany', as James Joyce called these moments. They are referred to as 'momentary deities' by Ernst Cassirer in *Myth and Language*, and are the prime subject of Eliot's *Four Quartets*. In this respect, ancient charms, riddles, spells, and even nursery rhymes have much of the magical character of 'catching in the act' some cosmic phase or power. The culture-hero as conceived in our time by James Joyce (*Stephen Hero*) is he who has learned the technique of intercession between the profane and the divine. He is the inventor of language, the one who can capture in his net the divine powers.

In her *Epyllion from Theocritus to Ovid*, Marjorie Crump comments on the passion for abstruse erudition which attached itself to the little epic forms:

> The fashion for learning affected not only the style but the choice of subject. Scholars searched their records for unknown myths, strange customs and marvels of all kinds. The idea of explaining some custom or ceremony which appears in certain of the Attic tragedies, took firm root in Alexandrine poetry, and gave rise to the *Aitia* of Callimachus and to various poems dealing with κτισεις or the founding of cities.

Here is an aspect of little epic which never leaves the form whether it is cultivated by Virgil, Dante, Chaucer, Spenser, or Marlowe. But its major phase is found in Joyce, Pound, and Eliot.

Digression is the principal artistic device by which little epic exists. The reason for this is quite simple. To transcend time one simply interrupts the natural flow of events. A recent study by B. A. Van Groningen (*In the Grip of the Past*, E. J. Brill, Leiden, 1953) is devoted to the peculiar time-sense of the Greeks. They preferred the past to the present, he says, because of their dread of the flux of the present, so that Herodotus interrupts the natural course of events by telling the outcome, or past thereof, in advance. This enabled the Greek 'to survey a fact or a series of facts from a later point of view . . . the reader does not progress at random, but is able to take up a position to which he sees everything approach. . . . The Greek does not like to be kept in suspense and accordingly does not strive after the excitement which faces him again and again with the question: What will happen next? . . . He is more sensitive to another emotion, the awareness of the inevitable and the tragic or comic irony present in so many tales. The tragedies, which constantly vary the same subjects, are a clear instance of this preference of the "how" of the narrative to its "what?" '. Thus, while Homer's Odysseus strives homeward to the known, Tennyson's Ulysses moves onward into the unknown. Homer chooses 'one point of view from which he can look back. This point is situated immediately before the end. Odysseus looks backward and not forward to tell the largest part of his tale.'

It would require a lengthy study to rehearse the adventures of the little epic among the Elizabethans and the Augustans. The strong linear pressures of the new science were very unfavourable to the existence of the double-plot and ironies natural to the form. With Thomson and the picturesque developments in poetic presentation, however, the tide turned strongly towards that intense visualization of situations which easily led the romantics toward the wall-painting style which the Alexandrine school had strongly developed. The work of George Crabbe, so much admired by Tennyson, would be a central area of study for any historian of the little or romantic epic.

Douglas Bush in *Mythology and the Romantic Tradition* notes of Shelley: 'On the side of poetic Shelley is generally as remote as possible from Aeschylus or anything Greek. . . . Instead of restrained and distinct images Shelley expands Aeschylean suggestions of nature's sympathy into a Turneresque panorama of atmospheric pageantry.' It is this fusion of outer and mental worlds that became the Romantic substitute for little epic narrative. For them the arresting of a vivid moment of experience, or 'spot of time' in Wordsworth's phrase, took precedence over any ritual order of events. And it is for this that Arnold indicted them in his 1853 *Preface*.

Fully acknowledging Tennyson's learning and skill in 'the placing of a miniature epic in a luxuriant natural background' for which he 'was indebted to the Alexandrian idyll and epyllion', Bush nevertheless finds no structure in his poems, but only a succession of splendid moments. Yet it is precisely his fidelity to the vivisection of isolated moments that links Tennyson to the greatest work of his time and of ours. This concern with the spectrum of the emotional life was linked with Newton and with Gainsborough on one hand and with the best art and archaeology of the nineteenth century on the other. It is to be related to the tendency to abandon succession for simultaneity when our instruments of observation acquired speed and precision. Looking back from the nuclear age it is easy to recognize the pattern of 'total field' forming in the concern with totality of implication in the aesthetic moment, or spot of time. Lineal succession as a concept of order cannot hold the same absolute position in our nuclear consciousness as it did in the great age of mechanism that stretches from Gutenberg to Darwin.

In 'Locksley Hall', as vision yields to vision, the speaker experiences a moment of ironic consciousness. And it is in the recognition of the timing and placing of such effects that much of the enjoyment of Tennyson consists. Yet it is exactly this location of effects as in the simultaneous order of a cabinet picture that Tennyson derived from the romantic or little epics of Alexandria. Today it is not necessary to look up these poems, since Pound and Eliot have given such familiar contemporary form to them.

J. W. Mackail shows how Theocritus applied the idyllic or picture method to lyric, epic, and dramatic alike. Tennyson adopted the same procedure. Moreover he followed Theocritus in adding the elegiac, or the poetry of reflection and sentiment to the little epic fusion of lyric, epic, and dramatic. It was natural then for Tennyson to use the term 'idyll' for almost all his poems. And 'he used the name as he used language always,' says Mackail, 'with precise accuracy and with a complete understanding of its Greek meaning.' Mackail goes on to point out the close correspondence between Tennyson's idyls (written in blank verse as those of Theocritus are in hexameters) and the poems of Theocritus:

> *Audley Court* is an English analogue of the seventh idyll of Theocritus, the *Thalysia*. *Walking to the Mail* gives a picture in finished verse of commonplace country talk, reproduced in detail with all its inconsequence and vulgarity, yet with a faint gleam over it which somehow or other makes its way into poetry . . . *Dora*, an idyllic narrative of rural life, shows the tendencies of the idyll to break its bounds; it points forwards to the longer poems in the same manner, *Enoch Arden* or *Aylmer's Field*, where the enriched idyllic treatment is applied on a larger scale, and not perhaps with the most successful result; for in these poems one cannot but feel that the balance between subject and treatment is on the point of being lost.

Mackail points to 'Come down, O maid' in *The Princess*—which Tennyson himself called 'a small Sweet Idyl'—as like the songs of Thyrsis or Lycidas in Theocritus. And of 'Tears, Idle Tears' he says: 'The style, the movement, the enriched, subtilised and refracted embodiment of emotion, though applied to a different subject, are precisely those of the twelfth idyll. . . . *Godiva* is an accurate reproduction or reincarnation . . . of the shorter epyllion, as we have it for instance in the twenty-sixth idyll (of uncertain authorship) dealing with the legend of Pentheus and Agave.'

At the head of his English Idyls Tennyson placed his 'Morte d'Arthur', and of the curious line in the epilogue about 'King Arthur like a modern gentleman' Mackail remarks that it is exactly such a line as Theocritus might have written in his aim of 'bringing the subjects of poetry into fresh touch with the actual modern world'. Both poets, says Mackail, 'have the same kind of sense of language; the same enriched and loaded sweetness of phrasing; the same sensitiveness to sights and sounds'.

The pervasiveness of the sense of romance in Theocritus and Tennyson, so closely woven into their idylls, needs much more attention if only for the sake of illumination of the work of Yeats, Pound, and Eliot. Such a study would avoid the illusion, still prevalent, of a sharp break between Victorian and modern poetry. Because of its most serious research and experiment, the Romantics, the Victorians, and the moderns were agreed in using the romantic epic as their major instrument.

1959

III

Symbol and Myth—
Modes of Indirection

TENNYSON'S GARDEN OF ART:
A STUDY OF *THE HESPERIDES*

G. Robert Stange

ONE OF the chief reasons the great Victorian poets are not read with the attention they deserve is that the modern reader is often baffled by the idiom of their more successful poems. We do not know just how to take them, and we find it difficult to do justice to the richness of their language. The case of Tennyson has been particularly unfortunate. In order to discover those poems capable of exciting the contemporary sensibility, one must first discount the adverse critical reaction. Though it may have been historically necessary, it managed to eclipse the Laureate for at least a generation. But having made this effort, one must still penetrate the formidable and misleading masks of household poet which the later Tennyson adopted.

The problem is exhibited in reading such a poem as *The Hesperides*. It is a neglected work, fascinating in itself, which has the additional interest of developing several motifs and sets of images which are central to much of the poet's early expression. It strikes Tennyson's recurrent note of longing for a vanished or unattainable paradise and explores the persistent theme of the inhuman fascination of isolation and retreat. Yet it was the poet himself who originally barred the reader's way. The poem was first published in the volume of 1833 and then, for reasons never given, was suppressed by Tennyson for the rest of his life.[1]

The Hesperides is a kind of incantation, in the young poet's most ornate strain. Traditionally it has been read (on the rare occasions when it *has* been read) as a piece of 'pure' music or delightful word painting, but to do justice to the work one must see how its verbal effects are reinforced by a complex and firmly handled structure of imagery and how its controlling symbols define a subject and covertly attack a problem in which Tennyson seems to have felt an almost obsessive interest. The poem seems in fact to be an interpretation of the spiritual conditions under which the poetic experience comes to life. It is in essence a symbolic statement of the situation of the artist, and the inner pattern of completely associated motifs and images may all be seen to lead towards and to enforce this core of meaning.

The Hesperides is short and its form is simple. The body of the poem is the 'Song of the Three Sisters', the Hesperidian maidens, which is introduced by a blank verse prologue that fuses historical allusion with myth and somewhat casually places the verses that follow in the familiar framework of vision poetry. The opening lines were suggested by a passage in the *Periplus* of the Carthaginian commander, Hanno, who navigated the west coast of Africa in the fifth century B.C.:[2]

> The North wind fall'n, in the new-starréd night
> Zidonian Hanno, wandering beyond
> The hoary promontory of Soloë,
> Past Thymiaterion in calméd bays
> Between the southern and the western Horn,
> Heard neither warbling of the nightingale,
> Nor melody of the Libyan Lotus-flute
> Blown seaward from the shore; but from a slope

[1] It was first reprinted by Hallam Tennyson (*Memoir*, i, pp. 61–5). Tennyson's son explained that it was republished 'in consequence of a talk I had with my father, in which he regretted that he had done away with it from among his "Juvenilia".' The poem may also be found in J. Churton Collins, ed. *Early Poems of Tennyson* (1900), and in W. J. Rolfe, ed. *The Poetic and Dramatic Works of Alfred Lord Tennyson*, Cambridge Ed. (Boston, 1898). My quotations from *The Hesperides* follow the text of the *Memoir* (chiefly because I prefer its punctuation).

[2] See *The Periplus of Hanno*, trans. Wilfred H. Schoff (Philadelphia, 1912). The passage which Tennyson seems to have had particularly in mind is para. 14, pp. 4–5.

That ran bloom-bright into the Atlantic blue,
Beneath a highland leaning down a weight
Of cliffs, and zoned below with cedar-shade,
Came voices like the voices in a dream
Continuous; till he reach'd the outer sea.

Tennyson sustains this dream-like air—of mystery combined with intense concreteness—which establishes the poem's peculiar tonality. The Sisters' song is incantatory in the literal sense; the magic of poetry is invoked in order that the poet's art may thrive and be protected.

The original myth is handled in a way characteristic of Tennyson's 'classical' poems; he does not rehearse the fable of the Hesperidian gardens, but uses some of its connotations to construct a dim allegory of personal and inward experience. The epigraph from *Comus*,

Hesperus and his daughters three
That sing about the golden tree,

reminds us that this nineteenth-century vision is to be compared with Milton's description (ll. 976–91) of the paradisaical home of the Attendant Spirit. Milton's Garden of the Hesperides is a place of repose and joyful freedom—the very source of regeneration. It has been best described by Professor A. S. P. Woodhouse as a symbol of life itself, or as 'the transfigured view of life which the practice of virtue and the experience of grace induce.' In Tennyson's version the religious implications of *Comus* are lacking. The chief resemblance of his poem to Milton's is in the parallel conception of the gardens as a restful abode for the privileged spirit and as a source of creativity—in Milton's case of the higher life, and in Tennyson's of the life of art.

All the elements of the myth upon which the highly individual structure of *The Hesperides* is built can be found in Hesiod's rendering of the fable. There the sisters are the daughters of 'murky Night', 'the Hesperides who guard the rich, golden apples and the trees bearing fruit beyond glorious Ocean'. They are said to be 'clear-voiced', and to dwell 'in the frontier land towards Night'.[1]

---

[1] Theog. 215; 274–5; 518. The reference to Hesiod in Servius on Virgil *Aen.* iv. 484 is also relevant. Somewhat different versions of the myth are given in Diodorus Siculus, iv. 27, and in Apollodorus, *Lib.* II. v. 11. There is an amplification of the legend in Hyginus, *Poet. Astron.* ii. 3. See *Hesiod*, trans. H. G. Evelyn-White, Loeb Ed. (1914), p. 95.

Tennyson's method was to take over these suggestions and adapt them to his own pattern of imagery.

The most direct way of getting at the meanings of the Sisters' song is to distinguish the several motifs of the poem, to see how they work in their context and how they acquire significance by their connection with the persistent imagery of some of Tennyson's other poems. The central motifs are all stated in the opening passage of the song:

> The Golden Apple, the Golden Apple, the hallow'd fruit,
> Guard it well, guard it warily,
> Singing airily,
> Standing about the charméd root. . . .
> If ye sing not, if ye make false measure,
> We shall lose eternal pleasure,
> Worth eternal want of rest.
> Laugh not loudly: watch the treasure
> Of the wisdom of the West.
> In a corner wisdom whispers. Five and three
> (Let it not be preach'd abroad) make an awful mystery:
> For the blossom unto threefold music bloweth;
> Evermore it is born anew,
> And the sap to threefold music floweth,
> From the root
> Drawn in the dark,
> Up to the fruit,
> Creeping under the fragrant bark,
> Líquid góld, hóneyswéet thró and thró.

One clear identification in this passage is of the golden apple as 'the treasure / Of the wisdom of the West', an analogy which faintly suggests the Miltonic fruit of the knowledge of good and evil which must be denied to man. Tennyson adds the essential fact that the golden fruit and the garden itself are to be protected from ordinary humanity. But 'wisdom' has here, as it so often did in Tennyson's work, a special connotation. His consciousness was so clearly centred on poetry and on the problems of art, that wisdom came to mean for him the artist's powerful insight, the poet's supreme attribute. The word is used in this way in 'The Poet', and indeed in all Tennyson's early descriptions of the vatic nature, the qualities of the poetic charism are termed 'wisdom'.[1]

---

[1] See, e.g., 'The Mystic', 'The Poet's Mind', and, for a negative statement, 'A Character'.

Another indication that *The Hesperides* treats of the nature of poetry is to be found in the suggestion that the fruit can be protected only by eternal singing; if the singing stops or 'if ye make false measure, / We shall lose eternal pleasure'. The relationship between the sacred fruit and the maidens' song is involved; the apple is the cause of their song, but unless they sing continually (and beautifully) it will be lost. The conception by which the burgeoning of the fruit depends on the charmed music of the Hesperides and they, in turn, draw their vitality and find the source of their song in the root and the tree, is a figure of the connection among the artist, his art, and his inspiration. The notion is complicated, but it is conveyed with precision because the symbols, though they expand and ramify, arouse only associations that are relevant to the central meanings of the poem. The golden apple may stand for the rare genius of poetry, but we need not exclude its meanings as 'the ancient secret', or even as the knowledge of good and evil.

The golden apple has also the virtue of being the treasure of the *West*. The notion of East and West had for Tennyson a special significance and, by means of reiterated images and allusions, became part of the private mythology of his earlier poems. In *The Hesperides* the varied associations of East and West establish a kind of symbolic geography which enforces the central duality of the poem and underlies its pattern of emotional contrasts. Etymologically the maidens are daughters of the West. The garden stands at the mysterious western edge of the world; Hesperus is the evening star, 'Looking under silver hair with a silver eye'. In the third part of the song the daughters address their father:

> Look from West to East along:
> Father, old Himala weakens, Caucasus
>   is bold and strong.
> Wandering waters unto wandering waters call;
> Let them clash together, foam and fall.
> Out of watchings, out of wiles,
> Comes the bliss of secret smiles.
> All things are not told to all,
> Half-round the mantling night is drawn.
> Purplefringéd with even and dawn
> Hesper hateth Phosphor, evening hateth morn.

The West, then, is a place of twilight, of rest, of warmth and secrecy. In the echoed words of Sappho's fragment on Hesperus, it is the home of 'all good things'. The attributes of this desirable state of being arise from a group of fundamental and sometimes unconscious feelings. Tennyson connects the West with images of the sea, of growth, and, paradoxically, of death. The antithesis to this condition he conceived as the land of dawn, bold and strong, full of activity and strife—the world of everyday life which is always plotting to steal the magic fruit.[1] The sharpness with which this antinomy is realized in *The Hesperides* enforces the effect of similar images in some of Tennyson's other poems.

This West, for example, is essentially the land of 'The Lotos-Eaters' and of 'The Sea Fairies'; it has affinities with the submarine world of 'The Merman' and 'The Mermaid'. The feelings that are associated with it are evoked whenever Tennyson expressed his enduring temptation to relinquish the struggle of life —as he did in 'The Two Voices' and *In Memoriam*. Wherever it is used Tennyson's development of this image-complex is based on a light–dark, evening–morning contrast, and incorporates the notion of a retreat to the past and an envisioning of the lost paradise.

There are several striking examples of this imagery in the early poems. In his undergraduate prize poem, *Timbuctoo*, Tennyson apostrophized the lost Atlantis and Eldorado:

> Where are ye,
> Thrones of the Western wave, fair Islands green?
> Where are your moonlight halls, your cedars glooms,
> The blossoming abysses of your hills?
> Your flowering capes, and your gold-sanded bays
> Blown round with happy airs of odorous winds?

And in the same poem the Spirit of Fable reveals to the poet that by furnishing him a vision of the lost city of Timbuctoo she has filled his lips with power and brought him closer to heaven, 'Man's first, last home.' Poetic inspiration is conceived, significantly, as dark and vegetative:

> I am the Spirit,
> The permeating life which courseth through
> All th' intricate and labyrinthine veins

---

[1] As it is put in the song: 'Guard the apple night and day, / Lest one from the East come and take it away' (41–2).

> Of the great vine of Fable, which, outspread
> With growth of shadowing leaf and clusters rare,
> Reacheth to every corner under heaven,
> Deep-rooted in the living soil of truth;
> So that men's hopes and fears take refuge in
> The fragrance of its complicated glooms,
> And cool impleachèd twilights.

An almost identical pattern of symbolism is developed in the curiously revealing poem, 'Youth', which Tennyson wrote in 1833 and never published. There the West finally comes to stand for the sheltering past and the East for the rigorous and uncertain future. The poet in this spiritual autobiography is paralysed by a divided will; feeling that he has lost his creative energy, he cannot choose between the voice of duty, the need to work for the future, and the 'low, sweet voices' of the past:

> Confused, and ceasing from my quest,
>   I loiter'd in the middle way,
> So pausing 'twixt the East and West,
>   I found the Present where I stay:
>
> Now idly in my natal bowers,
>   Unvext by doubts I cannot solve,
> I sit among the scentless flowers
>   And see and hear the world revolve.[1]

One other, much later example may help to illuminate the connotations of this chain of images. We know that for Tennyson the question of the social responsibility of the poet was an enduring problem. All through his career some poems announce a reasoned intention to participate in the world's work while others reveal a yearning for aesthetic detachment. The recurring antithesis of East and West is one means by which this conflict is expressed. *The Hesperides*, interpreted as a dramatization of the conditions of poetic creation, affirms the value of an art which is withdrawn, introspective, and sensuous. But one can usually find in Tennyson's work a counterstatement to every unequivocal description of the nature of poetry. At times the opposing viewpoint is expressed didactically, as in 'The Palace of Art' and 'The Poet', but on other occasions it involves a reversal of the values attached to a familiar image. The opposition between the symbolism of *The*

---

[1] *Memoir*, i. p. 113.

Hesperides and the later poem, 'Move Eastward, Happy Earth', illustrates this second process.

'Move Eastward', which was first published in the 1842 *Poems*, does not deal with the question of the poet's role. Its dominant note is one of joyful anticipation and acceptance of life—feelings which are imaged by the alternation of night and day. The basic figure of the poem is simply the rotation of the earth:

> Move eastward, happy earth, and leave
>   Yon orange sunset waning slow;
> From fringes of the faded eve,
>   O happy planet, eastward go. . . .
>
> Ah, bear me with thee, smoothly borne,
>   Dip forward under starry light,
> And move me to my marriage morn,
>   And round again to happy night.

Though the poem must be appreciated on its own terms, the effect of its imagery is enhanced by its association with the East–West duality of the earlier poems. In 'Move Eastward' the symbolism is analogous to that of *The Hesperides*, but the poet's attitude towards the antithetical conditions has altered. He rejoices in leaving behind the 'faded eve' of the West; the world moves through 'starry night' to the dawn of the marriage morn which is the joyful culmination of its cycle. The wedding very properly belongs to the East, the sphere of common social life. In another sense it is the dawn of new happiness. However, the lyric ends with a handsome paradox that reasserts the bond with the imagery of *The Hesperides*. For, the dawn achieved, the poet concludes by welcoming the coming night which is to bring the fulfilment of his love and joy. But by means of an ancient association, the image also suggests the night of death.

The sequence of ocean images in *The Hesperides* is another element supporting the affective pattern of the symbols of East and West. The garden is reached only by a voyage through unknown seas, and in the fourth part of the song the sea is described as the nurturing agent of the golden fruit:

> Every flower and every fruit the redolent breath
>   Of the warm seawind ripeneth,
>   Arching the billow in his sleep:

> But the land-wind wandereth,
>   Broken by the highland steep,
>   Two streams upon the violet deep. . . .
> The world is wasted with fire and sword,
> But the Apple of gold hangs over the Sea!

The sea of *The Hesperides* is typically Tennysonian; it is not fresh or splendid, but a sea that evokes feelings of quiescence, of the state of pre-existence which is analogous to death. Both the West and the warm sea may be said to illustrate the impulses that Freud called the Nirvana principle. Such images as that of 'Crocodiles in briny creeks [that] / Sleep and stir not', create the sense of a torpid and subliminal life, and remind us of the roots of being from which the poet's visions arise.

Two other suggestive motifs are developed in the opening passage of the maidens' song. The number symbolism, though it is intricately devised, is not of central importance; the pervasive image of the island-garden, however, works to modify and extend the meanings of the poem.

Tennyson's number references seem at first to be more puzzling than rewarding. The maidens sing: 'Five and three . . . make an awful mystery.' A simple meaning for the five is given later in the poem:

> Five links—a golden chain are we—
> Hesper, the Dragon, and Sisters three
> Bound about the golden tree.

It would appear, though, that the significance goes beyond this plain addition. For numerologists five is important as the first number which combines odd and even—the primary odd and the primary even—so that the number is the original unification of opposites.[1] To general experience, however, the natural associa-

---

[1] Donne's *Primrose* provides an elegant example of the poetic use of this conception:

> Since all
> Numbers are odde, or even, and they fall
> First into this, five, women may take us all.

In Donne's poem, however, the number is chiefly a representation of the senses, upon which love must be based, and in this respect his treatment offers an interesting gloss on Tennyson's symbolism.

tion is with the five senses, and this is perhaps its most important suggestion in *The Hesperides*. Interpreted in this way, the number symbolism contributes to a reading of the poem as a statement on the condition of art. Arthur Hallam reported that Tennyson was 'wont to say' that 'an artist ought to be Lord of the five senses',[1] and in 'The Palace of Art', the Soul, isolated in the life of Beauty, is described as,

> Lord over Nature, Lord of the visible earth,
> Lord of the senses five.

This identification is also relevant to the other images of the poem. The senses inhabit a twilight world, and through the charm they work and the ceaseless watch they keep, nourish, and protect the gift of poetry that grows only there. The senses do belong symbolically to the shadowy world of the unconscious, and certainly the image of sense as a golden chain made up of a dragon, a star, and three beautiful singing maidens is an effective one.

The other 'awful mystery' is three. This is, of course, first the three Hesperides, who are both sense and song. But there are again additional suggestions. For though the tree grows and blossoms to 'threefold music', it is itself a triune mystery. In the conclusion of the song the interdependence of the three parts of the magic tree is affirmed:

> Round about,
> All round about
> The gnarl'd bole of the charméd tree.
> The Golden Apple, The Golden Apple, The hallow'd fruit,
> Guard it well,
> Guard it warily,
> Watch it warily,
> Singing airily,
> Standing about the charméd root.

The root, the bole, and the fruit are the elements of a living unity. It would do violence to so concrete and expressive a symbol to try to limit its meaning; its success depends on the breadth of its

[1] From a letter of 1831, quoted in *Memoir*, i. p. 501.

associations. It not only symbolizes the process of growth and the nature of artistic creation, but also suggests the ancient distinctions among body, soul, and spirit, as well as the organic principle of multiplicity in unity.[1]

The garden-isle of the Hesperides is an archetypal image, and though it has a private significance for him, Tennyson preserves its mythological character. Remoteness and isolation are its most important features; it is both a type of the Garden of Eden and a figure of the poet's secret life. In this sacred grove, 'Honour comes with mystery; / Hoarded wisdom brings delight' (47–8). A parallel to this idea of an exclusive preserve of creativity is to be found in the final image of 'The Poet's Mind', which originally appeared in Tennyson's 1830 volume. There the poetic spirit is compared to a rare garden which must be protected from the intrusions of brash humanity:

> Dark-brow'd sophist, come not anear;
> All the place is holy ground;
> Hollow smile and frozen sneer
> Come not here.[2]

'The Poet's Mind' is an emphatic statement of the artist's sanctity; like *The Hesperides*, it defines the sources of art as hieratic, and expresses the necessity of the poet's separation from other men. The imagery of both poems may owe something to the writings of George Stanley Faber, one of the most widely read mythologists of the early nineteenth century. Faber described the holy gardens in which religious mysteries were celebrated, and observed that rites of purification usually took place in a garden or grove behind a sacred tree. This was 'that holy tree of immortality which makes so conspicuous a figure in the mythological systems of the east'.[3]

---

[1] Tennyson's tree symbol resembles the image in the concluding lines of Yeat's *Among School Children*: 'O chestnut tree, great rooted blossomer, / Are you the leaf, the blossom or the bole?' For Yeats the tree symbolized the state of glory in life and the reconciliation of antinomies—implications that might profitably be brought to bear on *The Hesperides*.

[2] I am quoting the final revision of 1842. In the original version the second line read: 'The poet's mind is holy ground'.

[3] *The Origin of Pagan Idolatry* (London, 1816), iii, p. 231. There is no convincing evidence that Tennyson read Faber. The possibility of an influence from this source was first suggested by W. D. Paden in his stimulating essay, *Tennyson in Egypt: A Study of the Imagery in His Earlier Work* (Lawrence, Kans., 1942).

Analogues to Tennyson's garden images also appear in some of Shelley's poems. In *Alastor*, for example, the final retreat of the poet is a 'green recess', reached by following a stream through dark caves. Shelley's garden is primarily a symbol of the solitary heart of poetic sensibility, but the fact that this 'recess' may also mean death helps to focus more sharply some of the final implications of *The Hesperides*.

We have been concerned thus far with the dominant themes of *The Hesperides* and with the nature of its poetic statement. Of the many remaining questions raised by the poem two, in particular, demand speculation: What, we are bound to ask, were Tennyson's motives in supressing it? And what is the relation of the poem to Tennyson's work as a whole?

The simplest answer to the first question would be that the poem was withdrawn in deference to the reviewers' attacks. Tennyson was peculiarly sensitive to criticism, and there are examples of extensive revisions made (particularly during the 1830's) as a result of the critics' suggestions.[1] It is true, too, that *The Hesperides* was roughly handled. In his condescending notice of the 1833 *Poems* Bulwer described it (as well as 'Œnone') as 'of the best Cockney classic and Keatesian to the marrow'. John Stuart Mill suggested that it be withdrawn, and the American critic, John Dwight, considered it one of the poems that was 'insulated as in a vacuum'.[2] However, Tennyson later admitted to his canon several less excellent poems that had been similarly attacked. *The Hesperides* touches on so many of Tennyson's central concerns that it is impossible to conceive his suppressing it out of complaisance to the critics.

I think it more likely that the poem was put aside because it expressed attitudes that the poet did not wish to make public later in his career. As a young man, Tennyson had assumed a position of artistic detachment and poetic independence, but as his reputation increased he became more strongly influenced by the public's demand for a *vates*. In his middle years we find him making a conscious effort to transmit to the people the ethos of his age, and to use his poetry as a didactic weapon. Yet, in a sense, Tennyson's

[1] See Edgar F. Shannon Jnr., *Tennyson and the Reviewers* (Harvard, 1952).
[2] *New Monthly Mag.*, xxxvii (1833), p. 72; *The London Rev.*, i (1835), p. 422; *The Christian Examiner*, xxiii (1838), p. 325.

will remained divided. In his more popular work there is an attempt either to suppress his conflicting desires for social engagement and for the life of art, or to resolve his conflict in favour of 'the whole life'—to treat the withdrawal to a palace of art or to a lotos-land as an aberration. *The Hesperides* is a statement of what 'the people's poet' came to feel was the devil's side in this continuing debate. So, for a variety of reasons, the socially responsible Tennyson may have found it desirable not to include *The Hesperides* in his later collections.

At the very end of his life I think (though there is not place for my evidence here) that Tennyson came to terms with his conflicting views on the function of the poet, and it would have been logical for him then to relax and to allow the poem to be published again.

Attentively read, *The Hesperides* acquires value as a fragment of the poet's spiritual history and, because it is so rich a poem, as a means of discriminating the kind of response which Tennyson's art demands. It can lead to a partial revaluation of the poet's earlier work and it displays in the most dramatic way the radical ambivalence of Tennyson's attitude towards the poetic life. Its imagery shares the sensuousness of Keats and Shelley, while its assertion of a desire to retreat from purposive moral activity suggests the doctrine of the Beautiful that Arthur Hallam formulated in his influential review of Tennyson's *Poems, chiefly Lyrical*.

The poem offers us a mystery, compels us to interpret; and the act of interpretation demonstrates some of the subtle ways in which Tennyson's poetry works upon us. The poem, we find, is not pure, wild song, but concentrated statement; its expressive meanings are found in the symbolic pattern that lies beneath its surface. Motifs that seem at first to be merely exotic are discovered to carry the weight of a major theme. The poet communicates through images that arouse feelings extrinsic to the subject matter of the poem—images that are significant to us because they correspond to elemental and general experience. They are of the sort that Dr. Jung called 'primordial' or 'archetypal', but in Tennyson's poetry they may be described as thematic. They are recurrent, and regardless of the context in which such an image appears, it always arouses the same kind of response and by its repetition defines persistent themes in the poet's work.

The Hesperides, in short, should help us to define Tennyson's poetic achievement. There are no evidences in it of those 'impurities' which Yeats and his fellow writers found characteristic of Victorian literature. It is a complex and allusive work that makes brilliant use of the resources of metaphor and the language of paradox. If it is not one of Tennyson's greatest poems, it at least shows him treating a difficult and meaningful subject with a strength and freedom that he did not always display.

1952

SYMBOLISM IN TENNYSON'S MINOR POEMS

Elizabeth Hillman Waterston

I

MANY OF Tennyson's mature poems follow the method of symbolism: they reinforce our direct attention to the 'subject' by dealing with another reality which will create emotional and intellectual responses in its own right but which is recognizable in the particular instance as a sign directing our interest back to the original subject. Using this tentative definition of the symbolic method as a touchstone, we observe in Tennyson's work a steady development in the technique of obliquity. In the present study I would first indicate certain general features of symbolic expression, as Tennyson practised it in the minor poems, and second, consider chronologically some minor poems that are typical in their symbolism.

The end result of a study of symbolism ought to be a clarification of the author's topic, not of his motivation, his psychoses, or his learning. Even a brief consideration of Tennyson's symbols will convince the reader that Tennyson was determined not to use his art for escape or for satisfaction of himself alone. Distressed by the atomism of his age, he sought societal symbols, rejecting images whose impact was guaranteed only by his private experience. Hence his life-long experiments with classical myth (in 'Œnone', 'Tiresias', and other poems) and with folk-lore (in poems using the legend of the swan-song, the Arthurian matter, and so on). Tennyson used familiar poetic parallels (of the sea to life, of rocks to death, of birds to escape, and so on), because of their proven ability to enrich the reader's response to the 'subject', and to deflect away from themselves the interest stirred by the emotional tension generated in reading poetry.

Mention of myth brings us at once to an epistemological problem. According to Whitehead, almost all adult mental response is to symbolic stimuli. This belief need not lead to solipsism; it may produce an interest, like Whitehead's, in the processes through which external reality, given in nature, is transposed into the mental flux, conditioned, 'intensified, inhibited, or diverted', by the nature of the receiver. Tennyson has a powerful recognition of the 'causal efficacy', the reality of the world without, and an equal interest in the relationship between that world and the world within the mind, particularly the world of dreams. He presents a psychological theory for the persistence in memory of certain emotionally-charged impressions in his 'Ode to Memory':

> . . . For the discovery
> And newness of thine art so pleased thee,
> That all which thou hast drawn of fairest
>   Or boldest since, but lightly weighs
> With thee unto the love thou bearest
> The first-born of thy genius. Artist-like,
> Ever retiring thou dost gaze
> On the prime labour of thine early days. . . .

He then lists as the realities of his own earliest memories, the realities most charged with emotional history for him, a narrow range of scenes which (as I shall show) recur throughout the poems with symbolic significance: high bushless fields, a sandy ridge, a cottage overlooking a marsh, a garden with dark alleys opening on plots of roses, lily, and lavender. Later in life, in tense moments, external nature provided other sense-impressions, stored in memory with emotional surcharge, ready for use as symbol when the emotion returned.

> Strange, that the mind, when fraught
> With a passion so intense
> One would think that it well
> Might drown all life in the eye,—
> That it should, by being so overwrought,

> Suddenly strike on a sharper sense
> For a shell, or a flower, little things
> Which else would have been past by!

This is the process, described in *Maud*, by which the mind stores up a private hoard of natural symbols. For Tennyson, the realities which most often served as symbols are: landscape, particularly when several levels sharply different can be seen; dark houses or halls with unusual lighting; rivers, usually with cataracts; mist rising; stars, particularly 'Hesper'; a family group of man, woman, and daughter; yellow colours, and rose; cheerful bells; rust; song-birds; ships at anchor; jewels. But these things do not form part of a private mythology; here, as in the case of folk-lore figures, the desire for a general impact has acted as a rigid censor, excluding the use as symbols of personal 'realities' not judged to be universally affective.

Tennyson is as aware as any modern philosopher of the categories of space and time. Several of his most effective symbols convey the sense of these realities: 'The Voyage', 'Recollections of the Arabian Nights', 'The Poet's Song'. A central theme of his work is the relationship between the poet's created world, 'out of space, out of time', and the world of mechanical time and measurable space. The links between these two worlds are forged by symbols, which have real significance, both as the effective stimulus or reminder of sense experience, and as 'things-in-themselves', crusted with the significance of the spaceless, timeless realm of dreams. Tennyson was impressed with the experiential reality of dreams, waking or sleeping:

> As when with downcast eyes we muse and brood,
> And ebb into a former life, or seem
> To lapse far back in some confused dream
> To states of mystical similitude. . . .

The mystical similitudes thus recognized in dreams correspond, as psycho-analysts show, to the pattern of myths; far back in the dream will be found symbols which rouse universal response. 'Men do not invent those mysterious relations between separate external objects, and between objects and feelings, which it is the function of poetry to reveal,' says Professor Owen Barfield. 'Those relations exist independently, not indeed of Thought, but of any individual thinker.' Psychology suggests the existence of historical strata in the mind, fossilizing primitive responses. In this respect, mythology is the ghost of concrete meanings. As Emerson says, there is a '*radical* correspondence between visible things and human thoughts'.

This brings us to the next phrase in the definition of symbolism: the other reality will create emotional and intellectual responses in its own right. We have already noticed the care with which Tennyson selected his symbols from familiar universal experiences. He lived before Freud produced his records of the many instances in which dreams of the sea obsess neurotics with a mother complex, and before popularization tagged ocean imagery as a 'regression symbol'. Consequently, the restlessness and infinity of the ocean sometimes suggested life in this world to him, sometimes (especially as he grew older) eternity. Similarly the rose may arouse gay and charming associations, or terrifying ones. And so, like most pre-Freudian poets, his symbolism rarely has a one-to-one ratio, an equation value; the symbol creates emotion, but it may be used in different poems to create different emotions. Nevertheless, the emotions will not be forced upon the symbol by the poet's mood; they will each in turn be appropriate and inevitable, because of the complexity of the reality chosen, and because of Tennyson's sensitivity to the great commonplaces and to the emotional and intellectual analogies between man's life and the patterns of the universe—of day and night, of restless sea and sterile rock, and so on. These analogies convey concepts and attitudes as well as emotions, ideas presented in totality for precision and speed.

Though we reject a Freudian key as the only clue to the symbols, we may note with interest that frequently fragmentary compositions embody a recognized symbol for some state of mind and emotion more directly discussed in another poem of the same date. For instance, 'The Merman' and 'The Mermaid' are exercises in form. Experimenting with rhythm, rhyme, and sound, Tennyson 'lets the sense look after itself', and produces the carefree vignettes of lust and laughter under the sea:

> . . . I would sit and sing the whole of the day;
> I would fill the sea-halls with a voice of power;
> But at night I would roam abroad and play
> With the mermaids in and out of the rocks,
> Dressing their hair with the white sea-flower;
> And holding them back by their flowing locks
> I would kiss them often under the sea. . . .

And in the next poem, 'Supposed Confessions of a Second-Rate Sensitive Mind Not in Unity with Itself', we find the open, direct confession of regressive impulse:

> Thrice happy state again to be
> The trustful infant on the knee!
> Who lets his waxen fingers play
> About his mother's neck, and knows
> Nothing beyond his mother's eyes.
> They comfort him by night and day;
> They light his little life alway. . . .

Again, death as a sea-monster ('The Kraken'), perfectly visual, but with intense emotional impact through verse movement and selection of details, follows a direct treatment of the theme of death's power, in 'Love and Death'. Tennyson was as interested as any modern psychologist in the source of such subconscious images, and in the pattern of undirected thinking; through Lucretius he asks:

> How should the mind, except it loved them, clasp
> These idols to herself? Or do they fly
> Now thinner, and now thicker, like the flakes
> In a fall of snow, and so press in, perforce
> Of multitude, as crowds that in an hour
> Of civic tumult jam the doors, and bear
> The keepers down, and throng, their rags and they,
> The basest, far into that council-hall
> Where sit the best and stateliest of the land?

Tennyson does not seem to me to rely much on the emotional implications of Christian symbolism, except in *In Memoriam* and the *Idylls of the King*—and here a more extended and intensive reference to the central figure of Christ would surely have solved many of the difficulties of conveying the message intended. Perhaps this merely tells us something about the state of Tennyson's own faith; perhaps again it is indicative of his cautious artistic avoidance of clouded symbols, and his preference for those to which he could expect unconfused response. The audience of his own day had been so confused intellectually and emotionally by the higher criticism that he could count on no certain or unified response to Christian symbol.

Now a clear symbol creates emotional response not only by its own meaning and connotation, but also by the fact of its being a symbol, by the aesthetic pleasure defined by Mr. Barfield as a 'felt change of consciousness'. A degree of sophistication heightens this pleasure, as, for example, in the symbolic closes of many of Tennyson's poems. Just because the reader's intellect has been so intensely engaged in the conceptual exposition of such a poem as 'On a Mourner', an exposition heightened, to be sure, by personi-fication and imagery, he experiences shock in the transition to the sudden final vision of the night when Troy's prince rises

> With sacrifice, while all the fleet
> Had rest by stony hills of Crete.

Abruptly, through the transitional phrase 'like a household god Promising empire', we are lifted to the sphere of symbolic pattern where the sacrifice of bereavement among the stony hills of sterile life is met by the promise and reminder of peace. The shock, the shift in responsive mode, carries with it the aesthetic pleasure of contrast which Burke characterized as sublime.

But this pleasure is not an end in itself. The symbols must not stand as the focus for the emotion they arouse. They must fill the next requirement set for symbolic method: the reality will be re-cognizable as in this instance a sign. Now this is true empirically of Tennyson's poetic symbols. Even insensitive readers recognize 'Ulysses', for instance, as not a simple story, not a dramatic mono-logue of individual character, but a series of clues to a hidden meaning. How does Tennyson force the reader to recognize the larger meaning in his poems? Not by adhering to a rigid system of symbols, as has already been shown. How then? Partly by enhanc-ing the mood with rhythm and tonal qualities, especially by the unique achievement of a slow-moving line, even in the usually choppy ballad metre, so that dignity and seriousness of movement suggest significance in the subject. (This can be illustrated even in a single line, such as 'Flow down, cold rivulet, to the sea.') Partly, the symbolic significance is emphasized by placing: the recurrence of closing passages in which the scene suddenly shifts, the pace changes, and the perspective widens soon leads the reader to suspect double intention, in 'Aylmer's Field', for example. Finally, we notice the habitual reference to levels. This will not affect us in a single poem, but we have hardly to read four or five pieces before becoming aware of how often Tennyson's scenery is stratified. Again and again our eyes will be led from plain to cliff to sky. Soon we begin to speculate whether Tennyson's intellectual eye moves in the same way, and whether he expects us to follow him from a simple literal level to a more difficult allegorical significance, and perhaps beyond that to anagogy, the dominant concept beyond the specific moral value.

Once recognized as a sign-post, the symbol must fulfil a final requirement: to direct our interest back to the original subject. How effectively do Tennyson's symbols succeed in enriching the significance of the thing symbolized? Does he increase in dexterity in shaping and placing his symbols? Is there any pattern in the kind of subjects which he considers fit for symbolic treatment? The answers to these questions involve an estimate of Tennyson's success and failure in this mode, and a chronological survey of his symbolic poems.

II

Even in the *Juvenilia* Tennyson showed an aptitude for oblique method. He was conscious from the first of the decorative value of the image, before he had any sense of its organic part in the total effect of the poem. In 'Isabel', for instance, the metaphors of 'golden' charity, Intellect's 'sword', the 'silver flow' of language, all serve to enrich the picture of his mother by turning on it the light of various analogies, military, religious, and natural. Metaphors are taken at random from conventional similes: the woman's heart is at one time a temple, at another a blanched tablet; and on the other hand flame is used once as an image of chastity, once as an image of love. But beneath the haphazard jumble we see that the poet is working toward another method of composition, for the images in each verse cluster around a central idea: that of religion in the first verse, of power in the second, and of nature's complexity in the third. The symbols of the Madonna, the Queen, and the flower (to be used often in Tennyson's later poetry) are latent in these image-clusters, not yet in focus, but ready for use when he has mastered the mechanics of his craft, and is ready to experiment with more basic techniques.

In metaphysics, he was already obsessed with the problem of the relationship between appearance and reality. In 'The Two Voices' he left the question of final reality open:

... something is or seems,
That touches me with mystic gleams,
Like glimpses of forgotten dreams. ...

(Later, in *The Princess*, he was to recreate in the reveries of the Prince his own boyhood confusion between shadow and substance).

The *Juvenilia* also show that Tennyson accepted from older poets the implicit metaphor of animism, and introduced personification and the 'pathetic fallacy' into early poems as testimony of his assumption of a universal duality of appearance and essence.

Early mastery appears in the economy of treatment of Mariana's house, black, crusted, rusted, broken, sad, and strange, set on 'the level waste, the rounding grey', symbol of desertion by love. Contrast the impression indirectly achieved here with the more direct effect of 'Deserted House', where the same equation of the house to the human body is heavily underlined, explained by the abstractions of 'Life' and 'Thought'. A comparable pair of early poems, also from the 1830 volume, are 'The Poet', and 'Recollections of the Arabian Nights'. Both show Shelley's influence. In 'The Poet', Tennyson borrows Shelley's imagery of the seed of truth, the winged arrows of thought. He adds his own vision of golden sunrise in a garden (to recur in *Maud*), with 'wreaths of floating dark upcurled', then writes in the equation marks by entitling the foreground figure 'Freedom', and by embroidering on her robes the flaming tag, 'Wisdom'. The poem is an experiment in the stately mode of eighteenth-century allegory, but Tennyson later rejected the mode, with his usual sensitive perception of the changing tastes of his age. In 'Recollections of the Arabian Nights', we have a symbol of Tennyson's own early poetic experience. Probably 'Alastor' furnished the suggestion for that dreamlike voyage through sensuous impressions: citron shadows in the blue, embowered vaults of pillared palm imprisoning sweets, rosaries of scented thorn, and so on. The insistence on remoteness from the world of empirical reality, 'apart from space, withholding time', sets us speculating on the possible parallels between the voyage and the experience of imagination. We form conjectures about the final landscape, with its 'black grots', its strange lighting effects, its dark blue sky, wondering about the sudden emergence into the lofty hall with its two presiding deities. This is one of the few poems in which a personal mythology prevails; as if in reaction against the older form of stabilized, formalized parallels, the poet explored the realm of personal symbolism.

In the 1833 poems the poetic method matures. In 'The Lady of Shalott' we have what I interpret as another symbol of poetic experience: the silent isle apart from movement and life, the mysterious web, the charmed mirror which cracks when the lady turns to reality. We notice a groping towards symbolic colouring: the 'colours gay' of the magic web, set within 'four grey walls and four grey towers', duplicate the jewel colours of the knight as he rides through yellow fields, and 'pale yellow woods'. A comparable concentration on limited detail marks 'Mariana in the South'. In contrast with the jumble of poignant, but unselected, detail of the earlier 'Mariana' we have here the single magnificent vision of the house 'with one black shadow at its feet . . . and silent in its dusty vines'. Details of wasteland landscape are added with 'stony drought and steaming salt'. Yellow emerges as the colour of grief and loss, and the symbolic cycle of the day is used for time, with an apocalyptic vision at the close, of the end of time and of loneliness, when at evening comes 'a sound as of the sea' as Hesper rises, symbol of changeless love. In the ocean and the evening star Tennyson found realities which would evoke universal response.

In the same volume appeared 'Œnone', 'The Palace of Art', and 'The Lotos-Eaters', a group on the power of sensuous beauty over the heart, showing an interesting range of symbolic method. 'Idalian Aphrodite' in the first poem is a lovely static figure from classical myth. Her direct appeal is marred by the laboured and rather confused allegory of Hera's and Athene's speeches, but the symbolic power of the poem as a whole is restored by the controlled opening and closing, which contrast the early misty beauty in the Vale of Ida (the soul) before Aphrodite's triumph, with the final stripped and barren landscape, night without mist, 'cold and starless'. The follows a typical *coda*, Cassandra's prophecy of war which suddenly suggests the influence on external relations of the soul's conquest by sensualism. 'The Palace of Art' is baroque, more complex in its symbolism, using a tapestry technique of significant detail, both in the landscapes symbolizing the shifting moods of the self-pleasuring soul, and in the later recognition of dark corners, uncertain shapes, white-eyed phantasms. Again the end brings a shift in symbol, to the equation of the lost and isolated soul to a still salt pool, sand-locked, seeing waters withdraw, led by the moon, but hearing far off a roar, perhaps of the sea, perhaps of the barren rocks, or perhaps of the wild beasts of uncontrolled passion. As in 'The Lady of Shalott', the numeral four is used to denote a completed cycle. In degree of obliquity 'The Palace of Art' stands between 'Œnone' and 'The Lady of Shalott': the allegory is explained, but the explanation is at least kept outside the limits of the poem proper, relegated to a preface. Last of the 'sensuous soul' group is 'The Lotos-Eaters'. Here we have extended use of the contrast of land and sea: languid land in amber light, where the yellow lotus dust blows beneath three silent pinnacles— changeless land, contrasted with the warring, confused, time-filled, dark blue ocean. The tone of the three poems shifts from tenderness and fascination, through detachment, to weariness, the cloyed effect of satiated senses.

In the 1842 edition appear some new symbols, and several old ones. Birds recur, and illustrate the impossibility of systematizing the symbols. Rosalind is a 'frolic falcon'; the blackbird is the singer who cannot produce in happy times; the mob are 'wild hearts and feeble wings That every sophister can lime'. (Later, Commerce is to be a 'white-winged peace-maker'.) Bird-songs follow Launcelot and Guinevere along the yellowing river. Other symbols are more fixed 'Ulysses' recalls the contrasted symbolism of barren crags and rust, opposed to the thunder and sunshine of the deep. But now Telemachus offers a third alternative, to be developed later into the Arthur figure.

Three poems in this volume illustrate the use of the sudden symbolic close. In 'Audley Court', the two songs, of self and of love, end in a peaceful sunset, a green light in the harbour. In 'Walking to the Mail', the theme of pity, as against 'This raw fool the world, Which charts us all in its coarse blacks or whites', ends with the whimsical sight of 'as quaint a four-in-hand As you shall see—three piebalds and a roan!' Finally, 'The Two Voices' caps the plea for 'more life, and fuller' with the vision of sunrise, of the family trinity, and of the hopeful fields.

In 'The Day-Dream' we have another use of folk-lore, the reverse of allegorical didacticism, a vision presented (ostensibly at least) for its own sake, like 'the wildweed-flower that simply blows'. 'And is there any moral shut Within the bosom of the rose?' The answer is sportive:

   . . . liberal applications lie
In Art like Nature, dearest friend;
So 'twere to cramp its use, if I
Should hook it to some useful end.

But our next poem demands that we ignore this warning, for it is
'The Vision of Sin'. Here we move in successive levels, from the
voluptuous world of human sense, past the universe of nature
where the mist of sin and materialism rises, to a vision of God's
apocalypse, where He 'made Himself an awful rose of dawn'.
Then an interlude of the Dance of Death (its suggestion made too
explicit in the song) leads to a vision of increased intensity of the
decaying, shifting material universe, where 'Men and horses
pierced with worms' form a weird setting for babbling explanations of the causes of sin—original nature, malice, the souring
grain of conscience. Finally, as a tremendous chorus, comes the
answer in a tongue unknown, like the voice in 'On a Mourner',
this time giving intimations, not prophecy; and the second vision
of God's 'awful rose of dawn'. The poem is strange and strained.
It represents a last intrusion of direct statement into the core of a
poem whose major movement is oblique. A last poem in the 1842
volumes shows no such lack of tonal unity. 'Break, Break, Break'
represents the height of Tennyson's symbolic method. It holds in
perfect balance the 'subject' of death and the 'other reality' of
temporal stones and eternal sea. It diverts conceptual and emotional response from the shout and song of the boys to the sound-
less haven of death. Finally it intensifies the ultimate regret for
time past, by creating the unspoken contrast between the sea
(whose individual waves breaking on the shore lose their own
identity, but whose infinite nature is unchangeable) and the 'tender grace' of unreturning time.

More hopeful is the *coda* of 'The Golden Year', in which James's
words of praise for work are echoed in a dynamite blast from the
stone quarry, representing the breaking of sterility by a human
agency.

In conclusion, I shall examine four poems, appearing late,
which duplicate some of the characteristics noted in the early
work. 'The Higher Pantheism' and 'Flower in the Crannied Wall'
represent the old team of direct statement and oblique, in parallel
poems, here on the question of the essence of self. The world of
sense-experience is a proof of consciousness, says the higher

pantheist, and a mark of the division of man from the universe around him. But the flower, 'root and all, and all in all', denies the possibility of differentiating by sense conclusions from the flux of time and space, and restores the final mystery by using affective symbol. 'The Ancient Sage' and 'Merlin and the Gleam' show that Tennyson was not only using the same techniques of symbolism in his later years as in earlier times, but was also applying the mode to the same familiar topics. 'Merlin and the Gleam' presents a final fusion of the Arthurian elements of folk-lore with the theme of poetic experience. In 'The Ancient Sage' we return to the classical correlative for a last word on the appeal of materialism.

This poem may be studied in detail for a final comment on Tennyson's later symbolic method. The duet form of its verse is intended to indicate the tonal difference between sensualist and sage: decorative, fanciful snatches of song interrupt the measured musings of the sage. But the opposition of form does not extend to a contrasted use of direct and oblique techniques. The sage presents his case through a series of images: of the cave, whose fountain with its 'higher' source symbolizes the faith he represents; of the city, from which he has escaped to die, but to which the younger man must return, to act, to 'curb the beast', to live more charitably; of the mount, to which faith climbs. Clusters of images appear also in the song of the materialist: bird images, flower images, images of light and darkness, of animals, and of fruit ('The kernel of the shrivell'd fruit Is jutting thro' the rind'). The true contrast in the poem appears in the opposed interpretations which the two speakers apply to the images. Both sensualist and sage introduce symbols which focus the poem on the central concept of the cycle. There is the cycle of bloom and seed, symbol of hope to the sage, of imminent death to the materialist. There is the cycle of 'the lark within the songless egg'; 'the shell must break before the bird can fly', says the cheerful sage, but his young friend sees only the restrictions of 'this earth-narrow life'. There is the cycle of light and dark, cue for despair to the sensualist, but for the idealist a mark of the fusion of past and present, 'as if the late and early were but one'. Loss of identity, pictured by the materialist in human terms at first (in the ageing warrior, merchant, plowman, and poet), is finally symbolized by the 'ripple on the boundless deep That moves, and all is gone'. But the seer shifts the symbol:

> But that one ripple on the boundless deep
> Feels that the deep is boundless, and itself
> For ever changing form, but evermore
> One with the boundless motion of the deep.

Similarly, clouds, which mean doubt to the materialist, lead the sage into a different interpretation, this time based on the scientific lore on which Tennyson so often drew for his imagery: 'The clouds themselves are children of the sun.' Science furnishes also his interpretation of interdependent light and dark:

> . . . Earth's dark forehead flings athwart the heavens
> Her shadow crown'd with stars.

Obviously, this poem suggests the richness of symbolism: 'Idle gleams to you are light to me,' says the sage; and he deplores the questioner's desire to define, to analyse, to prove, to wage the endless war of 'counter-terms'. The close of the poem brings a final example of the level-climbing *coda*, and a final plea for vision, in the mountain ranges rising to 'the high-heaven dawn of more than mortal day'.

Few changes in range of symbols; few extensions in basic range of subject-matter; no radical departure from the initial double line of attack, direct and oblique—are we to conclude that Tennyson was timid, or conservative, or simply that, having established an effective range of indirect techniques astonishingly early in his career, he accepted the tool as forged, and concentrated his effort on enlarging and deepening the thought-content, the significance of the thing symbolized? Perhaps the most fruitful conjecture would be that Tennyson was aware that both direct and oblique methods have a poetic value, and that in his minor poems he made a consistent effort to fuse the powers of both.

1951

THE 'HIGH-BORN MAIDEN' SYMBOL IN TENNYSON

Lionel Stevenson

IN SPITE of the wide range of topics and techniques in the poetry of Tennyson, a reader is apt to become aware of certain recurrences which eventually assume an air of familiarity. The present study deals with one of the most persistent of these recurrences, which is especially significant because of a process of change that affected it over a period of years, symptomatic of a gradual shift in the poet's outlook.

At the beginning of Tennyson's career several of his poems were unmistakably influenced by Shelley. The two particularly noticeable specimens of this influence were sometimes linked together in Shelley's poems, as in two successive stanzas of 'To a Skylark':

> Like a Poet hidden
> In the light of thought,
> Singing hymns unbidden,
> Till the world is wrought
> To sympathy with hopes and fears it heeded not:

> Like a high-born maiden
> In a palace-tower,
> Soothing her love-laden
> Soul in secret hour
> With music sweet as love, which overflows her bower . . .

The first of these, the concept of the poet who remains personally inconspicuous and yet influences history and national destiny, is now best known through Shelley's extensive passage on the 'unacknowledged legislators' in the *Defense of Poetry*; this, however, was merely an elaboration in prose of an idea which Shelley had embodied in the episode of the old hermit in *The Revolt of Islam*, and in other poems, where Tennyson could have encountered it at the beginning of his career. In a paper already published I have suggested the relationship between this idea of Shelley's and such early poems of Tennyson as 'The Mystic' and 'The Poet'.[1]

The concept in the other stanza of 'To a Skylark', that of the imprisoned or otherwise isolated maiden, is more widely pervasive in Shelley's poetry. It is vividly employed in *The Revolt of Islam* in the episode of Cythna's incarceration in the island cave that can be reached only by an underwater passage. In terms of actual—though romanticized—experience, it becomes Emilia Viviani's imprisonment in her convent (*Epipsychidion*):

> Poor captive bird! who, from thy narrow cage,
> Pourest such music, that it might assuage
> The ruggèd hearts of those who prisoned thee,
> Were they not deaf to all sweet melody . . .

The same theme, more playfully treated, appears in *The Witch of Atlas*, wherein the enchantress eventually rebels against her seclusion in her mountain cavern.[2]

Echoes of these poems are to be recognized in the many passages in which Tennyson recurred to the image of an isolated and unhappy maiden with a persistence amounting almost to obsession. It is not possible, of course, to affirm that Tennyson derived his image solely from Shelley. No trace of it, however, can be found in his juvenile poems, written before he encountered Shelley's works.[3] Professor W. D. Paden, in his exhaustive study of the imagery of those boyhood writings and its sources in Tennyson's reading, brings out scarcely an item that might be identified as the 'high-born maiden' in any guise.

---

[1] 'Tennyson, Browning, and a Romantic Fallacy,' *Univ. of Toronto Quarterly*, xiii (Jan. 1944), pp. 175–95.

[2] The reclusive poet and the unattainable maiden appear also in *Alastor*.

[3] Of *The Lover's Tale*, composed when he was eighteen, Tennyson said, 'that was written before I had ever seen a Shelley, though it is called Shelleyan.' *Memoir*, ii, pp. 285, 498.

In his volume of 1830, however, after he had gone to Cambridge and found the literary undergraduates excited about Shelley, she made her first appearance, with a strange effect as though she had invaded the author's imagination without his knowing what to do with her. This poem, 'Mariana', stood out as the most effective in the volume, its detailed description and its unity of gloomy emotion being in strong contrast with the vague melodies about 'Adeline' and 'Margaret' and 'Eleanore'. Nevertheless, the subject of 'Mariana' remained curiously unidentified: no actual story was told in the poem to account for Mariana's loneliness, or to explain who 'he' was and why 'he' did not come.

The immediate inspiration for the poem, of course, while literary, was not Shelleyan. It originated with a phrase in *Measure for Measure*, 'Mariana in the moated grange', referring to her desertion by Angelo. But this does not adequately explain why the words captured Tennyson's imagination and suggested a dreamy, half-supernatural atmosphere, very different from Shakespeare's bitter comedy. The poem plainly implies that Mariana is totally alone and unattended, and such mundane questions as how she received food are left unconsidered. Obviously Shakespeare's phrase, with its connotations of remoteness and imprisonment, aroused memories of fairy-tales of the 'Sleeping Beauty' type, and became so vivid that it shaped itself in the landscape of Tennyson's native Lincolnshire.

To these elements, however, a distinct suggestion of Cythna in her cave was added, even to the use of a haunting, melancholy refrain line:

> But I was changed—the very life was gone
>   Out of my heart—I wasted more and more
> Day after day, and sitting there alone
> Vexed the inconstant waves with my perpetual moan . . .

> But all that cave and all its shapes, possest
> By thoughts which could not fade, renewed each one
>   Some smile, some look, some gesture, which had blest
> Me heretofore; I, sitting there alone
> Vext the inconstant waves with my perpetual moan . . .

Evidence of the strength with which this theme possessed Tennyson is the fact that his next book of poems, two years later, contained a companion piece, 'Mariana in the South', again with a refrain that seems to echo Cythna's lament. Like most sequels, it was inferior to its predecessor, partly because it merely reiterated the same effect, partly because the Mediterranean landscape was less real in the poet's mind. Other poems of the 1833 volume, however, gave the theme a fresh significance. The two 'Mariana' poems were merely studies in mood and scene; when the lady next appeared in a poem she had acquired a new literary source, a more detailed story, and a distinct symbolic meaning.

In 'The Lady of Shalott' Tennyson's newly-developing Arthurian studies had introduced him to another maiden in a palace tower soothing her love-laden soul in secret hour. Nevertheless, he did not completely adopt the story of Elaine as it was to be found in Malory (Book XVIII, Chapters 9–20); and the Italian *novella* of *La Damigella di Scalot*, which was presumably its more immediate source, had no tower, tapestry, mirror, or curse.[1] Like Spenser, Tennyson adapted the Arthurian material for his own ulterior purpose, omitting the girl's name, using an obscure form of the name of her residence, and introducing an element of the supernatural. The story, while much better developed than in 'Mariana', is still incomplete; there is no explanation as to why a spell has been laid upon the lady or how it causes her death.

The Shelleyan echoes in the poem connect it especially with *The Witch of Atlas*, whose solitary cave was visited by a procession of wild animals, mythological beings, shepherds, *et al.* To avoid dazzling these passers-by with her beauty, she became a weaver:

> . . . she took her spindle
> And twined three threads of fleecy mist, and three
> Long lines of light, such as the dawn may kindle
> The clouds and waves and mountains with; and she
> As many star-beams, ere their lamps could dwindle
> In the belated moon, wound skilfully;
> And with these threads a subtle veil she wove . . .

> All day the wizard lady sate aloof . . .
> . . . broidering the pictured poesy
> Of some high tale upon her growing woof . . .

When she grew weary of her seclusion she conjured up a magic boat and drifted down the rivers of the world to observe all its

[1] F. T. Palgrave said that the poem was based upon an 'Italian romance'. This has been convincingly identified by L. S. Potwin, 'The Source of Tennyson's *The Lady of Shalott*', *Modern Language Notes*, xvii (Dec. 1902), pp. 237–9.

wonders. She remained happy as an onlooker, isolated from human life; but Shelley adds:

> 'Tis said in after times her spirit free
>> Knew what love was, and felt itself alone—
> But holy Dian could not chaster be
>> Before she stooped to kiss Endymion,
> Than now this lady—like a sexless bee
>> Tasting all blossoms, and confined to none,
> Among those mortal forms, the wizard-maiden
> Past with an eye serene and heart unladen.

In Tennyson's poem this idea is grafted upon the Arthurian material to bring out a definite allegory. The lady of Shalott is an artist, weaving beautiful pictures which are supposed to reproduce real life but which are derived entirely at second hand through the mirror. At the beginning of the poem she is perfectly happy with her artificial, lifeless creations. When she catches a first glimpse of real emotion, even in the mirror (the young lovers) she suddenly begins to rebel, crying out, 'I am half sick of shadows!'[1] As soon as emotion touches her personally through her interest in Lancelot, she defies the curse, and enjoys her brief hour of genuine life, even though she knows it will be her last.

The personal application of this situation cannot have been ignored by Tennyson. In his secluded life at Somersby Rectory and at Cambridge he had written copious, facile poems woven out of the *Arabian Nights* and all the other reading that had appealed to him. The astringent reviews of his 1830 volume accused him flatly of being artificial and derivative. Like the lady of Shalott, he was deciding to discard all his previous serene creations and to face the painful experiences of real life.

A more explicit and remarkable treatment of the theme occurred in another poem of the 1833 volume, 'The Palace of Art'. The descriptive virtuosity in the first half of the poem has tended to obscure the intensity of the allegory, in spite of the prefatory lines *To* ——, which emphasized the symbolic significance. The poem originated in a remark by Tennyson's friend Richard Chenevix Trench, when they were both still at Cambridge, 'Tennyson,

---

[1] Tennyson stated positively to Alfred Ainger that 'the new-born love for something, for some one in the wide world from which she has been so long secluded, takes her out of the region of shadows into that of realities'. *Memoir*, i. p. 117.

we cannot live in art.'[1] As soon as this abstract opinion began to take specific form in the poet's mind it embodied itself in the familiar figure of the imprisoned maiden. This time no process of inference is necessary to convince us that the poet is symbolizing an inner experience of his own. Personifying his soul as a beautiful and arrogant woman, he tells how he built for her a palace on top of a precipitous mountain, where she dwelt in complete solitude. The decorations and furnishings of the palace represent the whole heritage of literature, art, philosophy, and science which makes up the culture of the modern world. From the windows the self-sufficient soul can look down contemptuously upon the primitive struggles of every-day life:

> O God-like isolation which art mine,
> I can but count thee perfect gain,
> What time I watch the darkening droves of swine
> That range on yonder plain.

> In filthy sloughs they roll a prurient skin,
> They graze and wallow, breed and sleep;
> And oft some brainless devil enters in,
> And drives them to the deep.

After achieving the supreme egotism of declaring, 'I sit as God holding no form of creed, but contemplating all,' the soul enjoys her solitary complacency for three years, and then abruptly falls into an insane agony of loneliness, in which she alternates between despair, sardonic self-ridicule, and terror of gruesome hallucinations. When she has finally suffered the illusion of actual death and burial, she realizes that her only salvation is to discard her royal robes and retire to 'a cottage in the vale' to practise penitence. In the final stanza she announces her hope that when she has purged her guilt she may return to the beautiful palace and bring companions with her.

The reminiscences of Shelley in the poems are particularly numerous. The description of the palace resembles that of the Elysian temple at the beginning of *The Revolt of Islam*:

> . . . through a portal wide
> We passed—whose roof of moonstone carved, did keep
> A glimmering o'er the forms on every side,
> Sculptures like life and thought, immovable, deep-eyed . . .

[1] *Memoir*, i, p. 118.

> And on the jasper walls around, there lay
> Paintings, the poesy of mightiest thought,
> Which did the Spirit's history display. . . .

Other parallels for the furnishings of the gorgeous palace, and for the lady's comfortable superiority towards all mortal conflicts and lusts, can be found in *The Witch of Atlas*:

> Her cave was stored with scrolls of strange device,
>   The works of some Saturnian Archimage,
> Which taught the expiations at whose price
>   Men from the Gods might win that happy age
> Too lightly lost, redeeming native vice;
>   And which might quench the Earth-consuming rage
> Of gold and blood—till men should live and move
> Harmonious as the sacred stars above . . .
>
> And wondrous works of substances unknown . . .
>   Were heaped in the recesses of her bower;
> Carved lamps and chalices, and vials which shone
>   In their own golden beams . . .
>
> At first she lived alone in this wild home,
>   And her own thoughts were each a minister . . .

The series of psychological stages endured by the soul while crazed by loneliness are reminiscent of Cythna in her cave. To find a prototype for the actual allegory of 'The Palace of Art', however, one must turn to another poem of Shelley's, *Queen Mab*. Ianthe's spirit was led into the 'Hall of Spells' in 'Mab's ethereal palace', with its 'floors of flashing light, its vast and azure dome', and its 'pearly battlements' which 'looked o'er the immense of Heaven'. Pointing to the gorgeous dome, Queen Mab declared severely:

> '. . . were it virtue's only meed to dwell
> In a celestial palace, all resigned
> To pleasurable impulses, immured
> Within the prison of itself, the will
> Of changeless nature would be unfulfilled.
> Learn to make others happy.'

Ianthe was then led to 'the overhanging battlement' and shown a universal panorama of human life and history, which was summed up by the Fairy in terms similar to the description of the soul's despair in 'The Palace of Art':

> 'How vainly seek
> The selfish for that happiness denied
> To aught but virtue! Blind and hardened, they,
> Who . . . sigh for pleasure they refuse to give,—
> Madly they frustrate still their own designs;
> And, where they hope that quiet to enjoy
> Which virtue pictures, bitterness of soul,
> Pining regrets, and vain repentances,
> Disease, disgust, and lassitude, pervade
> Their valueless and miserable lives.'

Tennyson's use of the high-born maiden symbol has therefore assumed a significant new implication in 'The Palace of Art'; she is no longer a pathetic, deserted creature who is the victim of external oppression, but a hard, arrogant egotist who has chosen isolation because she feels superior to her fellow-beings, and whose eventual misery is due not to the absence of one particular lover, but to her divorce from all human sympathy.

There remained one further step: consistent with his new determination to write about the actual affairs of human experience, Tennyson had to transfer his concept from allegory to objective portraiture. The poem which achieves this step is *Lady Clara Vere de Vere*. Most comments upon it are unfair through failing to mention that it is a dramatic monologue. The speaker is not Tennyson himself, but an idealistic country lad who suspects that the great lady of the manor is planning to break his heart for her amusement, as she has already broken the heart and caused the suicide of his friend. Lady Clara is the embodiment of pride and selfishness, regarding herself as set apart from her neighbours by the 'hundred earls' in her ancestry. And yet, like the lady of Shalott and the soul in 'The Palace of Art', she is finding her self-sufficiency inadequate for maintaining her happiness. Her effort to attract even the country bumpkins as admirers is a symptom of her unrest:

> I know you, Clara Vere de Vere,
>   You pine among your halls and towers:
> The languid light of your proud eyes
>   Is wearied of the rolling hours.
> In glowing health, with boundless wealth,
>   But sickening of a vague disease,
> You know so ill to deal with time,
>   You needs must play such pranks as these.

Therefore the youth advises her to undertake some social-service work:

> Clara, Clara Vere de Vere,
> If time be heavy on your hands,
> Are there no beggars at your gate,
> Nor any poor about your lands?
> Oh! teach the orphan-boy to read,
> Or teach the orphan-girl to sew,
> Pray Heaven for a human heart,
> And let the foolish yeoman go.

It is something of an anti-climax, just as the ending of 'The Palace of Art', but in both poems Tennyson is insisting that for the self-induced misery of isolation the only remedy is unselfish participation in human affairs.

Having thus transferred his high-born maiden from the cloudy realms of legend and allegory to the noonday of contemporary England, Tennyson varied her portrait in several other poems. In 'Locksley Hall' she is Amy, no longer coldly proud, but merely weak enough to sacrifice love in exchange for wealth and social prestige at the insistence of her parents. In *Maud* she becomes still less aloof; because she has been brought up amid wealth and flattery, at the beginning of the poem her moody admirer assumes that she will be cold and selfish; but Maud proves sincere enough —or perhaps wilful enough—to defy the family grandeur and keep tryst with her penniless lover.

Again the image may be found, multiplied into a whole institution-full of high-born maidens, in *The Princess*, with intellectual arrogance this time the barrier that must be broken down by love and all the demands of practical life. A playful variant of the same plot is provided in 'The Day-Dream', which retells the story of the Sleeping Beauty. This fairy tale, which had lurked vaguely in the background of 'Mariana' and 'The Lady of Shalott', is now presented for its sheer gay romanticism, with Tennyson half-ironically pointing out that this time it is devoid of allegory:

> Oh, to what uses shall we put
> The wildweed-flower that simply blows?
> And is there any moral shut
> Within the bosom of the rose?

But any man that walks the mead,
  In bud or blade, or bloom, may find,
According as his humours lead,
  A meaning suited to his mind.
And liberal applications lie
  In Art like Nature, dearest friend;
So 'twere to cramp its use, if I
  Should hook it to some useful end.

As final evidence that Tennyson had become the master of his symbol instead of its thrall, he later returned to the story of 'The Lady of Shalott' and retold it among the *Idylls of the King* as *Lancelot and Elaine*, eliminating all supernatural vagueness and inserting the explicit pseudo-historical details of the original chivalric romances.

The long persistence of the high-born maiden in Tennyson's poetry inevitably suggests a psychological interpretation. Indeed, the symbol conforms with amazing precision to the theory of Jung regarding the archetypal image of the *anima*, the most frequent unconscious symbol, which Jung regards as representing the unconscious itself, and which is always of the opposite sex. Tennyson himself forestalled Jung, in the key poem of the series, 'The Palace of Art', by explicitly identifying the lady as his own soul. A man usually 'projects' his *anima* emotionally upon an actual woman; but with progress towards complete maturity the projection can give place to a more rational relationship. This very difficult and painful process is the only way to psychological completeness. In the process the *anima* has to become recognized as a personified image of the unconscious, so that it can eventually be accepted as a normal psychological function. Jung says:

If the coming to terms with the shadow is the companion-piece to the individual's development, then that with the anima is the masterpiece. For the relation with the anima is again a test of courage and—more than that—a test by fire of all a man's spiritual and moral forces.

Since a poet, unlike other men, keeps an unintentional diary of his psychological evolution in his poems, the series of Tennyson's poems cited above can serve as illustrations of Jung's analysis.

In these poems the symbol went through three clear phases: (i) a vague, melancholy, and sympathetic picture of a girl imprisoned and isolated for no explicit reason, (ii) a bitter condemnation of the girl for being proud, selfish, and self-sufficient, (iii) a bland, objective use of the theme for its narrative value. The first of these phases, equivalent to an adolescent 'falling in love', showed the *anima* asserting itself without rational recognition. In the second phase Tennyson succeeded in labelling her clearly as the personification of his own unconscious, and therefore made her the scapegoat for the inner conflicts that were tormenting him. At last, as he gained emotional stability, he gradually transformed the mysterious maiden into a matter-of-fact literary stock-character.

A remarkable feature of the situation was that the early phases of the symbol in Tennyson's poetry were strongly affected by another poet whose work was almost equally permeated with it. Tennyson suddenly and temporarily fell under the spell of Shelley just when he was susceptible also to the stirring of the *anima* within himself. Thus he provides a clear instance of the way in which a poet's personal unconscious motivations can become linked with material that his imagination derives from his reading. He could certainly not have been so profoundly attracted to Shelley's high-born maiden passages unless they had accorded with conditions in his own inner life.

When the maiden first entered his imagination he was beginning uncomfortably to suspect, in spite of the adulation of fellow-students, that his narrow scope of poetry, based upon his reading, might be inadequate. The ideal of the poet, seductively depicted by Shelley as remaining hidden in the light of thought and converting the world to a millennium, seemed futile in the face of the utilitarian Victorian age. The bitter and almost masochistic poems came while Tennyson was grimly struggling to revise his work under the lash of the critics who had condemned his lack of 'power over the feelings and thoughts of men'. At the same time he was anxious about his engagement to Emily Sellwood, whom he could not marry until his financial circumstances should improve. Finally, his serene, objective representations of the high-born maiden were written when poetical success and—later—a happy marriage had justified the course he had elected.

1948

TENNYSON'S MYTHOLOGY
A STUDY OF *DEMETER AND PERSEPHONE*

G. *Robert Stange*

OUR PRESENT image of Tennyson's poetic career is well established; the pattern, in its broad outlines, is of a youthful burst of subjective lyricism followed by a half-century of suppression, propriety, and worldly success. As Harold Nicolson has ingenuously put it, Tennyson 'was intended to be a subjective poet, and was forced by circumstances into fifty years of unnatural objectivity'.[1] If we disregard its obvious inaccuracies such a view has much to recommend it. The reader of our time, influenced by the Aesthetic movement, nourished on the works of the French poets and novelists, is clearly more at home with a Tennyson who belongs to the band of *poètes maudits* than he would be with the Victorians' apotheosized Laureate. And since no total impression of a poet's life, no dramatic construction of his career, is ever likely to be accurate, we might well content ourselves with this image of Alfred Tennyson and be grateful to its originators for having made at least a small place for him in the modern pantheon.

But though we hold to the image of Tennyson as a poet of tortured sensibility, the voice of an ineffable despair, we must not

---

[1] *Tennyson: Aspects of His Life, Character, and Poetry* (London, 1923), p. 10.

permit this interpretation to be chronologically limited. The detached and almost hermetic qualities of the early poems did, it is true, give way to a tendency towards homely didacticism, and it is easy to assume that the Tennyson of the middle and later years found himself as a 'public' poet. The final fifty years, however, were not given over to an 'unnatural objectivity'; the tensions—and the richness—which mark Tennyson's early work can be found at the end as well as at the beginning of the collected poems.

Tennyson's poems, of whatever date, which seem to the modern reader efficient and expressive tend to display what can only be called the Tennysonian complex. They are ambiguous in tone; they exhibit the dialogue of the mind with itself; they circle round the anguished perception of the oppositions that rend the poet and his world. Tennyson's most typical conflict centres on his confusion as to the function of poetry. Throughout his career he sought to justify the saving power of poetry and expressed the ambivalence of the nineteenth-century artist, rejected by the world, who at one moment rejoices in his isolation, and at another struggles to assert himself as *sacer vates*.

Underlying this conflict is the poet's combined hatred for and acceptance of his age. He described it as 'an age of lies, and also an age of stinks',[1] yet he felt that the sober, energetic Victorian world somehow marked the threshold of a glimmering new existence in which all irreconcilables would be fused and faith and light have their day. Intermixed with these attitudes was the poet's characteristically Victorian religious conflict. Here too all was doubt and division. It was impossible for him to believe in conventional Christianity, yet that faith represented the only belief worth having. In this sphere Tennyson, as every reader of *In Memoriam* knows, attempted to affirm the value of doubt itself, to celebrate a weak faith in the 'one far-off divine event, To which the whole creation moves'.

Such a web of velleities and confusions would seem to offer the material not of great poetry, but of a poetry of passive suffering, of a wayward and individual despair. Tennyson nevertheless managed to create a body of great verse out of apparently defective materials. His achievement does not rest on an objectification or dramatization of his conflicts, nor on the strategies of ironic detachment and acute intellectual analysis. His tendency was rather

[1] *Memoir*, ii, p. 75.

to surround his personal subjects with the rich trappings of myth and legend, to suffuse them with a noble and melodious melancholy, to align his psychic ambivalences with the permanently affecting oppositions of the life of man and nature.

Stéphane Mallarmé, in trying to sum up his sense of Tennyson's nobility, had recourse to a comment of Villiers de l'Isle-Adam: 'En effet, la littérature proprement dite n'existant pas plus que l'espace pur—ce que l'on se rappelle d'un grand poète, c'est l'impression dite de sublimité qu'il vous a laissée, par et à travers son œuvre, plutôt que l'œuvre elle-meme'.[1] The impression of sublimity that Tennyson's poetry communicates does not, of course, exist independently of the work itself. He was above all a workman, and a close reading of his work would call attention not only to the peculiar climate of his poetry, but to the range of his interests and techniques, to the unexpected flexibility of his poetic instrument.

I intend to examine a very late poem of Tennyson's in the light of these generalizations. *Demeter and Persephone* recommends itself as a complex work which deals with the question of spiritual estrangement, which incorporates the poet's concern with his age and with religious belief, and which has the further interest of anticipating the reinterpretation of mythology which has informed some of the most distinguished poetry of our century.

Tennyson, who was eighty when *Demeter and Persephone* was published (in 1889), spoke of it afterwards in a pleasantly off-hand way. It is reported that his son Hallam suggested the subject because, he said, 'I knew that my father considered Demeter one of the most beautiful types of womanhood.' And the poet answered, 'I will write it, but when I write an antique like this I must put it into a frame—something modern about it. It is no use giving a mere *réchauffé* of old legends.'[2] He would cite as an example of the 'frame' the lines in which Demeter envisions a coming race of 'younger kindlier Gods', and iterates Tennyson's notion of the 'one far-off divine event'. The frame of modernism involved first a penetration of the essential meanings of the Greek legend, conceived not as allegory or symbol, but in the terms of myth itself, and then an assimilation of those meanings to the Christian hope

[1] Stéphane Mallarmé, 'Tennyson vu d'ici', *Divagations* (Paris, 1922), p. 113.
[2] *Memoir*, ii, p. 364.

of a New Jerusalem. The most striking achievement of the poem is the consistency with which the language of myth is used to include reflections on the nature of artistic creation, on the condition of the age, and on religious doctrine.

Tennyson derived his legend from the Homeric *Hymn to Demeter* and, except in the conclusion to his poem, was faithful to the spirit of the Greek original. However, the nature of his selection and variation of emphasis is in itself expressive. The expansive detail and the typal quality of the hymn are rejected in favour of a dramatic emphasis on the situation of the goddess and her daughter. Tennyson omitted the ritualistic background of the original; Zeus and Pluto appear only as symbols of the polarity of existence. The narrative is compressed to fit the exacting demands of the dramatic monologue form, and events are altered so that the scene of both Demeter's soliloquy and the reunion with her daughter is the Vale of Enna, from which Persephone was originally abducted.

With all these rearrangements, one discovers that the myth, though it retains its identity, has become a Tennysonian subject. Attempts have often been made to distinguish the 'classical' poems from Tennyson's other work and to find in them a firmer tone, an elevated impersonality. But the fact is that every Greek or Roman theme that the poet chose to treat became in his hands a symbolic narrative of separation, either from an object of love or from the natural course of life. Such dissimilar classical poems as 'Œnone', 'Ulysses', and 'Tithonus' share this central theme. In each case the subject offered an opportunity for a figurative expression of personal concerns, and the pattern of situation that emerges in the classical idylls is very little different from that of the poems based on history, medieval legend, or original narrative.

In a manner which is significant to the history of English poetry, Tennyson's reinterpretation of the myth of Demeter has affinities with that modern view of myth which is derived from the research of Sir James Frazer. The first volume of *The Golden Bough* was published in 1890, a year after Tennyson's *Demeter*. In the seventh volume of his study Frazer said:

... we do no indignity to the myth of Demeter and Persephone—one of the few myths in which the sunshine and clarity of the Greek genius are crossed by the shadow and mystery of death—when we trace its origin to some of the most familiar, yet eternally affecting aspects of nature, to the melancholy gloom and decay of autumn and to the freshness, the brightness, and the verdure of spring.[1]

Tennyson's centre of interest in Demeter is the scheme of related antinomies from which the imagery of the poem develops, and which are inherent in the myth. The poem's basic design is one of oppositions between brightness and gloom (compare Frazer's shadow and brightness). This pattern reflects the contrast between Persephone's joyful life on earth and her imprisonment in the underworld, and includes the antitheses of decay and fertility; of the ruling principles of life: God, 'the Bright one', and 'the Dark one', his brother; and finally the underlying duality of life and death.

Frazer interpreted the two goddesses as personifications of the corn in its double aspect—Persephone as the seed and Demeter as the ripe ear. Though Tennyson followed the nineteenth-century tradition of regarding Demeter as the Earth Mother,[2] his imaginative construction of the myth reveals the same insights as Frazer's scholarly study:

> Above all, thought of the seed buried in the earth in order to spring up to new and higher life readily suggested a comparison with human destiny, and strengthened the hope that for man too the grave would be but the beginning of a better and happier existence in some brighter world unknown. This simple and natural reflection seems perfectly sufficient to explain the association of the Corn Goddess at Eleusis with the mystery of death and the hope of a blissful immortality.[3]

Throughout his poem Tennyson stressed the theme of regeneration and related it to other threads of his imagery. The episodes are ordered and the change of emotions punctuated by the progression of the seasons—we follow Demeter through the phases of the year, from the melancholy of autumn, through the despair of winter, to the lightening hope of spring. The opening lines state some of the main motifs:

[1] 'Spirits of the Corn and of the Wild', *The Golden Bough; a Study in Magic and Religion*, 12 vols. (London, 1911–15), vii, p. 91.

[2] Frazer found no justification for this identification either in the rites of Demeter or in the artistic representation of the two goddesses. ibid., pp. 40 ff.

[3] ibid., p. 90.

Faint as a climate-changing bird that flies
All night across the darkness, and at dawn
Falls on the threshold of her native land,
And can no more, thou camest, O my child,
Led upward by the God of ghosts and dreams,
Who laid thee at Eleusis, dazed and dumb
With passing thro' at once from state to state,
Until I brought thee hither, that the day,
When here thy hands let fall the gather'd flower,
Might break thro' clouded memories once again
On thy lost self.

The passage exhibits the poem's characteristic quality of multiple suggestion and controlled ambiguity. The simile of the 'climate-changing bird' is typical; Persephone, like a bird, comes back
with the spring, but she is mythically the changer of the climate,
and her return *is* the spring. The darkness and the dawn represent
not only the days of the bird's flight and the passage from the
gloom of hell to the light of earth, but more profoundly, the birth
of a new day and a new season, symbolized by Persephone's
emergence from the underworld. The return to the native land is
the first suggestion of a succeeding discrimination among three
states of being; Hades marks one undesirable extreme and Heaven
the other; the earth, or more particularly, the Vale of Enna, symbolizes the middle state, the good place—but I shall have more to
say of this later.

It is implied that Persephone's abduction involved a losing of
the self; she is 'led upward' by Hermes out of the land of death and
carried by her mother to the place where the return of day will
bring her former self to light. In the lines that follow, Persephone's rebirth is expressed by images of light:

A sudden nightingale
Saw thee, and flash'd into a frolic of song
And welcome; and a gleam as of the moon,
When first she peers along the tremulous deep,
Fled wavering o'er thy face, and chased away
That shadow of a likeness to the king
Of shadows, thy dark mate. Persephone!
Queen of the dead no more—my child! Thine eyes
Again were human-godlike, and the Sun

Burst from a swimming fleece of winter gray,
And robed thee in his day from head to feet—
'Mother!' and I was folded in thine arms. (Lines 11–22)

The nightingale's song of welcome which partly dispels the
shadow of death, Persephone's likeness to her 'dark mate', may be
thought of as the greeting of nature. But Persephone does not
again become the child of Demeter until the day has fully dawned.
We are not allowed to forget that though the spirit of fecundity
may be re-united to her mother, the earth, she is married to the
god of darkness. In the second section of the poem this double
allegiance is more fully developed; Persephone has been permanently altered and to some extent estranged by what she has seen
in hell:

Child, those imperial, disimpassion'd eyes
Awed even me at first, thy mother—eyes
That oft had seen the serpent-wanded power
Draw downward into Hades with his drift
Of flickering spectres, lighted from below
By the red race of fiery Phlegethon;
But when before have Gods or men beheld
The Life that had descended re-arise,
And lighted from above him by the Sun?
So mighty was the mother's childless cry,
A cry that rang thro' Hades, Earth, and Heaven!
(Lines 23–33)

When we come to examine the third section of the poem we
shall see that the place of reunion, the Vale of Enna, closely resembles certain recurrent scenes in Tennyson's poetry, locations
which are symbolic of the proper home of the spirit. Anticipating
this interpretation, one might examine this section of the poem to
see if it reflects any of the poet's personal concerns. Persephone is
clearly the personification of fertility, but it is possible that she
may also express the principle of poetic creativity. The journey to
the underworld has frequently served as a figurative expression of
a poet's experience. The myth of Orpheus is the most notable
example of such an application; but early in his career Tennyson
used the figure of Ulysses (who had visited the underworld and
returned) to stand for the poet who had lived more fully than other
men and had consequently estranged himself from them. Tennyson also, and in this T. S. Eliot has followed him, found in the

myth of Tiresias an analogy to the suffering the poet must undergo as a result of the preternatural vision the gods had granted him. Both Tennyson and Eliot presumably based their interpretations on Homer, who accorded to Tiresias a special position in the underworld as the only shade that retained integrity of judgement and knowledge after death.

The description of Persephone's transformation, which is original with Tennyson, bears some resemblance to his treatment of mythical poet-figures. The changes that the 'human' goddess has suffered reflect the traditional conception of the terrible effects of visions that are not meant for earthly eyes. In the fires of hell she has seen revealed the secrets of death; she has become 'imperial'— that is, regnant over the spirits of the underworld—and 'disimpassioned'—remote from ordinary emotion. She is a 'human-godlike' personage who has become estranged from our life by the intensity of her dark experiences.

Tennyson was obsessed by the theme of penetration to secret wisdom. The seer—Tiresias, Lucretius, Merlin, the Ancient Sage —is vouchsafed a vision which is accompanied by both powers and dangers. The descent and resurrection of Persephone are related to this theme; one aspect of her legend conveys Tennyson's sense of the poet's penetration of the realm of the imagination, of the forbidden region of shadows which must be entered before the highest beauty or the highest meaning of experience may be perceived. Since the story of Persephone is a myth of generation, the poet includes in his treatment of it not only the fertility of the soil and the creation of new life, but his definition of the attributes of the artist—imperial, disimpassioned, who moves between divided and distinguished worlds.

Related to all the implications of the Persephone myth is the notion that only through union with the earth can the principle of creativity find its self. Demeter laments the change Persephone has suffered, but rejoices that her daughter has risen again; the experience is likened to the feeling of the sun's warmth, and conveyed by images that are instinct with the sense of vegetable growth. The idea of rebirth is emphasized by Demeter's 'childless cry', which recalls Persephone to earth. This is, of course, explicitly the wail of a deprived mother, but it suggests the pains of labour, and may be thought of as the Earth Mother's cry of agony as she brings forth new life from the world of death.

The third section celebrates the precarious triumph of life and fertility over death:

> So in this pleasant vale we stand again,
> The field of Enna, now once more ablaze
> With flowers that brighten as thy footstep falls,
> All flowers—but for one black blur of earth
> Left by that closing chasm, thro' which the car
> Of dark Aïdoneus rising rapt thee hence.
> And here, my child, tho' folded in thine arms,
> I feel the deathless heart of motherhood
> Within me shudder, lest the naked glebe
> Should yawn once more into the gulf, and thence
> The shrilly whinnyings of the team of Hell,
> Ascending, pierce the glad and songful air,
> And all at once their arch'd necks, midnight-maned,
> Jet upward thro' the midday blossom.
>   No!
> For, see, thy foot has touch'd it; all the space
> Of blank earth-baldness clothes itself afresh,
> And breaks into the crocus-purple hour
> That saw thee vanish.   (Lines 34–51)

The passage, I think, intentionally echoes some famous lines from Milton's description of the Garden of Eden:

> Not that faire field
> Of *Enna*, where *Proserpin* gathring flours
> Her self a fairer Floure by gloomie *Dis*
> Was gatherd, which cost *Ceres* all that pain
> To seek her through the world . . .
> . . . might with this Paradise
> Of Eden strive.

This passage of *Paradise Lost* (Book IV, lines 268 ff.) is one that Tennyson frequently read aloud,[1] and the parallel both indicates the traditional background of his description and suggests the conception of the Vale of Enna as the earthly paradise.

Imaginary places analogous to the Eden garden are abundant in Tennyson's poems; they usually suggest a refuge from active life, a retreat to the past (as in *The Hesperides* and *Maud*), or a sacred

[1] F. T. Palgrave reported that Tennyson was fond of reciting lines 305–11 of Book IV. See *Memoir*, ii, p. 503.

bower of poetic inspiration (as in 'The Poet's Mind'). In Tennyson's poetry both heights and depths suggest danger and death; the valley, the sheltered plain, represent the fruitful life. The secluded valley of Enna is reminiscent of the enclosed, shadowy gardens, or the tropical islands of the other poems.

An account of Demeter's long search for Persephone follows and contrasts with the description of the pleasant vale. The subject is the kind for which Tennyson felt a peculiar sympathy: an elevated spirit deprived of the sources of its power, wandering shelterless through a desolate landscape. The world through which Demeter moves is one that has lost its power of generation; without abandoning the mythical treatment, Tennyson expresses his characteristic melancholy and presents a vision of an age deprived of the principle of life and creativity.

The poet described himself in *In Memoriam* as 'an infant crying in the night'; Demeter expresses the same sense of hopeless despair. She called her daughter's name to the midnight winds and heard voices in the night; she peered into tombs and caves, and after following out 'a league of labyrinthine darkness', she saw a vision of the Fates, who could not tell her of her daughter since she was not mortal. All the images of this fourth section evoke blackness, desolation, and death.

> . . . I stared from every eagle-peak,
> I thridded the black heart of all the woods,
> I peer'd thro' tomb and cave, and in the storms
> Of Autumn swept across the city, and heard
> The murmur of their temples chanting me,
> Me, me, the desolate mother!
>   'Where?'—and turn'd,
> And fled by many a waste, forlorn of man,
> And grieved for man thro' all my grief for thee,—
> The jungle rooted in his shatter'd hearth,
> The serpent coil'd about his broken shaft,
> The scorpion crawling over naked skulls;—
> I saw the tiger in the ruined fane
> Spring from his fallen God, but trace of thee
> I saw not.   (Lines 67–80)

This wasteland is both a concrete extension of the mood of the bereaved Demeter and the image of a society without faith or hope. 'Evil', said Tennyson in 1887, 'will come upon us headlong, if morality tries to get on without religion.'[1] In this ruined world beasts swarm over the relics of civilization; the tiger springs from man's fallen God. The Moerae know nothing of the universal fate beyond them, which can be anticipated only when Demeter and Persephone are re-united.

The description of the search is the most 'Tennysonian' passage in the poem. It is in keeping with the original myth, yet it bears the weight of Tennyson's psychic, social, and religious concerns. It exemplifies what the poet, in another connection, called a 'parabolic drift'. The figure of Demeter is analogous to the sensitive mind searching for creativity. It is implied that there must be union between the mother and daughter before fecundity can be achieved; like the poet, Demeter wanders through endless deserts and dark places, crying out, demanding to know the secrets of nature, in order that she may summon Persephone back to life and to the dying world.

The lowest point of Demeter's despair is reached when she is greeted by the ghost of her daughter, which tells her:

> 'The Bright one in the highest
> Is brother of the Dark one in the lowest,
> And Bright and Dark have sworn that I, the child
> Of thee, the great Earth-Mother, thee, the Power
> That lifts her buried life from gloom to bloom,
> Should be for ever and for evermore
> The Bride of Darkness.'   (Lines 93–9)

Demeter learns that the two highest and opposite powers are related, and that both are heedless of the life of earth. The Earth Mother bears the same relation to the extremes of God and the king of the underworld that the Vale of Enna bears to heaven and hell; her power is the source of terrestrial life. She curses the cold and complacent gods of heaven:

> I would not mingle with their feasts; to me
> Their nectar smack'd of hemlock on the lips,
> Their rich ambrosia tasted aconite.
> The man, that only lives and loves an hour,
> Seem'd nobler than their hard eternities.
>
>   (Lines 101–5)

---

[1] *Memoir*, ii, p. 337.

The goddess' grief brings on the death of vegetation, and autumn gives place to winter; the course of the seasons is again a reflection of Demeter's emotions.

Then the god, 'who still is highest', relents, and decrees that Persephone may dwell,

> For nine white moons of each whole year with me,
> Three dark ones in the shadow with thy King.

And the narrative of Demeter's search is concluded by a Keatsian description of the return of fertility to the earth:

> Once more the reaper in the gleam of dawn
> Will see me by the landmark far away,
> Blessing his field, or seated in the dusk ·
> Of even, by the lonely threshing-floor,
> Rejoicing in the harvest and the grange.
>
> (Lines 121–5)

Here, insofar as the poem is an adaptation of a Greek myth, it may be considered to end. The cycle of the year is rounded and the season of fertility has returned. The concluding section of the poem is a bold attempt to extend the meanings of the classical myth by grafting on to it a hopeful vision of the future which embodies Tennyson's conception of the gentle humanism of Christian faith. Demeter proclaims the working of a 'Fate beyond the Fates' which is impenetrable to the Olympian gods. This universal fate decrees the eventual triumph of 'younger, kindlier Gods' who will bear down the Olympians even as they conquered the Titans. Will not the new Gods come, Demeter asks,

> To quench, not hurl the thunderbolt, to stay,
> Not spread the plague, the famine; Gods indeed,
> To send the noon into the night and break
> The sunless halls of Hades into Heaven?
> Till thy dark lord accept and love the Sun,
> And all the Shadow die into the Light,
> When thou shalt dwell the whole bright year with me.
>
> (Lines 131–7)

Tennyson was quite right in conceiving this section as the 'something modern' with which he surrounded the old legend. As an attempt to augment the implications of a vital myth the passage is in the great tradition of Spenser, Milton, and the Shelley of *Prometheus Unbound*. In its synthesis of the myths of more than one culture it anticipates the interpretation of mythology which later enriched the poetry of Yeats and Eliot. But what was 'modern' to Tennyson is Victorian to us, and it is this conclusion to *Demeter and Persephone* which now seems most dated.

The difficulty Tennyson faced was that of presenting a vision of the triumph of life and love without having the belief that would make that vision ring true. In stating his affirmation Tennyson lacked the assurance that one finds in such poets as Dante or George Herbert. For Tennyson the dream of faith soon reduces itself to a faint trust in 'the larger hope'. With so inadequate a base the poet was perhaps inevitably tempted to push his assertions farther than was appropriate. It is instructive to compare Tennyson's uplifting message with the modified hope expressed at the end of Eliot's *The Waste Land* (which also attempts a fusion of disparate mythologies), or with the vision of the future presented by Yeats's *The Second Coming*. Tennyson's desire for certainty, when he felt none, mars the last lines of *Demeter*, and though they are gorgeously coloured, they seem quite static. Demeter addresses her daughter:

> . . . thou that hast from men
> As Queen of Death, that worship which is Fear,
> Henceforth, as having risen from out the dead,
> Shalt ever send thy life along with mine
> From buried grain thro' springing blade, and bless
> Their garner'd Autumn also, reap with me,
> Earth-Mother, in the harvest hymns of Earth
> The worship which is Love, and see no more
> The Stone, the Wheel, the dimly-glimmering lawns
> Of that Elysium, all the hateful fires
> Of torment, and the shadowy warrior glide
> Along the silent field of Asphodel.

The myth of Persephone has been reinterpreted as an anticipation of the story of Christ. The conception of an unchanging life and a continual earthly fruition is, however, not entirely consistent with the notion of a union of opposites imaged by the buried grain. It is curious, too, that the best lines of the passage describe the Elysium that is to be abolished. The success of Tennyson's reinterpretation is not, I think, an unqualified one.

Whatever may be the flaws of *Demeter and Persephone*, they are not of the sort one finds in minor poetry. The poet may not have entirely succeeded in making his myth bear the modern implication, but of the creative energy and poetic skill he brought to his task there can be no doubt. Beneath the poem's elegant diction and its sharp, almost Pre-Raphaelite outlines one perceives the action of the sad, shadowy drama which is typical of Tennyson's poetry. The poem skirts the edge of excessive self-pity, of railing at the age, of pious reflection on faith and doubt, of the bathos which ruined many Victorian poems. But Tennyson's core of toughness saves him. His extraordinary insight into the nature of myth, his ability to relate a private or social distress to the radical dualities of human experience, makes a poetic triumph out of a personal despair.

1954

IV

Various Readings

I.

ULYSSES

It little profits that an idle king,
By this still hearth, among these barren crags,
Match'd with an aged wife, I mete and dole
Unequal laws unto a savage race,
That hoard, and sleep, and feed, and know not me.
I cannot rest from travel: I will drink
Life to the lees: all times I have enjoy'd
Greatly, have suffer'd greatly, both with those
That loved me, and alone; on shore, and when
Thro' scudding drifts the rainy Hyades
Vext the dim sea: I am become a name;
For always roaming with a hungry heart
Much have I seen and known; cities of men
And manners, climates, councils, governments,
Myself not least, but honour'd of them all;
And drunk delight of battle with my peers,
Far on the ringing plains of windy Troy.
I am a part of all that I have met;
Yet all experience is an arch wherethro'
Gleams that untravell'd world, whose margin fades
For ever and for ever when I move.
How dull it is to pause, to make an end,
To rust unburnish'd, not to shine in use!
As tho' to breathe were life. Life piled on life
Were all too little, and of one to me
Little remains: but every hour is saved
From that eternal silence, something more,

A bringer of new things; and vile it were
For some three suns to store and hoard myself,
And this gray spirit yearning in desire
To follow knowledge like a sinking star,
Beyond the utmost bound of human thought.
　　This is my son, mine own Telemachus,
To whom I leave the sceptre and the isle—
Well-loved of me, discerning to fulfil
This labour, by slow prudence to make mild
A rugged people, and thro' soft degrees
Subdue them to the useful and the good.
Most blameless is he, centred in the sphere
Of common duties, decent not to fail
In offices of tenderness, and pay
Meet adoration to my household gods,
When I am gone. He works his work, I mine.
　　There lies the port; the vessel puffs her sail:
There gloom the dark broad seas. My mariners,
Souls that have toil'd, and wrought, and thought with me—
That ever with a frolic welcome took
The thunder and the sunshine, and opposed
Free hearts, free foreheads—you and I are old;
Old age hath yet his honour and his toil;
Death closes all: but something ere the end,
Some work of noble note, may yet be done,
Not unbecoming men that strove with Gods.
The lights begin to twinkle from the rocks:
The long day wanes: the slow moon climbs: the deep
Moans round with many voices. Come, my friends,
'Tis not too late to seek a newer world.
Push off, and sitting well in order smite
The sounding furrows; for my purpose holds
To sail beyond the sunset, and the baths
Of all the western stars, until I die.
It may be that the gulfs will wash us down:
It may be we shall touch the Happy Isles,
And see the great Achilles, whom we knew.
Tho' much is taken, much abides; and tho'
We are not now that strength which in old days
Moved earth and heaven; that which we are, we are;
One equal temper of heroic hearts,
Made weak by time and fate, but strong in will
To strive, to seek, to find, and not to yield.

THE DILEMMA OF TENNYSON

W. W. Robson

I BEGIN BY quoting one of the most familiar passages of nineteenth-century English poetry.

> The lights begin to twinkle from the rocks:
> The long day wanes: the slow moon climbs: the deep
> Moans round with many voices. Come, my friends,
> 'Tis not too late to seek a newer world.
> Push off, and sitting well in order smite
> The sounding furrows; for my purpose holds
> To sail beyond the sunset, and the baths
> Of all the western stars, until I die.
> It may be that the gulfs will wash us down:
> It may be we shall touch the Happy Isles,
> And see the great Achilles, whom we knew.
> Tho' much is taken, much abides; and tho'
> We are not now that strength which in old days
> Moved earth and heaven; that which we are, we are;
> One equal temper of heroic hearts,
> Made weak by time and fate, but strong in will
> To strive, to seek, to find, and not to yield.

That is the close of Tennyson's 'Ulysses'. It is a very beautiful
poem; and I think you will agree that those closing lines derive
part of their beauty from a sense we have of a whole history of
European imagination and aspiration to which Tennyson is giving

voice through the lips of Ulysses. For although he speaks with the accent of Tennyson, the speaker is unmistakably the Ulysses of Dante. In the eleventh book of the *Odyssey* it is foretold to Ulysses that, after his return to Ithaca and the slaying of the suitors, he is to set off again on a mysterious voyage. This voyage, and its sequel, is described by the tragic figure in Dante's *Inferno*. His most famous lines are these, which exhort his companions on his last voyage, beyond the Pillars of Hercules:

> 'O brothers', said I, 'who are come despite
> Ten thousand perils to the West, let none,
> While still our senses hold the vigil slight
> Remaining to us ere our course is run,
> Be willing to forgo experience
> Of the unpeopled world beyond the sun.
> Regard your origin,—from whom and whence!
> Not to exist like brutes, but made were ye
> To follow virtue and intelligence'.
> (*Considerate la vostra semenza:*
> *fatti non foste a viver come bruti,*
> *ma per seguir virtute e conoscenza.*)

Tennyson's Ulysses is Homer's Odysseus felt through Dante; but the vibration of this poem of Tennyson is not due merely to a modern poet's response to the Renaissance. The emotion to which it gives this dramatic expression is something personal to the poet, as a man alive in his own time. What the poem meant to Tennyson we know. He tells us that 'Ulysses' was written soon after Arthur Hallam's death. 'It gives the feeling [he says] about the need of going forward and braving the struggle of life more simply than anything in "In Memoriam".' As so often in Tennyson, the resolve, the will, to undertake responsible public action and effort, is linked with the need to find release from an overwhelming personal sorrow. This message, then, about 'the need of going forward and braving the struggle of life', is the point of juncture between the poet as a private individual, with his private sorrows, and the poet as a responsible social being, conscious of a public world in which he has duties. The poet in the first place is exhorting himself, to seek consolation in 'going forward'; but he exhorts himself as a responsible social being, and his exhortation—as the tone of the verse so plainly indicates—is equally aimed at a whole moral community of which he is one member.

And it found a response in that community. 'Ulysses' seems to have been what converted Carlyle to a belief in Tennyson. Edward Fitzgerald tells us:

> This was the Poem which, as might perhaps be expected, Carlyle liked best in the Book. [The 1842 volumes.] I do not think he became acquainted with Alfred Tennyson till after these Volumes appeared; being naturally prejudiced against one whom everyone was praising, and praising for a *Sort* of Poetry which he despised. But directly he saw, and heard, the Man, he knew there was A Man to deal with: and took pains to cultivate him; assiduous in exhorting him to leave Verse and Rhyme, and to apply his Genius to Prose and *Work*.

This exhortation of Carlyle, the amusing starkness of the antithesis between 'Poetry' and 'Work', helps us to bring into focus a curious anomaly in 'Ulysses'. It is an anomaly which in various forms must often trouble the reader of Tennyson—the reader whose interest is in poetry as poetry, and not merely in the explicit intentions of the poet or the paraphraseable content. No one can doubt that that admirable Victorian seriousness, which Carlyle saluted in 'Ulysses', is really there; the desire to express it is manifestly an important part of the poem's inspiration. And yet, when we restore that heroic close of the poem to its context—and even when we examine the passage I quoted by itself—there is something to be said about the quality of the verse, the poetic texture, which is strikingly at odds with the judgement—so obviously true —that Tennyson is here at one with an aspiration of his age.

> The lights begin to twinkle from the rocks:
> The long day wanes: the slow moon climbs: the deep
> Moans round with many voices . . .

That slow movement, still further retarded by the characteristic lingering on the vowel-sounds ('. . . mouthing out his hollow o'es and a'es') pervades the poem.

> Yet all experience is an arch wherethro'
> Gleams that untravell'd world, whose margin fades
> For ever and for ever when I move.

Matthew Arnold said of these lines that they take up as much time as a whole book of the *Odyssey*. And it seems to me that even at the point where Tennyson's Ulysses rouses himself finally from his

lethargy, and sounds the call to action, the effect of the verse as
verse is not radically different.

> Come, my friends,
> 'Tis not too late to seek a newer world.
> Push off, and sitting well in order smite
> The sounding furrows; for my purpose holds
> To sail beyond the sunset, and the baths
> Of all the western stars, until I die.

There is not here the same obvious preoccupation with a decorative effect that we see in 'The long day wanes: the slow moon
climbs', and so on, but the prevailing quality, as it were of a
language or medium that is too conscious of itself, is not really
different. T. S. Eliot has remarked on the contrast, in one important respect, between Tennyson's Ulysses and Dante's; Dante's
character, whatever else he may be, is certainly in the first place a
seaman telling a yarn; Tennyson's speaker is a self-conscious poet.
This contrast considered by itself does not imply that Tennyson's
poem is inferior; there is no critical rule about the degree of trans-
parency permitted to a poet's *persona*. But the contrast remarked
by Eliot does bring out the effect of which, I think, Tennyson's
attitude to his language is the cause. There is a radical discrepancy
between the strenuousness aspired to, and the medium in which
the aspiration is expressed.

This discrepancy points to no insincerity here, at any level, in
Tennyson. It is not true to say, as is sometimes said—and I think
in Tennyson's own time, Edward Fitzgerald at least implied something like this—that Tennyson was essentially a lyric poet, with a
true gift only for the decorative, the evocative, and the elegiac,
who made himself express the attitudes of his age to large public
subjects not because he really wanted to do this or was capable of
doing it but because he felt he ought to. This is not, I think, a true
account of Tennyson's development in general, and it is certainly
not fair to 'Ulysses'. The unsatisfactoriness—if there is unsatisfactoriness—in 'Ulysses' is more interesting than that. My point is
this: there is a real ring of conviction in those last lines of the
poem:

> . . . that which we are, we are;
> · One equal temper of heroic hearts,
> Made weak by time and fate, but strong in will
> To strive, to seek, to find, and not to yield.

If Tennyson was expressing here a feeling that can be called 'typically Victorian', it was a feeling in which he himself shared to the full; we do not need biographical evidence in order to see that the theme is personally felt. But the more we recognize this, the more strongly are we conscious of that anomaly I spoke of: how could a Tennyson who is so deeply concerned with what he is saying—and we will be making a big mistake if we underrate the scope and reality of Tennyson's intellectual and moral preoccupations—how *could* a poet of that intelligence have been content with the style of a minor poet?

The incongruity of 'Ulysses' may be summed up like this: 'Tennyson, the responsible social being, the admirably serious and "committed" Victorian intellectual, is uttering strenuous sentiments in the accent of Tennyson the most un-strenuous, lonely, and poignant of poets.' That this incongruity does not spoil the poem, that it remains very beautiful and, in its way, perfect, I infer from my own experience and the attested experience of generations of readers. But to appreciate its beauty—and at the same time to recognize its limitations—that is useful in reminding us of how complex the 'poet–public' relationship is in Tennyson's more interesting verse. There is plenty of evidence that Tennyson felt himself compelled, as Laureate and mouthpiece of Society, to write things in which his peculiar genius was not involved; we dismiss those things, or put them in their place—they are dated—just because the 'poet–public' relationship, in their case, so plainly is a simple one: the 'public' addressed is external, Tennyson is speaking from a platform. The poems—'Ulysses', for example—that concern the literary critic and the lover of poetry, allow no such easy analysis of ends and means.

In 'Ulysses' the 'public' in the first place is Tennyson himself: and its exceptional interest lies in the fact that both Tennyson the responsible social being, and Tennyson the depressed private poet, are really there in the poem: while its limitation, I think, lies in there being no conscious relationship, manifested at the poetic level, between them. But there is no crude antithesis. In the obviously unsatisfactory or bad poems of Tennyson—I mean, such of them as are more than mere official utterances or popular anthology-pieces—there is a patent disharmony. Indeed, it often looks as if Tennyson the moralist and Tennyson the artist are functioning on entirely separate planes. Certainly it is possible for the reader to take an interest in the skill, the technique, which is quite distinct from any interest he may have in what is being said. I am thinking of things like the bad parts of *Maud*. Technique, in a sense, and in a sense that was important to Tennyson, never fails him in those parts; it can be analysed and appreciated, independently of one's sense of the value of what is being done; but that this should be so is a comment on the quality of the technique— which in the good parts can so perfectly serve the emotional and moral purposes of the poet. And the presence of this technique, cultivated apart from the particular demands of any particular subject-matter, is perhaps what makes the bad parts of *Maud* seem so desolatingly bad:

> And the vitriol madness flushes up in the ruffian's head,
> Till the filthy by-lane rings to the yell of the trampled wife . . .

> And Sleep must lie down arm'd, for the villainous centre-bits
> Grind on the wakeful ear in the hush of the moonless nights,
> While another is cheating the sick of a few last gasps, as he sits
> To pestle a poison'd poison behind his crimson lights.

It is true that in *Maud* the narrator is not avowedly Tennyson, but a dramatic figure who is supposed to be hysterical and neurotic. But there is no evidence in that poem that the poet has firm criteria by which the hysteria and neurosis are judged to be so. The hero of *Maud* is sometimes a dramatic figure, and sometimes a mere subterfuge; he is, and is not, Tennyson. The result is such passages as

> And the vitriol madness flushes up in the ruffian's head

strike us, not as the product of dramatic imagination, but as a self-indulgence, and (because the show of drama is there to protect it) they strike us as self-indulgence of an exceptionally disagreeable kind.

These things are disagreeable, I think, because of the insistent presence of that technique—a technique practised everywhere in the poem—which compels us all the time to recognize, as some more ragged imprecation would not, that all this violence is being willed. But the critical interest of such things is more than that: they make us begin to wonder whether some of the exasperation they proclaim so stridently is due to the poet's own partial awareness that something is going wrong: his skill is not producing the

effect which, at one level of his being, is what he wants. I would
like to consider this further in its bearings on the whole critical
problem of Tennyson's poetry.

The decline of Tennyson is to me a much more painful spectacle
than the decline of Wordsworth. This is because, in Tennyson's
case, the difference between his living work and the work of his
decadence is not simply the difference between life and death.
There is often a curious unpleasant life in the later Tennyson that
compels some reaction from the reader, as the later Wordsworth
so rarely does.

I would like to look at one of the poems produced by the
elderly Tennyson—'Locksley Hall Sixty Years After'. This is a
poem that was famous in its day. Nowadays, I think it can safely
be said, there is no poem in the whole Tennyson canon which is
more damagingly and damningly dated; and yet, looked at without prejudice, can it be denied to have considerable power?
Effects like this are not at all uncommon:

. . . war will die out late then. Will it ever? late or soon?
Can it, till this outworn earth be dead as yon dead world the moon?

Dead the new astronomy calls her . . .

Poor old Heraldry, poor old History, poor old Poetry, passing hence,
In the common deluge drowning old political common-sense!

Tennyson is writing with unusual power, when he is able, as he is
here, to get his intellectual and scientific interests into poetry. And
yet 'Locksley Hall Sixty Years After' is disastrously bad, and in
the same way as *Maud* is bad where it is bad: this is a representative bit:

Is it well that while we range with Science, glorying in the Time,
City children soak and blacken soul and sense in city slime?

There among the glooming alleys Progress halts on palsied feet,
Crime and hunger cast our maidens by the thousand on the street.

There the Master scrimps his haggard sempstress of her daily bread,
There a single sordid attic holds the living and the dead.
There the smouldering fire of fever creeps across the rotted floor,
And the crowded couch of incest in the warrens of the poor.

We cannot mistake the genuine anguish of the agonized social conscience; these horrors are realities to Tennyson, and he labours to render them with all he can summon of dramatic (and melodramatic) power. But—that tone of voice, and that movement:

> There among the glooming alleys Progress halts on palsied feet,
> Crime and hunger cast our maidens by the thousand on the street.

It is like bad Dickens. I expect no one now would dispute either of two judgements: Tennyson is deeply stirred here; and here Tennyson is not a poet; the verdict on the later Tennyson is pronounced by the almost total neglect of him. But I am surprised how unquestioningly both literary historians and amateurs of his poetry accept this failure as a matter of course. The meaningless judgement that Tennyson was 'outside his range' is all the critical help one is given. But Tennyson was one of the most intelligent and morally concerned men of his time, and I cannot see why it should be so complacently granted that he could not, in the nature of the case, write poetry about these things.

I think the main value of contemplating 'Locksley Hall Sixty Years After' is that it shows us in an extreme and crude form what went wrong with the poet–public, or public–private, relationship in Tennyson's poetry. There were no doubt many reasons why this went wrong, some of them lying quite outside Tennyson's personality or the short-comings of the Victorian poetic tradition, but I am concerned here only with what bears on the essential, the individual Tennyson. What I trace as a growing awareness in his poetry that he could not meet the needs of the public which he had helped to create, and to which, as a social being, he himself belonged—this awareness becomes open and complete in this poem. The *persona* here is in no such equivocal relation to Tennyson as the hero of *Maud*: he *is* Tennyson in all that matters, and it is significant that he relapses at last openly into what he has been essentially throughout: a futile old reactionary, half-pathetic, half-defiant in his sense of his futility:

> Poor old voice of eighty crying after voices that have fled!
> All I loved are vanish'd voices, all my steps are on the dead.

> All the world is ghost to me, and as the phantom disappears,
> Forward far and far from here is all the hope of eighty years.

There is, of course, a special poignancy in remembering the closing lines of 'Ulysses' when one reads this poem of the old Tennyson. But it is not merely that Tennyson is old and embittered; a certain violent irresponsibility about the writing suggests that he is getting a kind of gloomy satisfaction out of his feeling of powerlessness: while expressly admitting his final inability to engage his talents upon these themes that both fascinate and horrify him, he produces a picture of the 'public' world which has a queer nightmare life; the nightmare in his own; public and private are neither separate, as in some of his earlier poetry, nor consciously and critically related, but just confused.

In 'Locksley Hall Sixty Years After' we have an extreme case of the breakdown of relation between Tennyson's 'art' and his 'social conscience'. But this breakdown had occurred, in milder forms, long before. I think the difference at the end is merely that Tennyson was more aware of it, and this gave him a paradoxical energy of despair. His true greatness lay elsewhere; but, in concurring with the judgement that things like the lyrics in *Maud*, the lyrics in *The Princess*, are among his supreme achievements, we must recognize that without the earnestness, the sense of responsibility towards the world outside the poet, they could not have been written; while at the same time their peculiar sadness seems tacitly to acknowledge the inability of their author to confront that world as a poet.

1957

TENNYSON'S 'ULYSSES'—
A RE-INTERPRETATION

E. J. Chiasson

I T H A S long been recognized that Tennyson's *Idylls* are, among
other things, the allegorical presentation of ideas which had found
their place in a large number of poems, from 'The Palace of Art' to
'Lucretius' and 'The Ancient Sage'. Such fidelity to a set of ideas
need not surprise us in a poet who had always felt that 'only under
the inspiration of ideals, and with his "sword bathed in heaven"',
can a man combat the cynical indifference, the intellectual selfishness, the sloth of will, the utilitarian materialism of a transition
age.'[1] Yet despite this willingness on the part of critics to arrange
much of the Tennyson canon in this perfectly convincing pattern,
little attention has been paid to the intractability of 'Ulysses', that
is to say, to its virtual refusal to submit to such an arrangement.
As a result 'Ulysses' continues to be, what it has always been,
something of a 'sport' in Tennyson criticism. Although I do not
intend to fit 'Ulysses' into such a pattern by detailed references to
the *Idylls*, I shall try to show that critical attention to the poem has
stopped short of placing it precisely where it belongs, namely
among the many expressions of Tennyson's conviction that religious faith is mandatory for the multitudinous needs of life.

Lacking such a view of the poem, critics of 'Ulysses' (no longer

---

[1] *Memoir*, ii, p. 129.

enthusiastically restricting themselves to an admiration of its 'gleam' qualities) think of it generally as a poem of relatively un-resolved antinomies. One critic, regarding it as, at least intention-ally, a 'gleam' poem, is of course struck by the familiar disturbing Dantean conception of Ulysses's character, and concludes that 'Ulysses' is a brilliant failure in which the 'details are inconsistent, the reasoning specious, the whole a kind of brilliantly whited sepulchre. . . .'[1] Another critic,[2] most perceptive on the whole, sees in the poem evidence of a certain ambivalence in Tennyson's thinking; while still another detects a dichotomy between 'Tenny-son's own account of his meaning' and the 'desolate melancholy music of the words themselves. . . .'[3] Charles Tennyson in his recent *Life* returns to the non-committal view that in 'Ulysses' Ten-nyson 'expressed his realization of the need for going forward and braving the battle of life, in spite of the crushing blow of Arthur's death'.[4]

While it is true that 'Ulysses' was written as a result of Hallam's death, the assumption has too quickly been made that this fact is by itself helpful to an understanding of the poem. The purpose of this essay, therefore, is to suggest as an alternative that in 'Ulysses' Tennyson is elaborating the belief, which was to become perennial with him, that life without faith leads to personal and social dis-location. Briefly stated, the position of this writer is that Tennyson is writing here not a mismanaged 'gleam' poem or a poem which gives evidence of 'the operation of private insights' though 'ostensibly addressed to a Victorian audience', but a dramatic portrayal of a type of human being who held a set of ideas which

---

[1] P. F. Baum, *Tennyson Sixty Years After* (Chapel Hill, 1948), p. 303.

[2] E. D. H. Johnson, *The Alien Vision of Victorian Poetry* (Princeton, 1952). Johnson recognizes, of course, not only Tennyson's suspicion of the anti-social devotion to the life of activity, but also the fact that Tennyson was too much of his time 'to put the life of contemplation above the life of doing' (p. 40). His references, however, to 'ambivalence' (p. xi) and 'divided will' (p. 12) as conditioning elements in Tennyson's poetry, and his view of 'Ulys-ses' and other poems as giving evidence 'of the operation of private insights within poems ostensibly addressed to a Victorian audience' (p. 42), perhaps minimize the *positiveness* of Tennyson's answer in this poem to certain Vic-torian prepossessions, and ignore Tennyson's statement of purpose. The use of such words as 'ambivalence' at any rate seems to suggest the expectation of a somewhat simplistic and 'one-layer' synthesis.

[3] C. C. Walcutt, 'Tennyson's Ulysses', *Explicator*, iv (1946), p. 28.

[4] C. Tennyson, *Alfred Tennyson* (1949), p. 193.

Tennyson regarded as destructive of the whole fabric of his society.

It must be confessed that the celebrated passage from Hallam Tennyson's *Memoir* has assisted mightily in reinforcing the view of 'Ulysses' as a paean to heroic effort. For Tennyson is quoted in the *Memoir* as saying: ' "Ulysses" . . . was written soon after Hallam's death, and gave my feeling about the need for going forward, and braving the struggle of life *perhaps more simply than anything in "In Memoriam"*. '[1] Since this statement of purpose is, of course, somewhat cryptic, it is perhaps not surprising that most critics have taken it to mean that the character Ulysses is, in some measure at least, the spokesman of Tennyson, or that it is Ulysses who is to be construed as braving the struggle of life. It is possible, however, to interpret Tennyson's statement of purpose to mean simply that here he has given us his views on the general question of what an adequate pursuit of life means, and has given us no licence to assume that Ulysses is his spokesman, or that his architectonics have been obvious. That this wary reading of Tennyson's statement of purpose is not merely wilful is suggested by the italicized part of the above quotation wherein Tennyson asserts that his intention in writing 'Ulysses' was, in some sense at any rate, identical with his intention in writing *In Memoriam*. If this convergence of intention is a fact, 'Ulysses' will have to be re-examined in the light of *In Memoriam*. That is to say, we shall have to recall the answers which Tennyson, in *In Memoriam*, arrives at as solutions to his despair at Hallam's death, and remind ourselves in the process of what Tennyson means in that poem by braving the struggle of life.

In section 34 of *In Memoriam* and elsewhere, Tennyson expresses the pivotal doctrine of his creed, namely that life without immortality is not only meaningless but monstrous. It is indeed the conviction that immortality is a fact which enables him to rise above his despair. Certain corollaries, central to our purpose, follow from this belief. One of them, as we learn from section 35, is that without immortality love would become 'mere fellowship of sluggish moods' or at its coarsest, a bruising and crushing urge which 'bask'd and batten'd in the woods'. Another resultant of this pivotal discovery, as we see from section 66, is a new awareness in the poet of the value of the softer affections, especially within a fami-

[1] *Memoir*, i, p. 196. My italics.

lial context. Section 106, with its look into the future, is a measure of the more strictly social direction which his exaltation takes after he has conquered his despair. In section 109 he reflects on the great promise that Hallam had given of being 'A potent voice of Parliament A pillar steadfast in the storm.' But especially important to our purpose is Tennyson's statement of dissatisfaction with an extravagant intellectualism divorced from faith and love.[1] Guarding himself against obscurantism, he, none the less, in 114, deprecates knowledge which aims at 'Submitting all things to desire', and refers to such knowledge as but 'half-grown' and incapable of fighting 'the fear of death'. Finally the tribute to wedded love, in the latter part of the poem, focusses our attention, as it does in 'The Two Voices', on another detail of Tennyson's conception of a properly oriented life. The overriding ideas of *In Memoriam*, are, perhaps, that it is not knowledge but wisdom, a combination of faith and love, which is best calculated to serve the purposes of this life; and that pursuit of life and its values will take the form of religiously-motivated action.

If we examine 'Ulysses' in the light of this rather cursory analysis of certain features of *In Memoriam*, keeping in mind Tennyson's statement that *In Memoriam* and 'Ulysses' were written with much the same purpose in mind, we observe some of the familiar antinomies which, to this reader, need not go unresolved. Tennyson sets the tone early in the poem. Ulysses is speaking. There is a hard and incisive quality to his language, a hardness which includes the startling and un-Tennysonian connubial insensitivity of the phrase 'match'd with an aged wife'. His scorn for his people and for the essentially gradual character of government is made clear by the tonal quality of the words 'mete' and 'dole', and

---

[1] A statement from *Memoir*, i, p. 317, gives Tennyson's views on both the shirking of responsibility and arrogant intellectualism; 'If a man is merely to be a bundle of sensations, he had better not exist at all. He should embark on his career in the spirit of *selfless* and adventurous heroism; should develop his true self by not shirking responsibility, by casting aside all maudlin and introspective morbidities, and by using his powers cheerfully *in accordance with the obvious dictates of his moral consciousness*. . . . The real test of a man is not what he knows, but what he is in himself and in his relation to others.' My italics. Spedding's estimate (*Memoir*, i, pp. 192–3) of Tennyson's criticism of the Soul in 'The Palace of Art' as one which 'in the love of beauty, and the triumphant consciousness of knowledge, and intellectual supremacy, in the intense enjoyment of its power and glory, has lost sight of its relation to man and God', makes essentially the same point.

by his view of his people as a 'savage' race. The line of hard mono-syllables, 'That hoard, and sleep, and feed, and know not me', taken together with the context of the first lines, stamps Ulysses as a hard, self-contained individual, contemptuous of his people, impervious to the softer affections, the sheer incarnation of 'Re-naissance' *superbia*.

The Dantean conception of Ulysses's character continues as the poem proceeds. But the tone changes; the flat, contemptuous lan-guage becomes rhetorical. Whereas the first five lines have given us some insight into Ulysses's character by telling us what he de-spises, the next twenty-seven serve the same purpose by telling us of his enthusiasms. 'Drinking life to the lees' is but the obverse of the scorn of the opening lines, and gains reinforcement from the Byronic catholicity of the later line: 'I am a part of all that I have met.' The Faustian quality appears too, as it does in all Byronic heroes,[1] and one is reminded tonally of Milton's Satan, that arch-enemy of the prevailing hierarchy. It is well to remember that Ulysses establishes only the slightest hierarchical preference in his experiences. Though the thirst for the naked intellect is there, un-diluted with any of the softer affections, it exists, as we might expect from the Dantean conception of Ulysses' character, cheek by jowl with, for Tennyson, an alarming lack of selectivity. Drink-ing life to the lees, drinking delight of battle with his peers, fol-lowing knowledge like a sinking star—all render him abundantly lyrical. There is, moreover, no internal evidence that 'life piled on life' would have given Ulysses any increase of what Tennyson calls wisdom.[2]

---

[1] A passage from Mrs. Charles Randle's diary, quoted in *Memoir*, i, p. 277, provides us with a suggestion of how Tennyson felt, in 1848, towards the Faustian yearning for 'completeness'; '[Tennyson] Felt the grand intellec-tual power of *Faust*, but threw it aside in disgust at the first reading.' The *Memoir*, ii, p. 386, also tells us that Tennyson 'was dominated by Byron till he was seventeen, when he put him away altogether.'

[2] Tennyson seems determined to trip Ulysses up at every opportunity by making him subscribe to positions which, as we know from *In Memoriam*, Tennyson rejects. Ulysses's yearning for 'life piled on life' is not an idea con-genial to Tennyson. In *In Memoriam*, 41, the thought that he may never catch up to Hallam, and that he will be 'evermore a life behind' is 'spectral doubt which makes him cold.' In 85, again, Hallam's ascent into heaven is direct, without any intermediary steps to perfection. The *Memoir*, ii, p. 474, tells us that Tennyson asked Sterling if he would accept this life as the pre-paration of more perfect beings, and, receiving an affirmative, said, emphatic-

As the poem shifts to a new accent, we observe one of the more familiar 'disturbing' passages in it. At first view, this passage looks like a simple contrast between two ways of life—the life of infinite search as opposed to the life of conscientious absorption in duty. If we look at this passage in the light of the later *Idylls* with their studied juxtaposition of the active Arthur ideal and the Galahad mysticism, we can easily enough be misled into viewing 'Ulysses' as an early careful statement by Tennyson of the legitimacy of aspiration along with a recognition that the more humdrum attention to household and civic duties, if more pedestrian, is none the less equally essential. Such a view seems indeed reinforced by the line 'He works his work, I mine', which except for the inverted emphasis is essentially the view proposed by Arthur: ' "Ah Galahad, Galahad," said the King, "for such As thou art is the vision, not for these." ' The apparent position of the two poems would seem, except for the respective emphases, to be identical, i.e., both apparently recognize two modes of life.

But to lay such weight on the line, 'He works his work, I mine', as if Ulysses were capable of such moderation, is to accept Ulysses as a responsible and, so to speak, Tennysonian spokesman—a procedure rather risky if I am correct in my analysis of Ulysses's character up to this point. But the immediate context, too, suggests that we should be somewhat wary of regarding Ulysses as inclined to such judiciousness. For the line in question is preceded almost immediately by the line 'How dull it is to pause and make an end', and then by the scornful vibrations of 'as though to breathe were life'. The apparent, grudging respect which Ulysses has for Telemachus must be judged with this tonal vibration in one's ears.

For the scorn is evident not only in the tone of the words which remind us of Antony's damning praise of Brutus, but in the simple fact that Ulysses pretends to admire Telemachus for possessing the very qualities which we know he himself despises. He scorned, earlier, meting and doling 'unequal laws unto a savage race', i.e., the prudence required for the shaping of means to ends, and yet

ally, 'I would *not*. . . .' It would seem that Tennyson, mindful of his purpose, deliberately allows Ulysses to be enthusiastic about things that he himself repudiates. For Tennyson gains his strength in his hard-won acceptance of life, not from rationalizations or from any conviction of the satisfactoriness of this life, certainly not from any aspiration for life piled on life, but from the intuitively derived conviction that this life is explained by an after life.

professes to admire Telemachus for his 'slow prudence to make mild a rugged people'. The disingenuousness of Ulysses peeps out from behind this cynical inconsistency, as it does from behind his politic shift from 'savage' to 'rugged' as words to characterize his people.[1]

But Ulysses's disingenuousness is revealed more importantly in his movement from a denial of immortality ('that eternal silence') in the passage immediately preceding, to the thinly disguised irony of the later assurance that Telemachus, along with his other pedestrian virtues, may well be relied upon to pay 'meet adoration' to the household gods. Later he will reiterate that 'death closes all'. Ulysses's anticipation of some 'work of noble note' which will be 'not unbecoming men who strove with gods', merely reinforces the view that he is content to leave the duty of adoration (with its recognition of hierarchy) to Telemachus, while he will *strive* either in company with or against the gods (in terms of hierarchy, either interpretation is damaging to Ulysses). The 'comforting' assurance to his men, in the final section, that perhaps they shall reach the Happy Isles is tonally indifferent, and is uttered with the same equanimity which characterizes the admission that perhaps the gulfs will wash them down. Ulysses, it is clear, personally rejects, or is at least quite uninterested in, immortality, but remains capable of a kind of jovial agnosticism, designed perhaps to reassure some of his men.

The last section of 'Ulysses' ends with the well-known burst of oratory. However, we must beware of viewing the exalted language which ends the poem as the culmination of the poem's meaning. It is precisely this mistake, the reading of the poem in the light of its conclusion rather than in the light of its beginning, which has led to past misinterpretations.[2] For the person who

[1] Baum, *Tennyson Sixty Years After*, p. 301. What I view here as disingenuousness, perfectly consistent with Ulysses's previously known character, Baum views as simply another example of Tennyson's failure to maintain consistency in his characterization.

[2] Baum, ibid., thinks that the latter part of the poem represents Ulysses's 'real dignity and nobility'. He recognizes however that this nobility conflicts with the irresponsibility and contemptuousness of Ulysses in the beginning and middle of the poem. His conclusion is that Tennyson is guilty of 'muddled thinking', and that 'the Byronic was probably not intended for our ears, perhaps not entirely clear in the poet's'. Another inference, as the whole tenor of this essay suggests, is possible.

speaks this language is the person whom Tennyson has introduced to us as connubially insensitive, or as Roy Campbell would say, 'Too sensitively nerved to bear Domestication . . .', contemptuous of duty and the softer affections, proud in his relationships with the gods, disingenuous and contemptuous towards his own son and towards his own people; a man who pursues life with thoroughgoing indiscrimination, and who reaches at best a vague and undirected respect for the life of intellect. For Ulysses, in his last burst of oratory, is completely vague as to what he means by 'to strive, to seek, to find'. What it is he will not yield to is uncertain, unless it be the limitation inseparable from the orientation of his energies, affective and intellectual, towards some recognized hierarchical system.

It is incredible to suppose that Tennyson, in the light of his assertion that 'Ulysses' was a simpler statement than *In Memoriam* of the necessity of braving the struggle of life, should have contradicted himself so abysmally. For the Byronic catholicity of Ulysses, compounded as it is of marital and social irresponsibility, pursuit of sensation, and adoration of the naked intellect, is thoroughly opposed to *In Memoriam*'s glorification of the marriage bond as symptomatic of and contributory to social solidarity, and opposed to the refusal of Tennyson, in *In Memoriam*, to allow the naked intellect to arrogate all powers to itself to the exclusion of faith and love. The scornful neglect of duty in 'Ulysses' comes with a shock from the poet who had praised Hallam for the virtues which not Ulysses but Telemachus possesses. It is especially surprising that the pivotal doctrine of *In Memoriam*, namely the belief in immortality, the belief which serves as sanction for all other beliefs, and without which life becomes mere rutting and social disintegration, should become in 'Ulysses' at best a subject for the display of a kind of jovial agnosticism. If, as Tennyson says, *In Memoriam* was written to convey his conviction that fear, doubt, and suffering will find answer and relief only through faith in a God of Love, 'Ulysses' represents a rather curious coda to such an expression of faith.

To resolve such an apparent antinomy, we must bear in mind constantly the opening lines of the poem, and not expect Tennyson to wreck his poem by strident emphases. We know very early in the poem what kind of man Ulysses is, and no spate of impassioned rhetoric should make us forget that we must judge him in the light of that knowledge. We realize all along that there is nothing in this monologue which an exponent (ancient or modern) of the pagan *virtus*, with a capacity for guile, could not have said. The exaltation of the concluding lines, like that of Milton's Satan, is an exaltation predicated on rejection, and is but a measure of his misdirected energies. For just as Milton is not misled by Satan's courage, an essentially neutral quality, the value of which is to be determined by its object, so Tennyson, whose affinities are Virgilian and Dantean rather than Homeric, recognizes that Ulyssean determination and courage, necessary as they are at certain junctures, are to be valued only if they contribute to the good life, personal and social.

'Ulysses' becomes, then, not at all a curious coda to *In Memoriam* if we regard it as a poem which proceeds by the method of indirection. Viewed in this way, it falls into place as the expression of one of the perennial interests of Tennyson, and can be read as the dramatic presentation of a man who has faith neither in the gods nor consequently in the necessity of preserving order in his kingdom or in his own life. As Tithonus is permitted, without the intrusion of the author, to reject life simply because life without term cannot give him a never-ending titillation of the senses,[1] and as the mariners in 'The Lotos-Eaters' are permitted, with equal indifference on the part of Tennyson, to reject life and its duties because they see no sanction to life, so Ulysses is permitted

---

[1] The *Memoir*, i, p. 459, quotes a letter to the Duke of Argyll in which Tennyson says: ' "Tithonus", written upwards of a quarter of a century ago . . . was originally a pendant to the "Ulysses" in my former volumes. . . .' The *Memoir*, ii, p. 70, also quotes a conversation with Frederick Locker-Lampson; 'I spoke with admiration of his "Ulysses"; he said, "Yes there is an echo of Dante in it." He gave "Tithonus" the same position as "Ulysses".' Tennyson's use of the word 'pendant' rather than 'antithesis' would suggest that Tithonus and Ulysses are either partners in crime or victims of an identical lack of adequate 'theology'. There is, indeed, a great similarity between the predicaments of both. Tithonus, reduced totally to his own resources, which are gradually decaying, wants to die. Ulysses is not yet so desperate, for Ulysses, it might be said, is a younger Tithonus who is still, as Tithonus once was, buoyed up by the quotidian promise of 'growing dewy-warm'. But there is in Ulysses the somewhat disturbed awareness of the fact that 'We are not now that strength which in old days Moved earth and heaven,' and it will not be long before Ulysses will be doubly convinced (as Tithonus now is) that mere breathing is not living. The conclusion of both poems would seem to be that the absence of belief in an after life makes meaningful life impossible.

to express with irresponsible directness a yearning for limitlessness, predicated on the scornful rejection of the Telemachuses and the Hallams of this world. To Tennyson these three 'scorners of the ground' were only very superficially different. All three illustrated his constant conviction that disregarding religious sanctions and 'submitting all things to desire' lead to either a sybaritic or a brutal repudiation of responsibility and 'life'. Tithonus and Mark (in the *Idylls*) are the two ends of the spectrum. Ulysses lies between. 'Ulysses' then takes its place in the pattern which is woven throughout Tennyson's poetry, sometimes negatively and hesitantly, as he resolves his own spiritual conflicts, sometimes positively. Tennyson, in 'Ulysses', is well past the hesitancy of 'The Two Voices', and has reached the conviction of *In Memoriam*, if not the triumphant assertiveness of 'The Ancient Sage'.

1954

II.

'TEARS, IDLE TEARS'

Tears, idle tears, I know not what they mean,
Tears from the depth of some divine despair
Rise in the heart, and gather to the eyes,
In looking on the happy Autumn-fields,
And thinking of the days that are no more.

Fresh as the first beam glittering on a sail,
That brings our friends up from the underworld,
Sad as the last which reddens over one
That sinks with all we love below the verge;
So sad, so fresh, the days that are no more.

Ah, sad and strange as in dark summer dawns
The earliest pipe of half-awaken'd birds
To dying ears, when unto dying eyes
The casement slowly grows a glimmering square;
So sad, so strange, the days that are no more.

Dear as remember'd kisses after death,
And sweet as those by hopeless fancy feign'd
On lips that are for others; deep as love,
Deep as first love, and wild with all regret;
O Death in Life, the days that are no more.

THE MOTIVATION OF TENNYSON'S WEEPER

Cleanth Brooks

TENNYSON IS perhaps the last English poet one would think of associating with the subtleties of paradox and ambiguity. He is not the thoughtless poet, to be sure: he grapples—particularly in his later period—with the 'big' questions which were up for his day; and he struggles manfully with them. But the struggle, as Tennyson conducted it, was usually kept out of the grammar and symbolism of the poetry itself. Like his own protagonist in *In Memoriam*, Tennyson 'fought his doubts'—he does not typically build them into the structure of the poetry itself as enriching ambiguities.

Yet substantially true as this generalization is, Tennyson was not always successful in avoiding the ambiguous and the paradoxical; and indeed, in some of his poems his failure to avoid them becomes a saving grace. The lyric 'Tears, Idle Tears' is a very good instance. It is a poem which, from a strictly logical point of view, Tennyson may be thought to have blundered into. But, whether he blundered into it or not, the poem gains from the fact that it finds its unity in a principle of organization higher than that which seems to be operative in many of Tennyson's more 'thoughtful' poems.

Any account of the poem may very well begin with a consideration of the nature of the tears. Are they *idle* tears? Or are they not rather the most meaningful of tears? Does not the very fact that

177

they are 'idle' (that is, tears occasioned by no immediate grief) become in itself a guarantee of the fact that they spring from a deeper, more universal cause?

It would seem so, and that the poet is thus beginning his poem with a paradox. For the third line of the poem indicates that there is no doubt in the speaker's mind about the origin of the tears in some divine despair. They 'rise in the heart'—for all that they have been first announced as 'idle'.

But the question of whether Tennyson is guilty of (or to be complimented upon) a use of paradox may well wait upon further discussion. At this point in our commentary, it is enough to observe that Tennyson has chosen to open his poem with some dramatic boldness—if not with the bold step of equating 'idle' with 'from the depth of some divine despair', then at least with a bold and violent reversal of the speaker's first characterization of his tears.

The tears 'rise in the heart' as the speaker looks upon a scene of beauty and tranquillity. Does looking on the 'happy Autumn-fields' bring to mind the days that are no more? The poet does not say so. The tears rise to the eyes in looking on the 'happy Autumn-fields' *and* thinking of the days that are no more. The poet himself does not stand responsible for any closer linkage between these actions, though, as a matter of fact, most of us will want to make a closer linkage here. For, if we change 'happy Autumn-fields', say, to 'happy April-fields', the two terms tends to draw apart. The fact that the fields are autumn-fields which, though happy, point back to something which is over—which is finished—*does* connect them with the past and therefore properly suggests to the observer thoughts about that past.

To sum up: The first stanza has a unity, but it is not a unity which finds its sanctions in the ordinary logic of language. Its sanctions are to be found in the dramatic context, and, to my mind, there alone. Indeed, the stanza suggests the play of the speaker's mind as the tears unexpectedly start, tears for which there is no apparent occasion, and as he searches for an explanation of them. He calls them 'idle', but, even as he says 'I know not what they mean', he realizes that they must spring from the depths of his being—is willing, with his very next words, to associate them with 'some divine despair'. Moreover, the real occasion of the tears, though the speaker himself comes to realize it only as he approaches the end of the stanza, is the thought about the past. It is psychologically and dramatically right, therefore, that the real occasion should be stated explicitly only with the last line of the stanza.

This first stanza, then, recapitulates the surprise and bewilderment in the speaker's own mind, and sets the problem which the succeeding stanzas are to analyze. The dramatic effect may be described as follows: the stanza seems, not a meditated observation, but a speech begun impulsively—a statement which the speaker has begun before he knows how he will end it.

In the second stanza we are not surprised to have the poet characterize the days that are no more as 'sad', but there is some shock in hearing him apply to them the adjective 'fresh'. Again, the speaker does not pause to explain: the word 'fresh' actually begins the stanza. Yet the adjective justifies itself.

The past is fresh as with a dawn freshness—as fresh as the first beam glittering on the sail of an incoming ship. The ship is evidently expected; it brings friends, friends 'up from the underworld'. On the surface, the comparison is innocent: the 'underworld' is merely the antipodes, the world which lies below the horizon—an underworld in the sense displayed in old-fashioned geographies with their sketches illustrating the effects of the curvature of the earth. The sails, which catch the light and glitter, will necessarily be the part first seen of any ship which is coming 'up' over the curve of the earth.

But the word 'underworld' will necessarily suggest the underworld of Greek mythology, the realm of the shades, the abode of the dead. The attempt to characterize the freshness of the days that are no more has, thus, developed, almost imperceptibly, into a further characterization of the days themselves as belonging, not to our daylight world, but to an 'underworld'. This suggestion is, of course, strengthened in the lines that follow in which the ship metaphor is reversed so as to give us a picture of sadness: evening, the last glint of sunset light on the sail of a ship

That sinks with all we love below the verge.

The conjunction of the qualities of sadness and freshness is reinforced by the fact that the same basic symbol—the light on the sails of a ship hull down—has been employed to suggest both qualities. With the third stanza, the process is carried one stage

further: the two qualities (with the variant of 'strange' for 'fresh')
are explicitly linked together:

> Ah, sad and strange as in dark summer dawns . . .

And here the poet is not content to suggest the qualities of sadness and strangeness by means of two different, even if closely related, figures. In this third stanza the special kind of sadness and
strangeness is suggested by one and the same figure.

It is a figure developed in some detail. It, too, involves a dawn
scene, though ironically so, for the beginning of the new day is to
be the beginning of the long night for the dying man. The dying
eyes, the poem suggests, have been for some time awake—long
enough to have had time to watch the

> . . . casement slowly [grow] a glimmering square.

The dying man, soon to sleep the lasting sleep, is more fully
awake than the 'half-awaken'd birds' whose earliest pipings come
to his dying ears. We know why these pipings are sad; but why
are they *strange*? Because to the person hearing a bird's song for
the last time, it will seem that he has never before really heard one.
The familiar sound will take on a quality of unreality—of strangeness.

If this poem were merely a gently melancholy reverie on the
sweet sadness of the past, stanzas II and III would have no place
in the poem. But the poem is no such reverie: the images from the
past rise up with a strange clarity and sharpness that shock the
speaker. Their sharpness and freshness account for the sudden
tears and for the psychological problem with which the speaker
wrestles in the poem. If the past would only remain melancholy
but dimmed, sad but worn and familiar, we should have no problem and no poem. At least, we should not have *this* poem; we
should certainly not have the intensity of the last stanza.

That intensity, if justified, must grow out of a sense of the apparent nearness and intimate presence of what is irrevocably beyond reach: the days that are no more must be more than the conventional 'dear, dead days beyond recall'. They must be beyond
recall, yet alive—tantalizingly vivid and near. It is only thus that
we can feel the speaker justified in calling them

> Dear as remember'd kisses after death,
> And sweet as those by hopeless fancy feign'd
> On lips that are for others.

It is only thus that we can accept the culminating paradox of

O Death in Life, the days that are no more.

We have already observed, in the third stanza, how the speaker compares the strangeness and sadness of the past to the sadness of the birds' piping as it sounds to dying ears. There is a rather brilliant ironic contrast involved in the comparison. The speaker, a living man, in attempting to indicate how sad and strange to him are the days of the past, says that they are as sad and strange as is the natural activity of the awakening world to the man who is dying: the dead past seems to the living man as unfamiliar and fresh in its sadness as the living present seems to the dying man. There is more here, however, than a mere, ironic reversal of roles; in each case there is the sense of being irrevocably barred out from the known world.

This ironic contrast, too, accounts for the sense of desperation which runs through the concluding lines of the poem. The kisses feigned by 'hopeless fancy' are made the more precious because of the very hopelessness; but memory takes on the quality of fancy. It is equally hopeless—the kisses can as little be renewed as those 'feign'd / On lips that are for others' can be obtained. The realized past has become as fabulous as the unrealizable future. The days that are no more are as dear as the one, as sweet as the other, the speaker says; and it does not matter whether we compare them to the one or to the other or to both: it comes to the same thing.

But the days that are no more are not merely 'dear' and 'sweet'; they are 'deep' and 'wild'. Something has happened to the grammar here. How can the *days* be 'deep as love' or 'wild with all regret'? And what is the status of the exclamation 'O Death in Life'? Is it merely a tortured cry like 'O God! the days that are no more'? Or is it a loose appositive: 'the days that are no more are a kind of death in life'?

The questions are not asked in a censorious spirit, as if there were no justification for Tennyson's licence here. But it is important to see how much licence the poem requires, and the terms on which the reader decides to accord it justification. What one finds on closer examination is not muddlement but richness. But it is a richness achieved through principles of organization which many an admirer of the poet has difficulty in allowing to the 'obscure' modern poet.

For example, how can the days of the past be *deep*? Here, of course, the problem is not very difficult. The past is buried within one: the days that are no more constitute the deepest level of one's being, and the tears that arise from thinking on them may be said to come from the 'depth of some divine despair'. But how can the days be 'wild with all regret'? The extension demanded here is more ambitious. In matter of fact, it is the speaker, the man, who is made wild with regret by thinking on the days.

One can, of course, justify the adjective as a transferred epithet on the model of Vergil's *maestum timorem*; and perhaps this was Tennyson's own conscious justification (if, indeed, the need to justify it ever occurred to him). But one can make a better case than a mere appeal to the authority of an established literary convention. There is a sense in which the man and the remembered days are one and the same. A man is the sum of his memories. The adjective which applies to the man made wild with regret can apply to those memories which make him wild with regret. For, does the man charge the memories with his own passion, or is it the memories that give the emotion to him? If we pursue the matter far enough, we come to a point where the distinction lapses. Perhaps I should say, more accurately, adopting the metaphor of the poem itself, we *descend* to a depth where the distinction lapses. The days that are no more are *deep* and *wild*, buried but not dead—below the surface and unthought of, yet at the deepest core of being, secretly alive.

The past *should* be tame, fettered, brought to heel; it is not. It is capable of breaking forth and coming to the surface. The word 'wild' is bold, therefore, but justified. It reasserts the line of development which has been maintained throughout the earlier stanzas: 'fresh', 'strange', and now 'wild'—all adjectives which suggest passionate, irrational life. The word 'wild', thus, not only pulls into focus the earlier paradoxes, but is the final stage in the preparation for the culminating paradox, 'O Death in Life'.

The last stanza evokes an intense emotional response from the reader. The claim could hardly be made good by the stanza taken in isolation. The stanza leans heavily upon the foregoing stanzas and the final paradox draws heavily upon the great metaphors in stanzas II and III. This is as it should be. The justification for emphasizing the fact here is this: the poem, for all its illusion of impassioned speech—with the looseness and *apparent* confusion of unpremeditated speech—is very tightly organized. It represents an organic structure; and the intensity of the total effect is a reflection of the total structure.

The reader, I take it, will hardly be disposed to quarrel with the general statement of the theme of the poem as it is given in the foregoing account; and he will probably find himself in accord with this general estimate of the poem's value. But the reader may well feel that the amount of attention given to the structure of the poem is irrelevant, if not positively bad. In particular, he may find the emphasis on paradox, ambiguity, and ironic contrast displeasing. He has not been taught to expect these in Tennyson, and he has had the general impression that the presence of these qualities represents the intrusion of alien, 'unpoetic' matter.

I have no wish to intellectualize the poem—to make conscious and artful what was actually spontaneous and simple. Nevertheless, the qualities of ironic contrast and paradox *do* exist in the poem; and they *do* have a relation to the poem's dramatic power.

Those who still feel that 'simple eloquence' is enough might compare 'Tears, Idle Tears' with another of Tennyson's poems which has somewhat the same subject matter and hints of the same imagery, the lyric 'Break, Break, Break'.

> Break, break, break,
> On thy cold gray stones, O Sea!
> And I would that my tongue could utter
> The thoughts that arise in me.
>
> O well for the fisherman's boy,
> That he shouts with his sister at play!
> O well for the sailor lad,
> That he sings in his boat on the bay!
>
> And the stately ships go on
> To their haven under the hill;
> But O for the touch of a vanish'd hand,
> And the sound of a voice that is still!
>
> Break, break, break,
> At the foot of thy crags, O Sea!
> But the tender grace of a day that is dead
> Will never come back to me.

It is an easier poem than 'Tears', and, in one sense, a less confusing poem. But it is also a much thinner poem, and unless we yield comfortably and easily to the strain of gentle melancholy, actually a coarser and a more confused poem. For example, the ships are said to be 'stately', but this observation is idle and finally irrelevant. What relation has their stateliness to the experience of grief? (Perhaps one may argue that the term suggests that they go on to fulfil their missions, unperturbed and with no regard for the speaker's mood. But this interpretation is forced, and even under forcing, the yield of relevance is small.)

Again, consider the status of the past as it appears in this poem: the hand is vanished, the voice is still. It is true, as the poem itself indicates, that there is a sense in which the hand has not vanished and the voice is yet heard; otherwise we should not have the poem at all. But the poet makes no effort to connect this activity, still alive in memory, with its former 'actual' life. He is content to keep close to the conventional prose account of such matters. Memory in this poem does not become a kind of life: it is just 'memory'— whatever that is—and, in reading the poem, we are not forced beyond the bounds of our conventional thinking on the subject.

In the same way, the elements of the line, 'the tender grace of a day that is dead', remain frozen at the conventional prose level. The day is 'dead'; the 'tender grace' of it will never 'come back' to him. We are not encouraged to take the poignance of his present memory of it as a ghost from the tomb. The poet does not recognize that his experience represents such an ironical resurrection; nor does he allow the metaphors buried in 'dead' and 'come back' to suffer a resurrection into vigorous poetic life. With such phenomena the poet is not concerned.

Of course, the poet *need* not be concerned with them; I should agree that we have no right to demand that this poem should explore the nature of memory as 'Tears, Idle Tears' explores it. At moments, men are unaccountably saddened by scenes which are in themselves placid and even happy. The poet is certainly entitled, if he chooses, to let it go at that. Yet, it should be observed that in avoiding the psychological exploration of the experience, the poet risks losing dramatic force.

Mere psychological analysis is, of course, not enough to insure dramatic force; and such analysis, moreover, carries its own risks: the poem may become unnatural and coldly rhetorical. But when the poet is able, as in 'Tears, Idle Tears', to analyze his experience, and in the full light of the disparity and even apparent contradiction of the various elements, bring them into a new unity, he secures not only richness and depth but dramatic power as well. Our conventional accounts of poetry which oppose emotion to intellect, 'lyric simplicity' to 'thoughtful meditation', have done no service to the cause of poetry. The opposition is not only merely superficial: it falsifies the real relationships. For the lyric quality, if it be genuine, is not the result of some transparent and 'simple' redaction of a theme or a situation which is somehow poetic in itself; it is, rather, the result of an imaginative grasp of diverse materials—but an imaginative grasp so sure that it may show itself to the reader as unstudied and unpredictable without for a moment relaxing its hold on the intricate and complex stuff which it carries.

1944

'TEARS, IDLE TEARS'

Graham Hough

THIS TENNYSONIAN lyric has been skilfully dissected by Mr. Cleanth Brooks, and its *disjecta membra* added to the rich stock of paradoxes, ironies, and ambiguities boiled up so merrily together in *The Well-Wrought Urn*. What follows is an attempt to put the poem together again.

The theme is an almost objectless regret, rising in the last stanza to something troubled and tumultuous. The very slow movement of the opening suggests a heavy and uncontrollable emotion—the spontaneous and unrestrainable welling-up of tears. But it is not a pleasing-melancholy indulgence: the imagery uses all the most poignant suggestions of regret for the irretrievably lost, arranged in a crescendo—autumn fields (happy in themselves, but including the suggestions of lost summer and winter to come), departed friends (the ship disappearing below the horizon), lost life (life beginning again with the birds and the dawn, but lost to the beholder, since he is dying), lost love (the melancholy dead remembering human kisses in the grave; and still more unhappy, the living hopeless lover remembering kisses that once seemed possibilities and are now known to be unattainable). All obvious and powerful sources of irremediable pain—the pathos of autumn, of parting, of death, of hopeless love; all the things that make you cry, suggesting as overtones all the poetry about nostalgia and separation and about being dead when you don't want to be dead:

O western wind when wilt thou blow,
That the small rain down can rain?
Christ that my love were in my arms
And I in my bed again . . .

My mouth it is full cold, Margaret,
And my breath smells earthy strong.
If you have ae kiss of my clay-cold lips
Your time will not be long . . .

and the ghosts in Virgil stretching out their hands to the farther shore. This is not the elegiac feeling, not like the 'Elegy in a Country Churchyard' or Valéry's 'Cimetière Marin', where the limitations of human life are swallowed up in the will of God or some more metaphysical consolation. Nor is it the romantic commonplace 'I have been half in love with easeful death'. Are we to take the sorrow for 'the days that are no more' in a personal way (last summer when I was happy, the days when my friends were with me, the days when I still thought that she might love me)? I do not think so. I think the poem gets its power over the feelings from the way that these strong and clearly realized individual sources of sorrows are used to suggest another kind of sorrow, more inevitable and more universal. But we shall see.

Formally the poem is remarkable for being rhymeless. Very few people notice this. Yet if such a usual and expected element in a lyric poem is missing there must be some reason; and if people do not notice its absence something must be very skifully put in to supply its place. If we ask why rhyme is absent, we first have to say why it is usually present. What does rhyme do? Commonly it emphasizes the conventional verse form, by pointing the ends of the lines and so helping to give an effect of completeness and definition. The extreme cases are the heroic couplet, with its effect of separable, detached epigrammatic observations; or the Italian sonnet, where the intricate rhyme reinforces the intricacy of thought or emotion, but all self-contained, centred on some specific situation. Why then is this poem rhymeless? Because it is not about a specific situation, or an emotion with clear boundaries; it is about the great reservoir of undifferentiated regret and sorrow, which you can brush away, if you like to be brisk about it, but which nevertheless continues to exist.

Why do we not notice the lack of rhyme? A great deal no doubt is due to the variety and richness of the vowel sounds, in the handling of which, as Mr. Eliot has remarked, Tennyson is an unequalled master. It is easy to feel these effects, but to me they remain quite unanalyzable.

There is also just sufficient end-stopping to emphasize the line-structure; and the refrain provides a formal stress at the ends of the stanzas. And although there is no 'jingling sound of like endings', the end-sounds of the lines are not purely fortuitous; they are all either open vowels, or consonants or groups of consonants that can be prolonged in reading. The result is that each line is self-contained—yet does not end with a snap, but trails away, suggesting a passage into some infinite beyond: just as each image is extremely clear and precise, yet is only an instance or an analogy of something more inclusive. This is true of all except the penultimate line, which ends with a sharp closed syllable—*regret*—a phonetic stop to this hitherto fluent emotion, heralding and isolating the final refrain, which appears here in a much richer and more powerful form than before—'O Death in Life, the days that are no more'.

Why is Death in Life so powerful? Of course they are big words; and the phrase brings to mind 'In the midst of life we are in death'; and Coleridge's Life-in-Death in *The Ancient Mariner*. But the first of these is meant to suggest the awful proximity of the Four Last Things—Death, Judgement, Hell, and Heaven; and Coleridge's Life-in-Death symbolizes the *misère de l'homme sans Dieu* —the state of man who is fallen and powerless to save himself without supernatural aid. I think these associations are both wrong here. This is a quite pagan poem. We have already noted the absence of any of the quasi-Christian or supernatural consolations common in elegy. The tears are idle because they spring from despair; a situation you cannot do anything about. (When are tears ever other than idle? They may be useful if they relieve the feelings and leave you free for further action. But no action is going to cure this sorrow.) Despair is a sin in Christian moral theology, and this despair is therefore not divine in the Christian sense, but only in the sense of being something daemonic, some more than personal force, with some more than private cause.

The 'daemonic' suggestion comes up again with the 'underworld' of the second stanza. The primary sense of this is clearly the geographical one of antipodes, but the suggestion of the classical underworld, the land of the shades, is so strong that it almost swamps the other meaning. But of course Tennyson doesn't really mean an underworld inhabited by ghosts. What does the old symbol stand for in a modern consciousness? Surely for submerged memory from which our friends and other fragments of the past can and sometimes do emerge with such moving and embarrassing freshness. Similarly the next two lines are first a concrete geographical parting, and then the realization that the shades are only shades, that memories are going to disappear again into oblivion. The connection between the coming up of the friends from the underworld and their sinking below the verge is not obvious on the surface; it is only by the secondary meanings—the appearance and disappearance of buried memories—that they are linked. Ghosts appearing from the past—the incursion of the dead into the land of the living.

The same death and life antithesis is in stanza three—the birds waking up and the dawn breaking, the day coming to life, as the man is dying. These lines seem very painful, because the two movements are so utterly out of sympathy with each other: to the man who is dying it is strange that the day should be coming to birth: to the birds and the daylight it is merely indifferent that a man is dying. The words recall too the haunted chilly suspense of the hour before dawn, when vitality is at its lowest: death in life again.

Remembered kisses after death call up Clerk Saunders's ghost and Isabella's Lorenzo, and the Shropshire lad, and all the unquiet graves and all the dead lovers who have had to leave their mistresses above ground: and the next lines, another kind of death in life—a love that has no hope of fruition, but still feigns kisses in imagination: and this in turn calls up the idea of first love—a kind of love that is half-composed of imagination, and therefore has no fruition in actuality.

These situations are all analogies to 'the days that are no more', which are sad and fresh and strange in the same way. We can see now where the final form of the refrain 'O Death in Life' gets its force: it is the conceptual summing up of what has been presented in images in the preceding stanzas.

We have still left one of our questions unanswered. Are all these personal situations the stuff out of which the days that are no more are composed—thus making the poem one about personal love and sorrow? Or are they only similes for a general, not a private past,—thus making the poem one about the pathos of history, like Wordsworth's Mutability sonnet. Genetically, there is little doubt that the first, the private interpretation is the right answer. Tennyson said of the poem (*Memoir*, i, p. 253) 'The passion of the past, the abiding in the transient, was expressed in "Tears, Idle Tears", which was written in the yellowing autumn-tide at Tintern Abbey, full for me of its bygone memories.' The memories could be historical ones, naturally called up by a monastic ruin; but in fact they seem to link the poem with *In Memoriam* 19, also said to have been written at Tintern Abbey (v. Bradley, Commentary on *In Memoriam*, p. 100), whose theme is Arthur Hallam's burial at Clevedon close by. This almost certainly, as a matter of historic fact, gives us the clue to the particular 'days that are no more' that gave rise to the poem, and accounts for the poignancy of its images of death and lost love; accounts even for the ships in stanza two (v. *In Memoriam*, 60 and 10). It is as foolish to refuse such extraneous historical evidence as to overwork it. Values are not explained by their material origins; and poems are not explained by the circumstances that gave rise to them. But we are the less likely to understand either values or poems if we decline to take note of their genesis. Of course in the growth of this poem, the specific past has lost its private associations, and the passion has ceased to be any private grief. Tennyson's note equates 'the passion of the past' with 'the abiding in the transient'. The transient is events, objects, which were once present and are now past: the abiding is the essence of these events, presented to the mind as a passion, as a memory charged with emotion—but not reducible to longing, regret, sense of loss, or any specifiable emotion.

Dramatically the poem has its place in *The Princess*. It is one of the interspersed lyrics, all of which embody useless, irrational or instinctive emotions, and so oppose the active intellectualism of the Princess Ida herself. Naturally she is very impatient with it, and reproves the girl-singer:

> If indeed there haunt
> About the moulder'd lodges of the Past
> So sweet a voice and vague, fatal to men,
> Well needs it we should cram our ears with wool
> And so pace by: but thine are fancies hatch'd
> In silken-folded idleness.

The voice of the past is a siren song: the defence is to put wool in your ears and get on with the fight about votes for women. But of course the Princess loses in the end, and capitulates to all the soft, unreasonable siren voices, as Tennyson intended she should do from the start. What song the sirens sang is a notoriously unanswerable question. We nevertheless have a fairly good idea of what song they sang to Tennyson: it was something about absence, distance, desolation, partings, forsakings; and its echoes can be heard in all his verse, from 'Mariana' in 1830 to 'Far, Far Away' almost sixty years later. The sense of dereliction—arising perhaps from who knows what childish experience—formed a tangled and aching knot somewhere deep in Tennyson's being, a small patch of death in the midst of his life, inaccessible to Princess Ida's raps over the knuckles, or to what the age demanded. When rudely touched, as by the death of Hallam, this tangle of emotions could produce positively psychopathic results. But perhaps it was fortunate that it was not accessible to positivist therapeutics. For it is closely bound up with his greatest successes, which again and again are found to lie in his power of taking an extremely vague and unspecific and objectless emotion, and giving it form, not indeed by intellectualizing it, but by embodying it, partly in images, partly in sound-patterns, of which he is one of the greatest masters in the language. Sometimes he even so orders these private and morbid emotions that they come to correspond with the general experience of the human species: and we have a poem like 'Tears, Idle Tears', abounding in those 'images which find a mirror in every mind, and with sentiments to which every bosom returns an echo' of which Dr. Johnson so justly approved.

1951

'TEARS, IDLE TEARS' AGAIN
Leo Spitzer

I MUST DISAGREE with Mr. Graham Hough's sensitive and
thoughtful interpretation of Tennyson's poem 'Tears, Idle Tears';
insofar as he seems, in my opinion, to have failed sufficiently to
clarify the nature of the element which Tennyson calls (line 2)
'some divine despair' and which contains the principle on which
the structure of the whole poem rests. As for the epithet 'divine',
Mr. Hough limits himself to paraphrasing this by 'daemonic'
which term he defines as 'some more than personal force, some
more than private cause') and to pointing out a reflection of
this daemonic element in the mention of the 'underworld' in the
second stanza. According to my own interpretation, 'some divine
despair' means quite literally 'the despair of *some God*' (the Latinate
use of the adjective instead of a noun in the genitive, is paralleled
by the phrase 'the Aeolian harp' = the harp of Aeolus): of a God
as yet unnamed, but who will be clearly revealed (and named) in
the end of the poem as the God of 'Death in Life'. Our philo-
logical interpretation must then, in contrast to the procedure of
the poet, start with the definition of the nature and attitude of the
deity which is atmospherically ('*some* divine despair') present in
the poem from its very beginning. The particular god (or *Sondergott*, to use the classical scholar Usener's term) of Tennyson's
making is neither Life nor Death, but Death-in-Life; surely not

the Christian deity,[1] as Hough has felt; no more is he Thanatos or Pluto, the God of the underworld before whom man is doomed to appear after death, or even one of the aloof, serene Gods of Epicurus who dwell in the *intermundia*, unconcerned with man. The God Death-in-Life, who, like Christ, has his dwelling-place among the mortals as his name indicates, while sharing the aloofness of the Epicurean Gods, is an impressive and sterile dark God wrapped in his own 'despair' (his *intermundium* is life itself), 'idle' as are the tears of the poet. With the invocation of the name of the God who had been 'somehow' present, or latent, in the poem from the start, the poet's sad 'thinking' has come to an end, but not, we must surmise, his despair and his idle tears. To find a name (or intellectual formula) for the source of our sorrows is not necessarily to free ourselves from their impact. The poem 'Tears, Idle Tears', full of intellectual groping as it is, remains to its end an idle complaint—for the God Death-in-Life who in the end is revealed as the personification of the *lacrimae rerum* will not be able to quench the tears.

And now that I have clarified the 'particular theology' underlying our poem—are our modern critics deaf to the claims of any God?—I would point out that our poem, from beginning to end, is conceived from the point of view both of the 'remembering' poet and of the God 'Death in Life' (for remembrance to our unProustian poet is just that: Death in Life). The latter aspect explains, for instance, the order in which the various melancholy pictures of life are enumerated in our poem: in stanza two the first example is that of the sail 'that brings our friends up from the underworld': this is not only a poetic symbol for 'submerged memory from which our friends and other fragments of the past can and do emerge' (Hough), but also the actual vista before the eyes of the God Death-in-Life; he must see both the memory of friendship and the death of friends (next line) only in terms of the to-and-fro movements of Charon's bark. For him friendship is ephemeral, tinged with the mourning of death; for Death-in-Life it is death that is the normal course of events. Again, consider the picture of birds as they awake to life in the morning through song, but who, as seen by our God, awake and sing at the moment when

---

[1] It is, however, striking that Tennyson's pagan god bears a name derived from a *topos* of the Christian sermon ('in the midst of life we are in death'). This Christian reminiscence serves only to underline his non-Christian nature.

a human being dies. And finally, this god will give precedence, among remembrances of love, to 'remember'd kisses *after death*': 'first love' will appear in the wake of kisses after death and of unhappy love (since, in the view of the dark god and of the melancholy poet, the former must share the mortality of the latter experiences). All the pictures we are offered in our poem—happy autumn fields, friendships, morning birds, first love—are full of brightness on the surface, but suffused with the deep dark shadows of mourning. It is death that is called upon here to interpret life.

The dual principle 'Death in Life'[1] must needs be represented also in the structure of the poem; it is in this principle that the formal unity of the poem resides. (I find it strange that Mr. Hough, who judges Mr. Cleanth Brooks's treatment of 'Tears, Idle Tears' so severely [*disjecta membra* which Hough must put together again!], should not have welcomed the New Critic's emphasis on the structural aspect of the contradictory, or, as I would say, dualistic character of the epithets used by Tennyson in order to characterize the different remembered pictures: cf. particularly Brooks's statement: 'Tennyson cannot be content with *saying* that in memory the poet seems both dear *and* alive; he must dramatize[2]

[1] The dualistic inspiration of our poem is also reflected in the lines of canto IV of *The Princess* into which Tennyson has inserted it:

> 46 so *sweet* a voice and vague, *fatal* to men
> 69 a *death's-head* at the *wine*

Compare also the terms used by Tennyson himself in the autobiographic note: '*The passion of the past*, the *abiding* of the *transient* was expressed in "Tears, Idle Tears".'

The idea of personified Death-in-Life may have come to Tennyson by way of Coleridge's poem *The Ancient Mariner*, in which we find the opposite personification 'Life-in-Death', the 'spectre-Woman' mated with Death, 'the Nightmare' with yellow lips, golden hair, and a skin 'as white as leprosy', who dices with Death about the fate of the ship's crew and wins, as a result whereof the Ancient Mariner who has killed the Albatross must live on, like Cain, to endure a life worse than death. Coleridge's figure Life-in-Death is an elemental spirit related to the vague romantic world of folklore, Tennyson's Death-in-Life a near-classical deity.

[2] The word 'dramatize' is perhaps better chosen than Brooks himself may have known (with him it means no more than 'say dramatically, emphatically'): for in our short lyrical poem we have before us true dramatic development, with two protagonists of whom the first (the poet who sheds idle tears) becomes aware in the *dénouement* of the encompassing power of the second (the god wrapped in idle despair): the poet at the end of the poem comes to realize, in a manner reminiscent of ancient tragedy, that his personal act (of

its life-in-death for us ... The dramatization demands that the antithetical aspects of memory be coalesced into one entity which ... is a paradox, the assertion of the union of opposites.') Mr. Hough, rather than studying this clear-cut dualistic structure of the poem, would have recourse to a vague, for himself opaque[1] sound symbolism he feels to be present in the poem and to replace the rhyme usual in modern poetry; but is it not true of all ancient-classic (and also of ultra-modern) poetry that the place of rhyme is generally taken by an inner architecture of the poem, involving the repetition of patterns or motifs, rhythmical, ideational or verbal?

The dualistic structure of our poem is, in my opinion, twofold: first, as Brooks has seen, there is a dualism within the epithets chosen by the poet in his impotent revolt against remembered sensations:

> fresh but sad
> sad but strange
> dear, sweet, deep, but wild—

a dualism which, finding no final resolution in harmony, ends in a wild, 'tumultuous' (Hough) discordance of despair which breaks out at the moment of the epiphany of the God (and of the realization by the poet of the principle that underlies remembrance of the past). The accumulated, contradictory or disparate epithets (and here indeed sound symbolism is involved: all these simple, familiar, monosyllabic adjectives tend naturally to be prolonged and intensified in emotional speech)[2] leave us indeed in deep despair as

---

remembering) is nothing but a manifestation of an impersonal supernal power. (Brooks has taken cognizance only of the poet-protagonist, whom he calls 'the weeper'.

[1] Let us, however, not forget his excellent remark about the end-sound of all the lines, either open vowels or consonants or groups of consonants that can be prolonged in reading (so that each line 'trails away ... into some infinite beyond'), with the exception of the penultimate line whose end-word *regret* offers a 'phonetic stop to this hitherto flowing emotion, heralding and isolating the final refrain'. The 'trailing away into the infinite' represents the still shapeless musing of the poet, while the 'stop' manifests his clear realization of the disconcerting principle that informs our life. I feel here, as in the whole poem, a certain kinship of Tennyson with the Italian romantic-classical poet of melancholy, Leopardi.

[2] Such coupling of monosyllables which in spite of their shortness invite the imagination to wander is frequent in English: Penn Warren, *All the King's Men* (p. 57) writes: 'It is life sniffing ether, and everything is sweet and sad and far away.'

to the irrevocably antithetic nature of the Janus-like God: no
mortal can, by taking thought, exhaust the oceanic 'depth' of the
experience embodied in him.

But there is in existence besides what I would call a horizontal
dualistic structure, a second, a vertical dualism. The poet's 'thinking of the days that are no more' takes the form of an exclama-
tional pattern in which the refrain-words would serve again and
again as subjects of elliptic sentences consisting mainly of
emotionally-ejaculated adjectives which describe the remembered
bygone days:

> St. II: Fresh . . .
>> Sad . . .
>> So sad, so fresh, the days that are no more!
>>> (I shall supply each time the exclamation point evidently
>>> intended by the poet, but reserved for the last stanza—
>>> in which I shall use a double exclamation mark.)
> St. III: Ah, sad and strange . . .
>> So sad, so strange the days that are no more!
> St. IV: Dear . . .
>> And sweet . . .
>> . . . deep . . .
>> Deep . . . and wild . . .
>> . . . the days that are no more!! [1]

An American friend writes to me from France: 'Chartres was so *deep* and
dark and bright' (the underlining is found in the original letter; similarly,
Tennyson has exploited, by repetition, the phonetic dimension of the depth
present in the English word 'deep'). If my friend had spoken, not written, to
me she would have used the emotional inversion and the ellipsis of the
copula: '*Deep*, dark, bright—the cathedral of Chartres!' And this latter pattern is exactly the *spoken* prose basis of Tennyson's poem, the contrasts remaining unresolved and emotionality being pressed into the simple, familiar
English monosyllables. Only in English, with its long, semi-diphthongal
vowels, is such an effect possible: German epithets of the type of *lieb, tief,
schon* are rarer; and French monosyllabic adjectives cannot be prolonged at all
in pronunciation: *frais, doux, cher, frais* cannot trail away into the infinite.

[1] The construction in the last stanza should be the same as in the preceding
ones: just as we must interpret, for example, in St. III 'so sad, so strange [are]
the days that are no more' (the copula being omitted because of the exclama-
tory inversion of adjective and noun), so in the last stanza: 'Deep . . . deep . . .
deep . . . and wild . . . are the days that are no more.' According to this hypothesis 'O Death in Life' would be a vocative, interpolated by the poet who
now at last is able to address himself, directly, to that impassive deity who was
present from the start because only now he has found its name. But according
to the punctuation used by Tennyson which contradicts such an analysis we

From this syntactical-skeletal outline one cannot fail to grasp the vertical dualistic structure of our poem. The various epithets are contrasted with the ever self-same subject representing the harsh reality of 'no more'. A sensitive critic might perhaps find the repetitiousness of this refrain cumbersome in its folkloristic or melodramatic manner, were it not, as Mr. Hough takes pains to remind us, that the refrain has also a conceptual function: that of having us draw over and over again the same conclusion from the various pictures unfolded in the four stanzas; it is as though human agitation met repeatedly with a disillusioned refrain ('vanitas vanitatum!', 'mais où sont les neiges d'antan?'), or rather as though the tumultuous waves of ejaculations (the variation of adjectives bearing witness to the groping of the 'thinking' poet towards clarity) surged ceaselessly against the dam of doom: 'no more'. Is this periodic futile upsurge of life and emotion against the cold fact of death not, in itself, a manifestation of the Janus Death-in-Life?

Thus our poem is traversed, lengthwise and breadthwise, by structural antitheses or dualisms which form its 'contentual-formal' pattern: that of a certain mysterious harmony in disharmony, in accordance with an order of life which is far from cosmic harmony: 'the need for the beautiful mainly develops when man is in disaccord with reality, lives in disharmony and struggle, when he lives, that is, with greater intensity,' wrote Dostoyevsky. Tennyson, living in intense disharmony with reality, has created in the poem an artistic form which, while itself harmonious, bears the imprint of the basic disaccord in which he lived.

There is still another remark about the structure of our poem which needs to be made. For the sake of clarity I must here have recourse to a paraphrase of the poetic text, which procedure in Mr.

---

would have to assume a change of construction: it would be Death in Life that is identified with the days that are no more, the latter being 1., dear, 2., deep, 3., wild, 4., Death in Life. I suspect that the grammatical ambiguity is here intentional and that the first as well as the second of my interpretations can stand: it is the very nature of the *Sondergott* Death-in-Life that although one may invoke him (in the vocative) as a god who presides over the flux of life he *is* in reality identical with or immanent in that flux.

Mr. Brooks has asked himself the same grammatical question ('And what is the status of the exclamation "O Death in Life"? Is it merely a tortured cry like: "O God! the days that are no more"? or is it a loose appositive: "the days that are no more are a kind of death in life?" ')—without, however, finding any definite answer beyond the possibility of poetic licence.

Brooks's opinion is sheer 'heresy'. But since poetry creates, with material borrowed from our life (including our language) a new poetic world, it will sometimes be in order to use prosaic paraphrase (of course, not so as to reduce the poetic to our prosaic world) to appraise the distance from the workaday world which the poet has achieved in his creation. Tennyson has built our poem on the basis of a collection of pictures, all, as we have said, brought to a common denominator; we may suspect that spontaneous prosaic statements, not yet shaped into the unity of a poem, about the different 'pictures' would have been of the type:

> (Remembered) birth of friendship is *fresh*
> (Remembered) loss of friends is *sad*
> (Remembered) death in spring is *sad and strange*
> Remembered kisses after death are *dear*
> (Remembered) vain hope of kisses is *sweet*
> (Remembered) first love is *deep and wild*.

(It does not matter that 'remember'd' actually occurs only once in the text, in the last stanza, which draws the conclusion—it is to be supplied in all previous statements). Now it is obvious that by this very subordination of all the pictures of remembered detail to the concept 'the days that are no more', the epithets pertaining to each picture (fresh, sad, sad and strange, etc.) have all been applied to the superior concept (and the pictures of detail have been offered only as possible comparisons or examples: 'fresh *as* birth of friendship, sad *as* loss of friendship', etc.: each image is extremely clear and precise, yet is only an instance or analogy of something more inclusive, as Mr. Hough writes.) By an additive or cumulative, and very intellectual, procedure somewhat reminiscent of two devices of baroque poetry (*versus rapportati*[1] and *Summationsschema*[2]), the concept 'the days that are no more' has

---

[1] cf. Curtius, *Europäische Literatur und lateinisches Mittelalter* (p. 288): Milton, 'Aire, Water, Earth by Fowl, Fish, Beast, was flown, was swam, was walkt'.

[2] ibid., p. 289: the device known from the famous monologue of Segismundo in Calderon's 'Life is a dream':

> 1st stanza: What crime have I committed by being born?
> 2nd stanza: Why are other creatures not punished in the same manner for being born?
> 3rd stanza: The bird is born to enjoy freedom.
> 4th stanza: The beast of prey is born to enjoy freedom.
> 5th stanza: The fish is born to enjoy freedom.
> 6th stanza: The brook is born to enjoy freedom.

been made to appear all-inclusive, since it has appropriated all the epithets predicated of the single pictures; the remembered past is at once fresh and sad and strange and dear and sweet and deep and wild. Thus the encroachment of Death in Life appears as a quantitatively as well as qualitatively predominant, mysterious, and inexhaustible factor of our existence.

Our discussion, like that of Cleanth Brooks, has insisted on the clarity of design of a poem otherwise famous for its sombre irrationality: perhaps its very diaphanousness is apt to add to its melancholy beauty. Can there be anything more moving than the description of man's unhappy condition performed with all the intellectual craftsmanship of which man is capable, than a thing of beauty made out of human despair, than the mournful triumph of art?[1]

It is instructive to compare the treatment of a similar theme in former centuries more bound by the tradition of the *topoi*: for instance a sonnet of Quevedo, the seventeenth century Spanish baroque poet, entitled 'To show how all things warn us of death'.

> *Miré los muros* de la patria mia,
> si un tiempo fuertes, ya desmoronados,
> de la carrera de la edad cansados,
> por quien caduca ya su valentia.
>
> *Salíme al campo:* vi que el sol bebia
> los arroyos del hielo desatados,
> y del monte quejosos los ganados
> que con sombras hurtó su luz al dia.
>
> *Entré en mi casa:* vi que, amancillada,
> de anciana habitacion era despojos;
> mi báculo, más corvo y menos fuerte.
>
> Vencida de la edad *sentí mi espada,*
> *y no hallé cosa* en que poner los ojos
> que no fuese *recuerdo de la muerte.*

7th stanza: What justification is there for man to be deprived of the divine gift enjoyed by brook, fish, beast of prey, and bird?

[1] William Empson, in *The Kenyon Critics* (1951), p. 134, writes: 'It is naive . . . to imagine that in a "pessimistic" poem . . . the despairing assertions are meant to be accepted quite flatly. The art-works which can be viewed as glorifying death-wishes cover a large field . . . It seems to be a general rule, however, that if the effect is beautiful the lust of death is balanced by some impulse or interest which contradicts it.'

This is a skeletal outline of the sonnet:

> St. 1: I looked at the walls of my country, once so strong, now weighted down by the years;
> St. 2: I went out into the country-side and saw that the sun had dried out the brooks and, by throwing shadows, had darkened the daylight for the grazing cattle;
> St. 3: I went into my house and saw it deteriorated by age; my staff was bent and weak;
> St. 4: I felt my sword conquered by age, and I could not set my eyes on any object that would not be a reminder of death.

One immediately sees that the baroque *sic transit gloria mundi* motif (particularly apparent in the first stanza) is meant as a Christian lesson to be learned by the reader (*recuerdo de la muerte = memento mori*) who should extract it from the fact of ageing (not from the manifestations of youth: love, friendship); the poet who is speaking is an old man looking back at his life and seeing in it pictures *reminiscent* of death (not of Death in Life). The different pictures, expressed by syntactical homologies (*Miré* 'I looked'—*salí* 'I went out'—*entré* 'I went in'—*sentí* 'I felt'), as with Tennyson, add up to one common denominator: *recuerdo de la muerte*; but with Quevedo the order of the universe is not yet shattered: we progress from public life to nature—to the house—to the self (which is seen as that of a public servant: with the sword). On the contrary, the theme of Tennyson is the existential despair of the single, lonely human individual—with the worm of death in the centre of his life.

The source of Quevedo's sonnet is obviously Ovid's *Tristia*: its end corresponds textually to the line I/11, 23: *quocumque aspexi nihil est nisi mortis imago* 'wherever I look there is nothing but reminders of death', and the listing of dreary aspects of life is an ever recurring *topos* in that ancient work. Ovid was, of course, pointing only to threats of death given with his personal situation as an exile in a barbarous country, with a sea voyage which came close to shipwreck, etc. (cf. the parallel wording I/2, 23 *quocumque aspicio nihil est nisi pontus et aer* 'wherever I look there is nothing but [choppy] sea and [stormy] wind'). The baroque poet Quevedo took such statements of Ovid in an existential meaning, as referring to human life in general, and expressed thus his total disenchantment (desengaño) in a series of *imagines mortis*.

It may be suggested that Tennyson's disenchantment fed on the same literary source as Quevedo's: the pictures of death unfolded by the exile of Tomi in the first decade of our era. But while Ovid, on the brink of death, was still hoping for life (his basic pagan optimism told him: 'if one god persecutes you another god brings you help' and 'who can forbid *some deity* [*aliquod numen*] to protect us against the wrath of another god?' I/2, 4 and 12), the disillusioned English romantic finds himself persecuted by *some divine despair*, by some desperate god who must refuse to protect man. The expression *some divine despair* is surely derived from the Ovidian *aliquod numen*—only Tennyson presents the *numen* not as helping man but as itself helpless.

Our comparison then has demonstrated the continuity of an Ovidian influence which inspired once a seventeenth-century baroque poet of Spain, later one of nineteenth-century Romantic England.

Nor is the theme of death-in-life dead in our own time. This idea, without the hypostasis of a transcendental god, but as an immanent principle of organic life, has been poetically paraphrased in the speech weighted down by doom of a somewhat Schopenhauerian Doctor in Hofmannsthal's 'Das kleine Welt-theater':

> Ich sehe einen solchen Lauf der Welt:
> Das Übel tritt einher aus allen Klüften;
> im Innern eines jeden Menschen hält
> es Haus und schwingt sich nieder aus den Lüften . . .
> Denn eingeborn ist ihr eignes Weh
> den Menschen: ja, indem ich es so nenne,
> verschleir ich schon die volle Zwillingsnäh,
> mit ders dem Sein verwachsen ist, und trenne,
> was nur *ein* Ding: denn lebend sterben wir.
> Fur Leib und Seele, wie ich sie erkenne,
> gilt dieses Wort, für Baum und Mensch und Tier . . .

> This is the course of the world which I can detect:
> woe comes out of crevices,
> it sets house in every man's inside
> and descends on him from the air . . .
> For his own woe is inborn
> to man; nay, in calling it thus,
> I am veiling somewhat its full twin identity
> whereby it has coalesced with being, and I am

severing what in reality is one: *for, living we die.*
This dictum is valid for body and soul, as I see them,
for tree and man and beast.

Whereas Tennyson's procedure was that of recreating a variety of
carefully observed phenomena in order to extract therefrom the
principle of death-in-life, Hofmannsthal's physician, a representative of the modern positivistic, scientific mind, begins by predict-
ing the principle which he corroborates with his final factual
enumeration of mortal beings.

Again, we may find our theme represented in a still more
modern author, this time surely under the direct influence of
Tennyson, however strange such an influence may seem at first
glance in the case of an author as fresh in inspiration and direct in
expression as Hemingway, who, as it seems to me, has inserted
in his novel *For Whom the Bell Tolls* a prose-paraphase of the
Tennysonian poem. The action of this novel is located in contemporary Spain, that European country which is characterized by
what Pedro Salinas has called 'a culture of death'; and the period
chosen is that of the Civil War, an event in which the American
protagonist as participant was able to find the realization of his
being by assuming a duty which entails his death: throughout the
novel Robert Jordan is shown to us steadying and steeling himself
against death. In a lengthy harangue which has the exuberance of
a prose poem (and from which I am extracting a skeletal outline)
the Gipsy woman Pilar, the representative of the spirit of Spain,
enumerates the different occasions on which Robert Jordan may
learn about the 'smell of death':

(1) by staying below deck, with the portholes tightly closed
on a ship that is pitching and rolling in a storm.

(2) by kissing the mouth of one of the old women who, early
in the morning, at the Puente de Toledo in Madrid, come out of
the slaughter house after having drunk the blood of the
slaughtered beasts, the mouth of one of those old women with
'pale sprouts in the death of their faces',

(3) by smelling in the city streets 'a refuse pail with dead
flowers in it',

(4) by smelling the sweepings of the brothels in the Calle de
Salud: the 'odor of love's labor lost mixed with soapy water and
cigarette butts',

(5) by inhaling in the Botanical Garden an 'abandoned gunny sack with the odor of the wet earth, the dead flowers, and the doings of that night': 'in this sack will be contained the essence of it all, both the dead earth and the dead stalks of the flowers and their rotted blooms and the smell that is both the death and birth of man', 'when thou inhalest deeply, thou wilt smell the odor of death-to-come as we know it'.

Hemingway, this modern poet of metaphysical sensuousness, has chosen to centre on sensations accessible to the nostrils, to the most drastically realistic, the olfactory sense (unlike Tennyson, the visual is here secondary, intended only to intensify the olfactory impressions). Moreover, with the exception of the first experience, the olfactory portents of death chosen by Hemingway are limited to a single background, the streets of Madrid, and to a single moment: morning, when indeed one should rather expect signs of awakening life. Morning soiled by the vestiges of the night—what symbol could be more expressive of death-in-life? Hemingway does not reminisce about a past become evanescent; he has us 'smell' the remainders of last night's debauch: by choosing as culmination the smell of the earth after fornication at night he has suggested to us birth under the sway of death; birth of life is infected, according to him, with smell of death, just as with Tennyson the sight of life implies the sight of death.

If we consider the historical line which leads from Ovid to Quevedo to Tennyson to Hofmannsthal to Hemingway we must conclude that the sensation of fear of approaching death is rendered with greater dramatic forcefulness in our first and our last poetic text. Quevedo and Tennyson appear more reflective in comparison with Ovid and Hemingway, though of the first two Tennyson is more desperate than Quevedo. Surely our contemporary American is the most virile poet among the four enumerated, since he considers death-to-come as an experience which we must, like soldiers before battle, anticipate by steadying our nerves and training our senses—without the vain hopes of Ovid, or the Christian consolations implied by Quevedo, or the idle tears indulged in by Tennyson, or the scientifically-detached hopelessness expressed by a character of Hofmannsthal.

1952

V

In Memoriam

IN MEMORIAM

T. S. Eliot

TENNYSON IS a great poet, for reasons that are perfectly clear. He has three qualities which are seldom found together except in the greatest poets: abundance, variety, and complete competence. We therefore cannot appreciate his work unless we read a good deal of it. We may not admire his aims: but whatever he sets out to do, he succeeds in doing, with a mastery which gives us the sense of confidence that is one of the major pleasures of poetry. His variety of metrical accomplishment is astonishing. Without making the mistake of trying to write Latin verse in English, he knew everything about Latin versification that an English poet could use; and he said of himself that he thought he knew the quantity of the sounds of every English word except perhaps *scissors*. He had the finest ear of any English poet since Milton. He was the master of Swinburne; and the versification of Swinburne, himself a classical scholar, is often crude and sometimes cheap, in comparison with Tennyson's. Tennyson extended very widely the range of active metrical forms in English: in *Maud* alone the variety is prodigious. But innovation in metric is not to be measured solely by the width of the deviation from accepted practice. It is a matter of the historical situation: at some moments a more violent change may be necessary than at others. The problem differs at every period. At some times, a violent revolution may be neither possible nor desirable; at such times, a change which may appear very slight, is the change which the important poet will make. The innovation of Pope, after Dryden, may not seem very great; but it is the mark of the master to be able to make small changes which will be highly significant, as at another time to make radical changes, through which poetry will curve back again to its norm.

There is an early poem, only published in the official biography, which already exhibits Tennyson as a master. According to a note, Tennyson later expressed regret that he had removed the poem from his Juvenilia; it is a fragmentary *Hesperides*, in which only the 'Song of the Three Sisters' is complete. The poem illustrates Tennyson's classical learning and his mastery of metre. The first stanza of 'The Song of the Three Sisters' is as follows:

> The Golden Apple, the Golden Apple, the hallow'd fruit,
> Guard it well, guard it warily,
> Singing airily,
> Standing about the charmèd root.
> Round about all is mute,
> As the snowfield on the mountain peaks,
> As the sandfield at the mountain-foot.
> Crocodiles in briny creeks
> Sleep and stir not; all is mute.
> If ye sing not, if ye make false measure,
> We shall lose eternal pleasure,
> Worth eternal want of rest.
> Laugh not loudly: watch the treasure
> Of the wisdom of the West.
> In a corner wisdom whispers. Five and three
> (Let it not be preach'd abroad) make an awful mystery:
> For the blossom unto threefold music bloweth;
> Evermore it is born anew,
> And the sap to threefold music floweth,
> From the root,
> Drawn in the dark,
> Up to the fruit,
> Creeping under the fragrant bark,
> Liquid gold, honeysweet through and through.
> Keen-eyed Sisters, singing airily,
> Looking warily,
> Every way,
> Guard the apple night and day,
> Lest one from the East come and take it away.

A young man who can write like that has not much to learn about
metric; and the young man who wrote these lines somewhere between 1828 and 1830 was doing something new. There is something not derived from any of his predecessors. In some of Tennyson's early verse the influence of Keats is visible—in songs and in
blank verse; and less successfully, there is the influence of Wordsworth, as in *Dora*. But in the lines I have just quoted, and in the
two Mariana poems, 'The Sea-Fairies', 'The Lotos-Eaters', 'The
Lady of Shalott', and elsewhere, there is something wholly new.

> All day within the dreamy house,
>   The doors upon their hinges creak'd;
> The blue fly sung in the pane; the mouse
>   Behind the mouldering wainscot shriek'd,
>   Or from the crevice peer'd about.

The blue fly sung in the pane (the line would be ruined if you substituted *sang* for *sung*) is enough to tell us that something important
has happened.

The reading of long poems is not nowadays much practised: in
the age of Tennyson it appears to have been easier. For a good
many long poems were not only written but widely circulated;
and the level was high: even the second-rate long poems of that
time, like *The Light of Asia*, are better worth reading than most
long modern novels. But Tennyson's long poems are not long
poems in quite the same sense as those of his contemporaries.
They are very different in kind from *Sordello* or *The Ring and the
Book*, to name the greatest by the greatest of his contemporary
poets. *Maud* and *In Memoriam* are each a series of poems, given
form by the greatest lyrical resourcefulness that a poet has ever
shown. The *Idylls of the King* have merits and defects similar to
those of *The Princess*. An *idyll* is a 'short poem descriptive of some
picturesque scene or incident'; in choosing the name Tennyson
perhaps showed an appreciation of his limitations. For his poems
are always descriptive, and always picturesque; they are never
really narrative. The *Idylls of the King* are no different in kind from
some of his early poems; the *Morte d'Arthur* is in fact an early
poem. *The Princess* is still an idyll, but an idyll that is too long.
Tennyson's versification in this poem is as masterly as elsewhere:
it is a poem which we must read, but which we excuse ourselves
from reading twice. And it is worth while recognizing the reason

why we return again and again, and are always stirred by the
lyrics which intersperse it, and which are among the greatest of all
poetry of their kind, and yet avoid the poem itself. It is not, as we
may think while reading, the outmoded attitude towards the relations of the sexes, the exasperating views on the subjects of matri-
mony, celibacy, and female education, that make us recoil from
The Princess.[1] We can swallow the most antipathetic doctrines if
we are given an exciting narrative. But for narrative Tennyson
had no gift at all. For a static poem, and a moving poem, on the
same subject, you have only to compare his 'Ulysses' with the
condensed and intensely exciting narrative of that hero in the
XXVIth Canto of Dante's *Inferno*. Dante is telling a story. Tennyson is only stating an elegiac mood. The very greatest poets set
before you real men talking, carry you on in real events moving.
Tennyson could not tell a story at all. It is not that in *The Princess*
he tries to tell a story and failed: it is rather than an idyll pro-
tracted to such length becomes unreadable. So *The Princess* is a dull
poem; one of the poems of which we may say, that they are beautiful but dull.

But in *Maud* and in *In Memoriam*, Tennyson is doing what every
conscious artist does, turning his limitations to good purpose. Of
the content of *Maud*, I cannot think so highly as does Mr. Humbert Wolfe, in his interesting essay on Tennyson which is largely
defence of the supremacy of that poem. For me, *Maud* consists of
a few very beautiful lyrics, such as 'O let the solid ground', 'Birds
in the high Hall-garden', and 'Go not, happy day', around which
the semblance of a dramatic situation has been constructed with
the greatest metrical virtuosity. The whole situation is unreal; the
ravings of the lover on the edge of insanity sound false, and fail,
as do the bellicose bellowings, to make one's flesh creep with sin-
cerity. It would be foolish to suggest that Tennyson ought to have
gone through some experience similar to that described: for a poet
with dramatic gifts, a situation quite remote from his personal
experience may release the strongest emotion. And I do not believe for a moment that Tennyson was a man of mild feelings or
weak passions. There is no evidence in his poetry that he knew

---

[1] For a revelation of the Victorian mind on these matters, and of opinions
to which Tennyson would probably have subscribed, see the Introduction by
Sir Edward Strachey, Bt., to his emasculated edition of the *Morte D'Arthur*
of Malory, still current. Sir Edward admired the *Idylls of the King*.

the experience of violent passion for a woman; but there is plenty of evidence of emotional intensity and violence—but of emotion so deeply suppressed, even from himself, as to tend rather towards the blackest melancholia than towards dramatic action. And it is emotion which, so far as my reading of the poems can discover, attained no ultimate clear purgation. I should reproach Tennyson not for mildness, or tepidity, but rather for lack of serenity.

> Of love that never found his earthly close,
> What sequel?

The fury of *Maud* is shrill rather than deep, though one feels in every passage what exquisite adaptation of metre to the mood Tennyson is attempting to express. I think that the effect of feeble violence, which the poem as a whole produces, is the result of a fundamental error of form. A poet can express his feelings as fully through a dramatic, as through a lyrical form; but *Maud* is neither one thing nor the other: just as *The Princess* is more than an idyll, and less than a narrative. In *Maud*, Tennyson neither identifies himself with the lover, nor identifies the lover with himself: consequently, the real feelings of Tennyson, profound and tumultuous as they are, never arrive at expression.

It is, in my opinion, in *In Memoriam*, that Tennyson finds full expression. Its technical merit alone is enough to ensure its perpetuity. While Tennyson's technical competence is everywhere masterly and satisfying, *In Memoriam* is the most unapproachable of all his poems. Here are one hundred and thirty-two passages, each of several quatrains in the same form, and never monotony or repetition. And the poem has to be comprehended as a whole. We may not memorize a few passages, we cannot find a 'fair sample'; we have to comprehend the whole of a poem which is essentially the length that it is. We may choose to remember:

> Dark house, by which once more I stand
> Here in the long unlovely street,
> Doors, where my heart was used to beat
> So quickly, waiting for a hand,

> A hand that can be clasp'd no more—
> Behold me, for I cannot sleep,
> And like a guilty thing I creep
> At earliest morning to the door.

> He is not here; but far away
>   The noise of life begins again,
>   And ghastly thro' the drizzling rain
> On the bald street breaks the blank day.

This is great poetry, economical of words, a universal emotion in what could only be an English town: and it gives me the shudder that I fail to get from anything in *Maud*. But such a passage, by itself, is not *In Memoriam*: *In Memoriam* is the whole poem. It is unique: it is a long poem made by putting together lyrics, which have only the unity and continuity of a diary, the concentrated diary of a man confessing himself. It is a diary of which we have to read every word.

Apparently Tennyson's contemporaries, once they had accepted *In Memoriam*, regarded it as a message of hope and reassurance to their rather fading Christian faith. It happens now and then that a poet by some strange accident expresses the mood of his generation, at the same time that he is expressing a mood of his own which is quite remote from that of his generation. This is not a question of insincerity: there is an amalgam of yielding and opposition below the level of consciousness. Tennyson himself, on the conscious level of the man who talks to reporters and poses for photographers, to judge from remarks made in conversation and recorded in his son's Memoir, consistently asserted a convinced, if somewhat sketchy, Christian belief. And he was a friend of Frederick Denison Maurice—nothing seems odder about that age than the respect which its eminent people felt for each other. Nevertheless, I get a very different impression from *In Memoriam* from that which Tennyson's contemporaries seem to have got. It is of a very much more interesting and tragic Tennyson. His biographers have not failed to remark that he had a good deal of the temperament of the mystic—certainly not at all the mind of the theologian. He was desperately anxious to hold the faith of the believer, without being very clear about what he wanted to believe: he was capable of illumination which he was incapable of understanding. The 'Strong Son of God, immortal Love', with an invocation of whom the poem opens, has only a hazy connection with the Logos, or the Incarnate God. Tennyson is distressed by the idea of a mechanical universe; he is naturally, in lamenting his friend, teased by the hope of immortality and reunion beyond death. Yet the renewal craved for seems at best but a continuance,

or a substitute for the joys of friendship upon earth. His desire for
immortality never is quite the desire for Eternal Life; his concern
is for the loss of man rather than for the gain of God.

shall he,

> Man, her last work, who seem'd so fair,
>   Such splendid purpose in his eyes,
>   Who roll'd the psalm to wintry skies,
> Who built him fanes of fruitless prayer,
>
> Who trusted God was love indeed
>   And love Creation's final law—
>   Tho' Nature, red in tooth and claw
> With ravine, shriek'd against his creed—
>
> Who loved, who suffer'd countless ills,
>   Who battled for the True, the Just,
>   Be blown about the desert dust,
> Or seal'd within the iron hills?

That strange abstraction, 'Nature', becomes a real god or goddess, perhaps more real, at moments, to Tennyson than God ('Are
God and Nature then at strife?'). The hope of immortality is confused (typically of the period) with the hope of the gradual and
steady improvement of this world. Much has been said of Tennyson's interest in contemporary science, and of the impression of
Darwin. *In Memoriam*, in any case, antedates *The Origin of Species* by
several years, and the belief in social progress by democracy antedates it by many more; and I suspect that the faith of Tennyson's
age in human progress would have been quite as strong even had
the discoveries of Darwin been postponed by fifty years. And after
all, there is no logical connection: the belief in progress being current already, the discoveries of Darwin were harnessed to it:

> No longer half-akin to brute,
>   For all we thought and loved and did,
>   And hoped, and suffer'd, is but seed
> Of what in them is flower and fruit;
>
> Whereof the man, that with me trod
>   This planet, was a noble type
>   Appearing ere the times were ripe,
> That friend of mine who lives in God,

That God, which ever lives and loves,
    One God, one law, one element,
    And one far-off divine event,
To which the whole creation moves.

These lines show an interesting compromise between the religious attitude and, what is quite a different thing, the belief in human perfectibility; but the contrast was not so apparent to Tennyson's contemporaries. They may have been taken in by it, but I don't think that Tennyson himself was, quite: his feelings were more honest than his mind. There is evidence elsewhere—even in an early poem, 'Locksley Hall', for example—that Tennyson by no means regarded with complacency all the changes that were going on about him in the progress of industrialism and the rise of the mercantile and manufacturing and banking classes; and he may have contemplated the future of England, as his years drew out, with increasing gloom. Temperamentally, he was opposed to the doctrine that he was moved to accept and to praise.[1]

Tennyson's feelings, I have said, were honest; but they were usually a good way below the surface. In Memoriam can, I think, justly be called a religious poem, but for another reason than that which made it seem religious to his contemporaries. It is not religious because of the quality of its faith, but because of the quality of its doubt. Its faith is a poor thing, but its doubt is a very intense experience. In Memoriam is a poem of despair, but of despair of a religious kind. And to qualify its despair with the adjective 'religious' is to elevate it above most of its derivatives. For The City of Dreadful Night, and the Shropshire Lad, and the poems of Thomas Hardy, are small work in comparison with In Memoriam: it is greater than they and comprehends them.[2]

In ending we must go back to the beginning and remember that In Memoriam would not be a great poem, or Tennyson a great poet, without the technical accomplishment. Tennyson is the great master of metric as well as of melancholia; I do not think any poet in English has ever had a finer ear for vowel sound, as well as a subtler feeling for some moods of anguish:

  [1] See, in Harold Nicolson's admirable Tennyson, pp. 252 ff.

  [2] There are other kinds of despair. Davidson's great poem, Thirty Bob a Week, is not derivative from Tennyson. On the other hand, there are other things derivative from Tennyson besides Atalanta in Calydon. Compare the poems of William Morris with The Voyage of Maeldune, and Barrack Room Ballads with several of Tennyson's later poems.

Dear as remember'd kisses after death,
And sweet as those by hopeless fancy feign'd
On lips that are for others; deep as love,
Deep as first love, and wild with all regret.

And this technical gift of Tennyson's is no slight thing. Tennyson
lived in a time which was already acutely time-conscious: a great
many things seemed to be happening, railways were being built,
discoveries were being made, the face of the world was changing.
That was a time busy in keeping up to date. It had, for the most
part, no hold on permanent things, on permanent truths about
man and God and life and death. The surface of Tennyson stirred
about with his time; and he had nothing to which to hold fast except his unique and unerring feeling for the sounds of words. But
in this he had something that no one else had. Tennyson's surface,
his technical accomplishment, is intimate with his depths: what
we most quickly see about Tennyson is that which moves between
the surface and the depths, that which is of slight importance. By
looking innocently at the surface we are most likely to come to the
depths, to the abyss of sorrow. Tennyson is not only a minor
Virgil, he is also with Virgil as Dante saw him, a Virgil among the
Shades, the saddest of all English poets, among the Great in
Limbo, the most instinctive rebel against the society in which he
was the most perfect conformist.

Tennyson seems to have reached the end of his spiritual development with In Memoriam; there followed no reconciliation, no
resolution.

And now no sacred staff shall break in blossom,
No choral salutation lure to light
A spirit sick with perfume and sweet night,

or rather with twilight, for Tennyson faced neither the darkness
nor the light, in his later years. The genius, the technical power,
persisted to the end, but the spirit had surrendered. A gloomier
end than that of Baudelaire: Tennyson had no *singulier avertisse-
ment*. And having turned aside from the journey through the dark
night, to become the surface flatterer of his own time, he has been
rewarded with the despite of an age that succeeds his own in
shallowness.

1936

VI

Maud

TENNYSON'S *MAUD*—
THE FUNCTION OF THE IMAGERY
John Killham

Shall I weep if a Poland fall? shall I shriek if a Hungary fail?
Or an infant civilization be ruled with rod or with knout?

THIS IS the despairing question which posed itself to one of the
literary outsiders of a century ago—to the speaker in Tennyson's
Maud. It is this sort of allusion to contemporary political and
social affairs which makes the poem so difficult to grasp as an
artistic unity. From its first appearance until today readers have
been embarrassed too by the conclusion wherein the speaker sails
to the Crimea:

And I stood on a giant deck and mixt my breath
With a loyal people shouting a battle cry.[1]

The modern historical view of the Crimean venture does not
coincide with that in the poem, that Nicholas I was a 'giant liar',
and that the cause was 'pure and true'. Moreover, the modern experience of the horrors of war forces us hopefully to seek for an
alternative to the view that Tennyson was a Jingoist and to argue
that the conclusion is to be read strictly in terms of a mind still

[1] See, e.g., E. D. H. Johnson, *The Alien Vision of Victorian Poetry* (Princeton, 1952), p. 31.

disordered, finding in war the only solution adequate to its needs.[1] The historical objections to the poem can thus be conveniently turned aside by arguing for psychological relativism being part of Tennyson's intention from the very beginning. Smaller objections can equally easily be disposed of in this way. For instance the complaint, forcefully uttered soon after the poem was published, that even if one admitted that the war was ethically justifiable it could hardly be expected to end the commercial malpractices against which the speaker rails at the beginning of the poem, cannot be sustained if one pleads that he is incapable of thinking logically.

One of the difficulties arising from using psychological concepts to counter historical ones is, whatever side we take, to cause us to consider the poem very largely in ideological terms—as propaganda or as a case-study. This is not to say that the issue can go unresolved. The poem, after all, deals directly with matters falling within the province of both history and psychology. But from the literary critic's point of view one important thing to emphasize is the dramatic nature of the poem: it deals with character and action. The historian's objections to the conclusion can be ruled out by simply asserting that the speaker's actions are governed by the beliefs he is shown to hold, and not by what other people may believe. The psychoanalytic view of the conclusion, which at first sight seems to resemble this, really bases itself upon the analyst's own feelings about war rather than upon those of the protagonist (if such a term is admissible in relation to a 'monodrama'). For it is not difficult to see that the conclusion, though perhaps not as inevitable as one would wish, is carefully prepared for throughout the poem. The hero's mind, as a result of the shock given it in childhood by the frightening circumstances of his father's death in the 'dreadful hollow behind the little wood', is obsessed by violence and death. He sees commercial competition to have led to a state resembling civil war, the spirit of Cain being paramount —an age

> When only the ledger lives, and when only not all men lie.

All about him

> . . . nature is one with rapine, a harm no preacher can heal;

[1] This is the view of Roy P. Basler in *Sex, Symbolism, and Psychology in Literature* (1945), p. 87 f.

The Mayfly is torn by the swallow, the sparrow spear'd by the shrike,
And the whole little wood where I sit is a world of plunder and prey.

The whole universe, in fact, seems to move without a conscience
or an aim: animal species die and are superseded: a 'sad astrology'
teaches that even the stars are tyrants,

> Innumerable, pitiless, passionless eyes,
> Cold fires, yet with power to burn and brand
> His nothingness into man.

What wonder that his whole desire is for withdrawal! He is cowed
by life and regrets that he ever came to possess the consciousness
which causes him to believe that life involves an unremitting resort to either violence or cunning, the struggle inevitably culminating in death.

Quite naturally introduced into the first part of the poem are
references to the war to come. The cruel suppression of Poland
and Hungary by Russia and Austria undertaken in 1848 and 1849
justifies his general mood of despair and quietism. International
affairs are seemingly conducted upon the same ruthless pattern of
violence, the suppression of the weak by the strong. Colonialism
too is but disguised tyranny. The mendacity of Czar Nicholas I
over the 'sick man of Europe' is no better than the petty untruth-
fulness of any working man:

> And Jack on his ale-bench has as many lies as a Czar.

Even those of the anti-war party seem to him to be motivated by
an ignoble self-interest, a concern for their profits:

> Last week came one to the county town,
> To preach our poor little army down,
> And play the game of the despot kings,
> Tho' the state has done it and thrice as well.
> This broad-brimm'd hawker of holy things,
> Whose ear is cramm'd with his cotton, and rings
> Even in dreams to the chink of his pence,
> This huckster put down war! can he tell
> Whether war be a cause or a consequence?

Ironically one of his earliest encounters with Maud is on the occasion of his passing near her unseen while she is singing,

> Singing of men that in battle array,
> Ready in heart and ready in hand,
> March with banner and bugle and fife
> To the death, for their native land.

This does not, as might have been expected, create in him a sense of revulsion against her, but rather a recognition that it is his own, and his age's baseness that is highlighted by her confident trust, as expressed by the words of the passionate ballad, that violent death for one's country in the cause of honour is not without positive value. As his love for Maud deepens his attitude towards violence and death changes: he is able to see that in some circumstances a resort to violence may not be without ethical justification. As his reasons for finding pleasure in life increase with his love, he paradoxically comes to see that death is not fearful and that the good may have to be defended by force. For Maud, for instance, he would die,

> for sullen-seeming Death may give
> More life to Love than ever is or was
> In our low world, where yet 'tis sweet to live;

though his aim now is to live,

> Not die, but live a life of truest breath,
> And teach true life to fight with mortal wrongs.

In Part II of the poem his killing of Maud's brother causes him to revert quickly to the mood of the opening lines, and it seems that he is again utterly revolted by violence. He sees the explosion of his pistol to have

> thunder'd up into heaven the Christless code
> That must have life for a blow,

and that the heavens are justified in destroying men who are but

> The feeble vassals of wine and anger and lust,
> The little hearts that know not how to forgive.

But even when he has succumbed to madness he sees clearly what he should have remembered before engaging in the duel: that violence, though never justified in the sphere of personal relations is permissible in defence of the *public* good:

Friend, to be struck by the public foe,
Then to strike him and lay him low,
There were a public merit, far,
Whatever the Quaker holds, from sin;
But the red life spilt for a private blow—
I swear to you, lawful and lawless war
Are scarcely even akin.

From this position it is a reasonably natural development to Part III wherein, exactly a year after, his mental disturbance righted, and his actions seemingly directed by a dream of Maud (some time dead), he faces the issue of imminent war. It appears to him as fulfilling the conditions which he earlier saw made a resort to force not merely justifiable but even an obligation imposed upon men who seek to direct their lives into good courses by upholding what they take to be right:

. . . it lighten'd my despair
When I thought that a war would arise in defence of the right,
That an iron tyranny should now bend or cease.

For I cleaved to a cause that I felt to be pure and true.

We should not allow our historical judgement of the merits of the Crimean War to enter here. The problem of what attitude we should take in face of tyranny can be related to any war which strikes the reader as offering the issue Tennyson presents. In other words, the rigidly historical approach can injure the poem if it takes no account of the dramatic development. On the other hand we should not attempt to disregard this dramatic development in another way by introducing the concept of psychological relativism as the proper counter to the historical approach. The high destructiveness of modern warfare makes us recoil from the use of violence, but unfortunately the basic problem is thereby made only more acute. Indeed it is a pity that the discussion of *Maud* turns so often upon such ideological problems, for its real value as a poem is consequently only partially considered. The historical and psychological aspects of the action have to be related to the work considered both as drama and a series of lyrics. Taken simply as a sort of drama it has admittedly to be recognized that it deals with a psychological-cum-philosophical theme in an historical setting. This theme is reducible ultimately to the notion that a psychic balance in man, who is obliged to accept that violence and death have to be faced as part of his lot on earth, is attainable through the experience of love, which with maturity can take the form of sexual love. (The various fantasy-worlds of each of the patients in the asylum is explicity stated to be meant to

> ... wheedle a world that loves him not.)

To body forth this theme (which is touched upon in the early (1830) poem 'Love and Death'), Tennyson devised the plot of *Maud*, a plot which, more than fifty years ago, Andrew Lang showed to resemble that of *The Bride of Lammermoor*.

But although the role of the dramatic plot is to develop this overall theme, it must not be forgotten that it was devised at the suggestion of Sir John Simeon as a setting for the poem 'O that 'twere possible' published long before in 1837, now forming (with slight changes) the fourth section of Part II. In addition, the poem as we now have it is not really a regular drama at all, but a series of lyrics and dramatic monologues. In fact, it is truer on the whole to say that the drama is subordinate to the lyrics, rather than the reverse; and this means that the critical techniques used to show the way in which a reader's response to lyric poems is controlled are just as applicable to *Maud* as are those used in relation to drama. In other words, the imagery is as important as the themes, and the portrayal of character in action serves Tennyson's lyric interests equally with his thematic ones.

All lyric poems, after all, are dramatic in the sense that something of the state of mind of the presumed utterer of their words is conveyed along with a certain amount of prose-meaning. Tennyson shows in 'Mariana' and 'The Palace of Art', not to speak of certain of his dramatic monologues, a penchant for 'art-characters' whose morbidity and loneliness allow him to achieve certain unusual effects by bringing into juxtaposition images possessed of unexpected reverberations.

> The blue fly sung in the pane; the mouse
>   Behind the mouldering wainscot shriek'd,
> Or from the crevice peer'd about.
>   Old faces glimmer'd thro' the doors,
>   Old footsteps trod the upper floors,
> Old voices called her from without.

The device employed in *Maud* of placing such a character in a dramatic movement allowed him to carry images from one lyric to another, thus creating ever richer associative contexts, but inevitably indicating the changes in the mind of the presumed utterer. Thus, although Tennyson may have had uppermost in his mind the problem of creating with words ever-rarer imaginative effects (the artist's preoccupation), he could not avoid the obligation of giving causes for the changes in his 'character's' mood by resort to a thread of narrative, kept so thin, indeed, as to be lost by some readers of the first edition. But *In Memoriam* should indicate that Tennyson could be preoccupied with lyric-effects first and connection afterwards, and that *Maud* shows that he had learned that a charge of insincerity and artificiality (still levelled against *In Memoriam* because the poet, notwithstanding his protest that he was not the 'speaker' in that poem, is *felt* to be personally involved) can only be evaded by resort to the greater artificiality of fiction. But the point to be made is that in *Maud* theme and story are secondary, and that the reader should concentrate upon poems and poetry.

Although I shall discuss the imagery and its effects in the poem, a word must be said about the rhythm in which it is enveloped, for at all times this is used, as generally in Tennyson, to reinforce the effects of other devices.

Sir Harold Nicolson wrote in 1923 of his surprise and revulsion on seeing that the splendid Section XXII of *Maud* opened to the rhythm of a Victorian polka.[1] Of course such dance-rhythms in verse are not unfamiliar today, but even so it is odd that no mention was made of the fact that Section XXII concerns the hero's vigil in the garden outside the ballroom where that very dance was in all likelihood being enjoyed. Tennyson floats his lyrics upon the rhythms appropriate to the mood and the occasion, varying from the monotonous, obsessive tone of the opening section to the excited flutter of the lover's expectancy. Some of his effects are beautifully contrived. Take this, for example:

> And suddenly, sweetly, my heart beat stronger
> And thicker, until I heard no longer
> The snowy-banded, dilettante,
> Delicate-handed priest intone.

[1] Harold Nicolson, *Tennyson*, p. 233.

or this:

> . . . a million horrible bellowing echoes broke.

This artistic precision is to be found in many other forms. So exactly described is the landscape in which the action occurs that it can be mapped: the seasons of a year are carefully integrated with the moods of the hero. But the brilliance of the lyric-effects mainly rests upon the imagery, which throughout the poem, despite this careful alluding to an English landscape and climate, is really highly artificial, even to the extent of being unnatural. Tennyson, often thought of as a poet limited in range by virtue of the fact that his imagery is often drawn from external nature, uses the circumstance of his hero's being unusually, indeed pathologically, sensitive to his environment, to communicate a novel imaginative experience to the reader. The hero's sensory world is over-brilliant, exaggeratedly alive: and we can imaginatively recognize his condition as much from this as from his hysterical denunciations of the evils springing from the commercial spirit. He is, for example, unusually responsive to scents and sounds, as well as to colours, so that the lyrics ostensibly displaying his responses to a normal English environment often have an exotic flavour. Colours, for instance, are given the unnatural glitter of precious stones—emeralds, sapphires, rubies:

> A million emeralds break from the ruby-budded lime
> In the little grove where I sit . . .

Sometimes unusual atmospheric tints are caught in a single phrase —'a bed of daffodil sky', 'yellow vapours', 'a dull red ball'. By these devices Tennyson can suggest something of the speaker's obsessive state of mind. The colour-imagery, hectic and of unusual energy, so exactly represents his mood that it can even be seen to possess a punning quality, as if his vision is unconsciously directed by his *idée fixe*. For example, at the beginning of the poem, when his mind is agitated by his recollection of his father's death as a result of a failed speculation, the landscape is made to share the notion of ruin.

> And out he walk'd when the wind like a broken wordling wail'd,
> And the flying gold of the ruin'd woodlands drove thro' the air.

The smallest sounds are magnified by his outraged consciousness into torturing cacophony. The shriek of a mouse in the wainscot, a clock's ticking, the scream of a madden'd beach, the 'grind-ing of villainous centre-bits', are all part of a living nightmare, in which hallucination is made to play an additional part:

> ... my own sad name in corners cried,
> When the shiver of dancing leaves is thrown
> About its echoing chambers wide.

The smell of flowers—of musk, of roses, of violets—is introduced so as to produce an almost eastern luxury of perfume.

> And the woodbine spices are wafted abroad
> And the musk of the rose is blown.

This eastern effect is reinforced by a use of pathetic fallacy, par-ticularly in Section XXII of Part I, a device employed by the Persian composers of the Ghazel, or Ode, an adaptation of which Tennyson introduced into *The Princess* some years earlier in the shape of the exquisite lyric, 'Now sleeps the crimson petal, now the white'. His study of the works of Sir William Jones could have given him the hint.

> All night have the roses heard
> The flute, violin, bassoon;
> All night has the casement jessamine stirr'd
> To the dancers dancing in tune;
> Till a silence fell with the waking bird,
> And a hush with the setting moon . . .

> I said to the rose, 'The brief night goes
> In babble and revel and wine . . .

(The justification for introducing this novel effect is, incidentally, provided by various allusions in the narrative. The speaker in the poem is predisposed to fit his ideas to the settings of the Arabian Nights. He almost thinks that his youthful 'betrothal' to Maud might be an echo of

> something
> Read with a boy's delight
> Viziers nodding together
> In some Arabian night,

and several times alludes to Maud's brother, who is over-fond of perfumes and personal jewellery, as 'the Sultan' or an 'oil'd and

227

curl'd Assyrian bull'. He would prefer to assume a Horatian posture of *nil admirari*

> Than to walk all day like the sultan of old in a garden of spice.

Maud's private garden of roses and lilies (she is 'Queen rose of the rosebud garden of girls') has obvious resemblances, too, to the forbidden gardens of the Sultan which Tennyson describes in 'Recollections of the Arabian Nights.')

Some readers may feel that what I have said about this imagery of scents, sounds, and colours is really nothing more than a familiar tribute to Tennyson's virtuosity, but that something more than this is demanded. What is really needed is evidence that he could use his verbal skill to explore an interesting human situation, or in other words, to cause it to reveal the genuine complexity of his theme. If it is accepted that his theme is the attainment through sexual love of a psychic balance, and that this must involve facing violence and death as part of the universal human lot, then it has to be shown that the imagery employed in the lyrics can, by its own mode of development, deepen and assist the dramatic movement. It is precisely this which can be illustrated from the changes undergone by a number of images relating to animals, stones, and flowers, which are themselves interrelated. These images have their natural right to be in the poem considered as drama because the mind of the hero is such that he is obliged to resort to them as the only means of expressing his feelings. Their function in the individual lyrics is that of controlling the associations in the reader's mind, though he may not consciously perceive the process. We can infer from the poem that despite his father's financial crash the speaker has had sufficient means to allow him to lead a life of leisure, even if in relative poverty. It is clear too that he is well-read (though Tennyson altered in the second edition the line 'I will bury myself in my books' to 'I will bury myself in myself'). At times he uses language which is coloured by that of Elizabethan drama and of pastoral poetry, and in one passage, as I shall show, recalls Marvell.

The opening sections of the poem show that the delayed effect of the traumatic experience in infancy has been to dispose him not merely to denounce the commercial spirit in all its manifestations but to see men in general to be no better than the vilest animals. This view is clearly supported by his awareness of the theory of development in species: his whole inherited system of beliefs and values has been destroyed. This attitude is reflected in the animal-imagery throughout the first and second parts of the poem. His father's partner had

Dropt off gorged from a scheme that had left us flaccid and drain'd.

Maud's official suitor is heir to a man who had

crept from a gutted mine
Master of half a servile shire,

and himself has

a rabbit mouth that is ever agape.

The English are represented in terms of a rat, a 'little breed', 'long-neck'd geese', and serpents. It is easy to see many other examples. The bull, the fly, the lean and hungry wolf, the raven, the drone, the venomous worm, the bird of prey, the titmouse, all represent various men. The speaker sees himself as 'a wounded thing with a rancorous cry'. What is of greatest interest is the development this imagery makes when Maud appears. At first she is also seen as a beast of prey from whom the hero is safe—'There are fatter game on the moor'. But gradually the imagery changes. First she is represented as a 'milk-white fawn', then he notices the 'Arab arch of her feet' and a grace as 'bright and light as the crest of a peacock'. Later she is seen as 'a bird with the shining head', a 'dove with the tender eye', equally exposed to birds of prey. Seeing her symbolized as a 'milk-white fawn' soon after her return, and while still on his guard, he is tempted to say of her:

You have but fed on the roses and lain in the lilies of life.

This line has been read in conjunction with the passionate feeling of Section XXII (the tone of which is quite distinct) and dubbed, proleptically, 'Swinburnian'.[1] But the allusion is clearly to Marvell's lines from 'The Nympth complaining for the Death of her Faun'.

I have a Garden of my own,
But so with Roses over grown,
And Lillies, that you would it guess
To be a little Wilderness.

[1] E. D. H. Johnson, 'The Lily and the Rose: Symbolic Meaning in Tennyson's *Maud*', *Publications of the Modern Language Association of America*, lxiv (1949), p. 1222.

> And all the Spring time of the year
> It onely loved to be there.
> Among the beds of Lillyes, I
> Have sought it oft, where it should lye;
> Yet could not, till it self would rise,
> Find it, although before mine Eyes.
> For, in the flaxen Lillies shade,
> It like a bank of Lillies laid.
> Upon the Roses it would feed,
> Until its Lips ev'n seem'd to bleed.

That this fawn was as white as milk is shown by other lines in the poem:

> With sweetest milk, and sugar, first
> I it at mine own fingers nurst.
> And as it grew, so every day
> It wax'd more white and sweet than they . . .
> There at my feet shalt thou be laid,
> Of purest Alabaster made:
> For I would have thine Image be
> White as I can, though not as Thee.

The image of the milk-white fawn, like that of Dryden's 'milk-white hind' amidst the jungle beasts in *The Hind and the Panther*, is not only a delightful one, but carries implicitly in it the power of softening the concept of nature red in tooth and claw which up to this point has filled the hero's mind. The pampered creature of Marvell's lines is an exact imaginative analogue for his first impression of Maud, who is thereafter associated in the verse with roses and lilies, though these flowers change their symbolic significance as the Marvellian use of the images is supplanted by that appropriate to Persian poetry, and are merged in allusions to flowers generally. Indeed it is the main characteristic of Tennyson's art in *Maud* that several groups of images develop simultaneously and show occasional interdependence. The introduction of the Marvellian line is a stage in a process by which the colour red, powerfully and neurotically associated with violent death and blood, is discharged of its baleful associations by being assimilated to the image of the rose, first mentioned contemptuously in a context (I.111.x) of poison flowers (source of the cruel madness of love), but progressively developed until at the end of Part I it represents sexual passion. Finally, as an indication of his being cured, the colour reverts to a reference to violence, but with the flower-image now serving along with it:

> The blood-red blossom of war with a heart of fire.

The painful associations of redness revealed at the beginning of the poem

> I hate the dreadful hollow behind the little wood;
> Its lips in the field above are dabbled with blood-red heath,
> The red-ribb'd ledges drip with a silent horror of blood,
> And Echo there, whatever is ask'd her, answers 'Death'—

have been neutralized. It is interesting to see that Tennyson fits the rose-symbol into the passionate last section of Part I (Section XXII) not only by using the devices familiar in the Persian ode, but also by blending with the description the erotic nuances familiar to the reader of Elizabethan poetry:

> For a breeze of morning moves,
> And the planet of love is on high,
> Beginning to faint in the light that she loves
> On a bed of daffodil sky,
> To faint in the light of the sun she loves,
> To faint in his light, and to die.

This fits the dramatic context perfectly, for it will be noticed that the early, disagreeable associations in the word 'die' have been replaced by others connected with sexual love. The imagery is deepening and enriching the dramatic (or psychological) development. The word 'blood' is similarly polarized:

> And the soul of the rose went into my blood.

The changes undergone by the imagery of animals and flowers, centring upon the fawn and the red rose, are paralleled by those of another cluster. These concern stones, and hard substances, and include dust, earth (with associations of death and burial) shells (and submarine life), and finally precious stones.

Just as, by a paradox, the 'cruel madness of love' causes him to return, via real madness, to a psychic balance, so his longing for a state of insensibility, imaged by way of becoming stony-hearted, or buried, or protected by water as in a womb, is ironically gratified by the terrible experience of believing himself buried alive;

though this does not occur before he has seen that he is naturally inviolate to the storms of life because protected by a hard shell of confidence, which leaves him sensitive (*not* stony-hearted) but still secure.

This train of imagery is introduced very early in allusions to stones, representing insensibility. Sooner or later, he feels, he will 'passively take the print' of his age,

> May make my heart as a millstone, set my face as a flint.

Meanwhile he smiles a hard-set smile, and sees

> a morbid eating lichen fixt
> On a heart half-turn'd to stone.

This endeavour to match the hardness of the age is thus symbolized later in the poem too. An interesting example is the way in which Maud's brother is alluded to (But then what a flint is he!). The hero relates that this brother

> Gorgonized me from head to foot
> With a stony British stare.

Just as the animal imagery is modified in reference to Maud, so similarly the stone images adapt themselves to a new attitude, showing a growth of a fresh sense of values. A glimpse of Maud as she returns to the Hall from abroad causes the speaker to seek for an image which will relate her to his regular mode of thinking. He sees her as a beautiful, yet distastely hard and cold, precious stone.

> . . . a cold and clear-cut face, as I found when her carriage past,
> Perfectly beautiful; let it be granted her; where is the fault?
> All that I saw—for her eyes were downcast, not to be seen—
> Faultily faultless, icily regular, splendidly null,
> Dead perfection, no more.

In a dream, her face comes before him again,

> Growing and fading and growing upon me without a sound,
> Luminous, gemlike, ghostlike, deathlike . . .

Gradually, as their acquaintance ripens into love, the image of diamond and pearl changes, and that of brilliantly-coloured precious stones, of sapphires, emeralds, rubies, extends through the descriptions. Maud becomes a jewel, her feet are 'like sunny gems on an English green', she lights her room with her presence like a precious stone. She even seems to him to take on the supernatural power long-attributed to gems:

> But now shine on, and what care I,
> Who in this stormy gulf have found a pearl
> The countercharm of space and hollow sky,

so that, for him,

> A livelier emerald twinkles in the grass,
> A purer sapphire melts into the sea.

Closely connected with this train of imagery is another which concerns protecting himself from the pain of his original condition by burying himself.

> I will bury myself in myself, and the Devil may pipe to his own.

His life in the empty house 'half-hid in the gleaming wood' is close enough to this, in all conscience: but as his love for Maud grows this morbid quietism is replaced by a desire to love. The image is of burial still.

> O, let the solid ground
> Not fail beneath my feet . . .
>
> Let the sweet heavens endure,
> Not close and darken above me . . .

Still later he comes to regard suicide as a form of selfishness, and then the image is dissociated from himself almost altogether and transferred to his feeling of hostility:

> So now I have sworn to bury
> All this dead body of hate,
> I feel so free and so clear
> By the loss of that dead weight . . .

Finally, in the 'Persian' Section XXII of Part I, the idea is treated in an appropriate tone of hyperbole, and incidentally connects with the image of the rose:

> She is coming, my own, my sweet;
> Were it ever so airy a tread,
> My heart would hear her and beat,
> Were it earth in an earthy bed;

> My dust would hear her and beat,
>   Had I lain for a century dead,
> Would start and tremble under her feet,
>   And blossom in purple and red.

In the next Part of the poem, the 'madness' section shows how this prophecy is travestied:

> Dead, long dead,
> Long dead!
> And my heart is a handful of dust,
> And the wheels go over my head,
> And my bones are shaken with pain,
> For into a shallow grave they are thrust,
> Only a yard beneath the street,
> And the hoofs of the horses beat, beat,
> The hoofs of the horses beat . . .

But an earlier section, where the speaker sees on the sea-shore a beautiful shell, gives an indication of his true condition. His noticing the shell at all in his shocked condition, is carefully explained as an example of a strange feature of an overwrought mind, that it develops a sharper sense

> For a shell, or a flower, little things
> Which else would have been past by!

But in reality the attention of the hero has, we may infer, been fastened on this object because it is an analogue, a symbol, of his own condition. Like it, he himself is a piece of detritus, washed up on the Breton shore (where he has fled to escape the consequences of the duel). And like it, too, he has developed a hard shell which protects his intensely vulnerable inner life. The love of Maud has given him a strength capable of withstanding the shocks and buffets of life:

> Slight, to be crush'd with a tap
> Of my finger-nail on the sand,
> Small, but a work divine,
> Frail but of force to withstand,
> Year upon year, the shock
> Of cataract seas that snap
> The three-decker's oaken spine
> Athwart the ledges of rock,
> Here on the Breton strand!

Here we see the symbol typically serving a double role. Dramatically, it reveals the mood and situation of the speaker: but it also enriches the imagery of the section considered simply as a lyric poem. But uniquely it controls the interpretation we are to put on what follows, the concluding sections of the poem.

The madness section exhibits one kind of spiritual storm which flesh is heir to. The imagery of beating (other forms of this image occur earlier in the poem) is a counterpart of the 'shock of cataract seas' which he is now able finally to withstand and recover from. Earlier he had long 'sighed for a calm' in the stormy gulf of life, and later he yearns for some deep cave in which to hide:

> Always I long to creep
> Into some still cavern deep,
> There to weep, and weep, and weep
> My whole soul out to thee.

But we are to see that his condition is really secure and his recovery assured by the fact that he has already and finally rejected the solution to his problem by way of seeking unnaturally to harden himself into insensibility (expressed through the images of stone). Rather he sees himself as still fundamentally weak and vulnerable, but nevertheless protected by a new source of strength which he unconsciously compares with a shell of great beauty, a 'miracle of design'. Accepting his weakness, but trusting his strength, he is finally able to enter a world where violence, rapine, and greed exist naturally in the hearts of men and nations, but are not unaccompanied by movings of a better spirit which can fulfil itself by trying to overcome evils as they appear, as they will appear, in different forms, in each man's lifetime. This is not an inadequate conclusion to the drama. But the conclusion is only a part of the total work. Poetic drama is not discussable in terms of a simple ideological proposition. The 'meaning' of *Maud* is diffused through its individual lyrics and monologues, each of which seeks to portray in words a singular human experience.

1958

VII

Idylls of the King—
A Fresh View

TENNYSON'S *IDYLLS*

F. E. L. *Priestley*

ONE OF the most persistent heresies in Tennyson criticism is the belief that the *Idylls* are literature of escape. Ever since Carlyle, with his usual vigour and not unusual critical myopia, greeted the first group with remarks about 'finely elaborated execution', 'inward perfection of vacancy', and 'the lollipops were so superlative', the myth has persisted that the poems are mere tapestry-work, 'skilfully wrought of high imaginings, faery spells, fantastic legends, and mediaeval splendours . . . suffused with the Tennysonian glamour of golden mist, . . . like a chronicle illuminated by saintly hands . . .'; 'a refuge from life'; 'a mediaeval arras' behind which Tennyson fled from 'the horrors of the Industrial Revolution'.

The *Idylls* are so far from being escape that they represent one of Tennyson's most earnest and important efforts to deal with major problems of his time. Their proper significance can only be grasped by a careful reading, not of separate idylls, but of the complete group in its final form. The misunderstandings by critics have, I think, arisen largely form the reading of detached idylls, a habit encouraged by Tennyson's mode of composition and publication.

The real deficiency of the *Idylls* grows out of their piece-meal composition; quite clearly Tennyson's intention, and with it his treatment, passed through three stages, introducing inconsistencies which only complete revision and a larger measure of rewriting of the earlier idylls could have removed. Tennyson began in the eighteen-thirties with 'Morte d'Arthur', which is conscientiously epic in style, and follows Malory very closely. But even at this stage he was not content merely to 'remodel models', and recognized that only the finding of a modern significance in the Arthurian material would redeem his poem 'from the charge of nothingness'. It seems evident, however, that he could see at this time no satisfactory way of continuing the epic treatment, and his next step was to abandon the 'epyllion' for the 'idyll'. The titles, *Enid and Nimuë: The True and the False*, of 1857, and 'The True and the False: Four Idylls of the King', in the proof-sheets of 1859, suggest a development of intention. The title of 1859 gives primacy to the exemplary and didactic function of the stories, with Enid and Elaine as types of fidelity, Nimuë (Vivien) and Guinevere as types of the false and unchaste. The moral message is, however, very general, and the treatment is for the most part rather like that of the 'English Idyls'; 'Nimuë' in particular offers a convincing portrayal of ordinary human psychology. Critics who approach these poems as typical of the *Idylls* may perhaps be forgiven for believing that the poet is concerned chiefly with a translation of the Arthurian material into a poetical variety of realistic fiction. But the style retains reminiscences of the epic, and 'Enid' and 'Nimuë' often suggest symbolic overtones, especially in Earl Doorm. Tennyson's final intention appears ten years later, with the provision of the main framework of symbolic allegory in 'The Coming of Arthur', 'The Holy Grail', and 'The Passing of Arthur'. 'Pelleas and Ettarre' and the later poems complete the pattern, but however unified the total structure has been made thematically, the treatment remains heterogeneous. 'Lancelot and Elaine' belong quite clearly to a different *genre* from 'The Holy Grail'—to the *genre* of 'Enoch Arden' or 'Aylmer's Field', not to that of 'The Vision of Sin.'

Nevertheless, the twelve poems do in fact form a pattern, and this pattern is best appreciated by interpreting the whole in terms of Tennyson's last intention, and recognizing that it is not his primary purpose to re-vivify Malory's story in a dramatic narrative, but to use the Arthurian cycle as a medium for the discussion of problems which are both contemporary and perennial. The *Idylls* are primarily allegorical, or (as Tennyson preferred to put it) parabolic. It is important to remember that the allegory is not simple. Tennyson himself, after reading reviews of the 1869 volume, complained: 'They have taken my hobby, and ridden it too hard, and have explained some things too allegorically, although there is an allegorical or perhaps rather a parabolic drift in the poem. . . . I hate to be tied down to say, "*This* means *that*," because the thought within the image is much more than any one interpretation.' Professor Cleanth Brooks's comment on *The Waste Land* applies with very little modification to the *Idylls*: 'The symbols resist complete equation with a simple meaning. . . . The poem would undoubtedly be "clearer" if every symbol had one, unequivocal meaning; but the poem would be thinner, and less honest. For the poet has not been content to develop a didactic allegory in which the symbols are two-dimensional items adding up directly to the sum of the general scheme.'[1] As Tennyson says elsewhere, 'liberal applications lie In Art like Nature.'

Tennyson himself tells us something. His earliest note identifies Arthur with religious faith, and the Round Table with liberal institutions. Much later, in conversation with Knowles, he said, 'By Arthur I always meant the soul, and by the Round Table the passions and capacities of a man.' Arthur's relationship to his knights is likened by Guinevere to that of the 'conscience of a saint' to his 'warring senses'. And again, Tennyson is quoted in the *Memoir* as saying, 'The whole is the dream of a man coming into practical life and ruined by one sin. Birth is a mystery and death is a mystery, and in the midst lies the tableland of life, and its struggles and performances. It is not the history of one man or of one generation but of a whole cycle of generations.' According to his son, Tennyson 'felt strongly that only under the inspiration of ideals, and with his "sword bathed in heaven", can a man combat the cynical indifference, the intellectual selfishness, the sloth of will, the utilitarian materialism of a transition age. . . . If Epic unity is looked for in the Idylls, we find it . . . in the unending war of humanity in all ages—the world-wide war of sense and soul, typified in individuals. . . .'[2]

Arthur is, then, in the most general sense, soul or spirit in action. It is significant that he is constantly associated with the

[1] *T. S. Eliot: A Study of His Writings by Several Hands*, ed. B. Rajan (London, 1947), pp. 34–5.
[2] *Memoir*, ii, pp. 127, 129–30.

bringing of order out of chaos, harmony out of discord. His city is ever being built to music, 'therefore never built at all, And therefore built for ever'. The life of man, the life of society—each depends upon a principle of order, upon the recognition of a set of spiritual values to which all is harmonized. Arthur as soul is a symbol of these spiritual values, ideals, aspirations, and is consequently for Tennyson identified with the religious faith which must animate man, society, and nation. The Round Table is the symbol of the order, individual or social, which the values create. It is 'an image of the mighty world', the cosmos created by spirit. The tragic collapse of Arthur's work in the *Idylls* is an allegory of the collapse of society, of nation, and of individual, which must follow the rejection of spiritual values.

But Tennyson is not so naïve as to think that the problem of retaining spiritual values is a simple one. From the first, we are faced with the most fundamental doubt of all: that of the validity of the values. What are the origins of our ideals? Some give to Arthur a naturalistic origin, saying that he is the son of Uther by Gorlois' wife; but Uther and Ygerve were both dark in hair and eyes, and 'this king is fair Beyond the race of Britons and of men'. Nevertheless many, among them Modred, deny the supernatural origin of Arthur, 'some there be that hold the King a shadow, and the city real'. Those who accept Arthur accept him in one of two ways. Bellicent, by knowing Arthur, has felt the power and attraction of his personality, and intuitively has known his kingship. (Arthur has comforted her in her sorrow; 'being a child with me', as she grew greater he grew with her, was stern at times, and sad at times, 'but sweet again, and then I loved him well'.) Gareth, on the other hand, accepts Arthur as proved by his works: to his mother's objection that Arthur is 'not wholly proven king' he replies,

> 'Not proven, who swept the dust of ruin'd Rome
> From off the threshold of the realm and crush'd
> The idolaters, and made the people free?
> Who should be king save him who makes us free?'

But the difficulty remains: the authenticity of Arthur's kingship is not established so that all *must* accept him. And even over those who acknowledge him king his power is not complete nor permanent. At the institution of the Order of the Round Table, a momentary likeness of the king flashes over the faces of the knights as they have the brief clear vision of Arthur's divine authority, but soon some are thinking of Arthur as merely human, others are recognizing his authority while they defy it, others are starting to complain that his system of vows is too strict for human nature to observe. Bound up in this fundamental problem of Arthur's authority is the whole set of fundamental problems of moral philosophy: the origin of our moral ideals, the sanctions attached to them, the nature of obligation, and so on.

Further problems are brought out by Arthur's marriage to Guinevere. Soul must act through Body; Thought must wed Fact; the Spirit must mix himself with Life; the Idea must be actualized:

> '. . . for saving I be join'd
> To her that is the fairest under heaven,
> I seem as nothing in the mighty world,
> And cannot will my will nor work my work
> Wholly, nor make myself in mine own realm
> Victor and lord. But were I join'd with her,
> Then might we live together as one life,
> And reigning with one will in everything,
> Have power on this dark land to lighten it,
> And power on this dead world to make it live.'

It is only through alliance with the temporal that the eternal can work in the temporal, and since for Tennyson the prime function of an ideal is to work in the temporal, the alliance is necessary. It nevertheless brings the inevitable danger of separation and of conflict.

From the start, then, the stability of Arthur's realm, of the reign of spirit, is threatened in two ways; its collapse occurs when the challenge to Arthur's authority becomes more widespread and open, and the rebellion of the flesh within the realm becomes more violent. The defection of Guinevere is by no means the sole, or perhaps the chief, cause of the failure of Arthur's plans. It is, to be sure, important, since it tends constantly to reinforce other influences operating towards the catastrophe. But the activities of Vivien, her capture of Merlin, the revolt against the vows typified by Tristram, the effects of the Grail quest, and the stealthy work of Modred are all profoundly significant.

Vivien and Tristram are both associated with the court of Mark, a court of active and irreconcilable evil. When Mark tries to bribe his way into the Order, he has his gift burned by Arthur and his petition indignantly rejected: 'More like are we to reave him of his crown Than make him knight because men call him king.' Mark, inasmuch as men *do* call him king, stands for a set of values accepted by many but absolutely opposed to the Christian values Arthur stands for. Mark's values are defined by Vivien and Tristram. Vivien's whole being is dedicated to one purpose, the destruction of the Order; she has no fleshly motive for her wickedness, nor does she need any; her motive is essentially the hate felt by evil for the good.

> 'As love, if love be perfect, casts out fear,
> So hate, if hate be perfect, casts out fear.
> My father died in battle against the King,
> My mother on his corpse in open field;
>   . . . born from death was I
> Among the dead and sown upon the wind. . . .'

Her song, 'The fire of heaven is not the flame of hell,' echoes Lucretian themes of materialist naturalism, and at once recalls the similar songs in 'The Vision of Sin' and 'The Ancient Sage'. Her values are thoroughly hedonist. 'I better prize the living dog than the dead lion.' 'What shame in love, So love be true.' Her weapons are slander and seduction. But it is to be noted that she succeeds only where some weakness already exists for her to exploit. She vanquishes Merlin only because he is already prey to 'a great melancholy', a sense of 'doom that poised itself to fall', a premonition of

> World-war of dying flesh against the life,
> Death in all life and lying in all love,
> The meanest having power upon the highest,
> And the high purpose broken by the worm.

He is overcome finally by weariness and Vivien's feigned repentance.

Merlin's surrender seems to signify more than the mere defeat of Reason by Passion, although this is undoubtedly in part what is meant. But Merlin, we are told, knew the range of all arts, was the king's chief builder, 'was also Bard, and knew the starry heavens'. His charm, the secret of his power and the preserver of his authority and indeed of his function, came to him from a seer to whom 'the wall That sunders ghosts and shadow-casting men Became a crystal'. If Merlin represents Reason, then, it is quite clearly not Reason in its empirical or even discursive sense; he is endowed with what Tennyson would call Wisdom, rather than Knowledge; like the poet, he threads 'the secretest walks of fame', and sees 'thro' life and death, thro' good and ill'. It is Vivien's complaint that he does not belong wholly to her; it is her boast finally that she has made Merlin's glory hers. The authority belonging properly to the intuitive reason, which is not bound to sensation and phenomena, but can penetrate to ideal reality, has been usurped by the senses. Reason has been reduced to 'empirical verification', and 'closed in the four walls of a hollow tower, From which was no escape for evermore'. The overthrow of Merlin means the rejection of that faculty which perceives the ideal, the faculty of the poet and seer.

With his removal, the task of Vivien becomes much simpler, for Merlin has been the chief support of Arthur's system, the chief witness of Arthur's kingship. After he is gone, the reality of the ideal, the validity of Arthur's kingship, is judged by other standards. Even Guinevere can question the value of the Round Table; she resorts to the false but comforting doctrine of the fallen: 'He is all fault who hath no fault at all', and glibly attributes to Arthur her own defection: 'A moral child without the craft to rule, Else had he not lost me.' The cause Vivien represents has won: Guinevere values imperfection and evil (since they are natural) above perfection and good; she admires craft more than virtue; and she judges worth by success in craft. These are the ethics of materialism, naturalism, utilitarianism. Once the higher ethical system is undermined, all codes go. The last virtues to be discarded are the merely barbarian 'sporting' virtues; Gawain breaks an oath readily, even when sworn by the honour of the Table Round, but it still stirs him to see three attacking one. Yet even these, when become a mere code of sportsmanship not based upon any deeper ideal, are abandoned, and the last tournament is simply a struggle for prizes. The change in attitude is symbolized by the absence of Arthur as president, and by the victory of Tristram, who now replaces Vivien as a symbol of 'Mark's way'.

In him the naturalist philosophy of the court of Mark has become more conscious and rationalized. He repeats the doctrines of hedonism, but his motivation is different from Vivien's. He is a sceptic. Vivien has always recognized the value of what she is attacking; she knows that Arthur is right, and that her own life is wrong and evil. But Tristram is prepared to defend by argument his own rejection of the vows: 'The vow that binds too strictly snaps itself— . . . ay, being snapt—We run more counter to the soul thereof Than had we never sworn.' He questions the foundation of Arthur's authority, of the authority of spiritual values, by an appeal to the 'natural':

>   'The vows!
> O, ay—the wholesome madness of an hour—
> They served their use, their time; for every knight . . .
> Did mightier deeds than elsewise he had done,
> And so the realm was made. But then their vows . . .
> Began to gall the knighthood, asking when
> Had Arthur right to bind them to himself?
> Dropt down from heaven? Wash'd up from out the deep?
> They fail'd to trace him thro' the flesh and blood
> Of our old kings. Whence then? a doubtful lord
> To bind them by inviolable vows,
> Which flesh and blood perforce would violate. . . .'

The only validity Tristram grants at any time to the vows is a pragmatic one: they served their use. He challenges their permanent validity by a naturalistic argument—Arthur cannot be traced 'thro' the flesh and blood Of our old kings', i.e., the spiritual values Arthur represents are not derived from the ruling elements of our physical nature. The morality Tristram seeks is one founded in those elements; he is the type of those who talk about making morality 'conform to the facts of human nature'. What he would advocate is an attitude which accepts the good and evil of human nature indifferently, which recognizes the naturalness of man's frailties, and which, making 'naturalness' the norm, gives free play to the passions. It is worth noting that Guinevere's sin occupies a subordinate place in Tristram's argument; he attributes the downfall of the Round Table primarily to the impossible strictness of the vows.

Guinevere had at one point also drawn comfort in her error from the belief (or hope) that goodness was impossible for ordinary human nature; she had spoken scornfully of Arthur,

> 'Rapt in this fancy of his Table Round,
> And swearing men to vows impossible,
> To make them like himself.'

Even the faithful fool Dagonet is moved to cry out bitterly that
Arthur is the king of fools, who

> 'Conceits himself as God that he can make
> Figs out of thistles, silk from bristles, milk
> From burning spurge, honey from hornet-combs,
> And men from beasts.'

All of these characters give strong expression to the naturalistic
argument and challenge the authority of religion and of systems of
ethics from the point of view of evolutionary naturalism.

But the problem is wider; it involves the whole difficulty of the
relationship of the ethical ideal to the humanly possible. And
Tennyson undertakes a solution. In the first place, he argues that
the vows are brought into disrepute, and indeed are made almost
impossible to follow, if they are exaggerated into an excessive
asceticism. Mark and Vivien recognize their first opportunity when
they hear that a few of the younger knights have renounced
marriage,

> So passionate for an utter purity
> Beyond the limit of their bond are these,
> For Arthur bound them not to singleness.

Sir Pellam shows another aspect of asceticism which has its dangers: he holds that heavenly things must not be defiled with
earthly uses; his heir is Garlon, the poisonous vessel of scorn and
slander. Some of the meaning of the Grail poem is to the same
general effect; ideals are for application to life, to human nature. If
they involve a turning of the back upon life, they are barren at
best, destructive at worst. The strict vow is for the exceptional,
for Galahads or perhaps even Percivales. But, asks Arthur,

> 'What are ye? Galahads?—no, nor Percivales
>   . . . but men
> With strength and will to right the wrong'd, of power
> To lay the sudden heads of violence flat. . . .
> Your places being vacant at my side,
> This chance of noble deeds will come and go,
> Unchallenged. . . .'

There is a special significance, perhaps, in the fact that the
chance of noble deeds was not being seized *before* the Grail vision.
Percivale's decision to pursue the Grail arose out of dissatisfaction
with the condition of the court,

> 'vainglories, rivalries,
> And earthly heats that spring and sparkle out
> Among us in the jousts, while women watch
> Who wins, who falls, and waste the spiritual strength
> Within us, better offer'd up to heav'n.'

The society is already pervaded with a sense of spiritual frustration; the ideal of service is already lost; the old order is already vastly changed. And the turning to the Grail quest marks for most of the knights a withdrawal from the everyday problems involved in Arthur's original purpose, to 'have power on this dead world to make it live', to inform the real with the ideal. For those who find the revelation, it is well, but few find it.

The Grail poem undoubtedly expresses, as most critics recognize, Tennyson's rejection of the ascetic way of life, at least as a normal vocation. But I think there is more in it. 'One has seen,' says Arthur, 'and all the blind will see.' And when the knights return, each has seen according to his sight.

> 'And out of those to whom the vision came
> My greatest hardly will believe he saw.
> Another hath beheld it afar off,
> And, leaving human wrongs to right themselves,
> Cares but to pass into the silent life.'

Quite clearly, the true purposes of ordinary life are not served at all by the Grail quest. Galahad, in his success, is as much 'lost to life and use' as Merlin; he has passed out on to the great Sea, beyond the limits of human life; he has been willing to lose himself to save himself. But the others, while wishing to stay in life, are seeking an easy way to spiritual certitude in the shift and clash of moral values. Without having any deep inward conviction, they insist on seeing the unseen. Arthur is content to let the visions come, and many a time they come. Not directly and deliberately seeking the vision, he sees more than most of the Grail adventurers. The restless quest for religious certainty, for most an inevitably fruitless quest, brings a paralysis of the will, as Tennyson had known as he wrote 'Supposed Confessions', and 'The Two Voices', and as Carlyle and Arnold had known. If man's proper task is undertaken, that of establishing the kingdom of the highest ideal on earth, then the 'visions' will come as a deep and passionate conviction that all pertaining to the flesh is vision, and 'God and the Spiritual the only real and true', and then will come to man the

> moments when he feels he cannot die,
> And knows himself no vision to himself,
> Nor the high God a vision, nor that One
> Who rose again.

(These lines, said Tennyson, are the central lines of the *Idylls*.) The proper way to faith is through works.

It is thoroughly consistent that those who seek to *know* Arthur's origins find no certainty. Arthur's royalty and holiness, and the holiness of the vows, are not to be empirically proved, 'Thou canst not prove the Nameless'; they are either recognized immediately, or not at all. Guinevere is for long blind to them; at the end it is as if a veil has been lifted:

> 'Thou art the highest and most human too,
> Not Lancelot, nor another. Is there none
> Will tell the King I love him tho' so late?
> Now—ere he goes to the great battle? None!
> Myself must tell him in that purer life. . . .
>   Ah my God,
> What might I not have made of thy fair world,
> Had I but loved thy highest creature here?
> It was my duty to have loved the highest;
> It surely was my profit had I known;
> It would have been my pleasure had I seen.'

The whole problem appears in that 'had I known', 'had I seen'. What had prevented her from knowing, and seeing?

> 'False voluptuous pride, that took
> Full easily all impressions from below,
> Would not look up, or half-despised the height
> To which I would not or I could not climb.'

The defect of recognition proceeds from a defect of will.

In Guinevere's repentant insight we are also given Tennyson's second answer to the naturalistic argument. The vows present the paradox: The highest is the most human too. A morality which merely conforms to our nature is based upon less than the highest possibility of our nature; we are most human when we transcend our ordinary selves. The ideal must not, like the ascetic ideal, be so remote that it seems obviously unattainable; nor must it, like the naturalistic ideal, be so close that it seems obviously attained. But it is the essence of ethics to be not descriptive, but normative; not to tell us how we behave, but how we ought to behave. The ethics of naturalism confuse the prescriptive end of ethics with the descriptive end of science.

The causes of Arthur's failure, then, are many. All round are the powers of the wasteland, powers of violence, hate, and lust. How far these and the powers of the North represent an active diabolic spirit of evil, and how far primitive atavistic forces within the individual soul and within society, does not matter—nor, I think, would Tennyson have felt it necessary to decide. Assisting them are the false philosophies represented by Mark, Vivien, and Tristram. These operate at two levels: as rationalizations in the individual, and as popular modes of thought in society. Both society and individual are secure against these powers of disintegration as long as there is a clear recognition of the spiritual values which give coherence to society and individual. This clear recognition is threatened in three ways: by doubts of the foundation and validity of the ideals; by a separation of the ideals from the actual, either in an exaggerated asceticism or in a withdrawal; and by the ignoring of the primary importance of action, and the abandonment of ethical problems in the quest for religious certainty.

The failure of Arthur's work presents the basic problem of the moral order. And here, in the last of the poems, whether deliberately or forced by the earlier pattern established in 'Morte d'Arthur', Tennyson changes the relationship of the king to the theme. He is no longer so much a symbol of Soul, or of the Ideal, as of defeated mankind asking a question. The poems have hitherto displayed how evil triumphs, how 'bright things come to confusion'; now Arthur asks the deeper question why.

> 'I found Him in the shining of the stars,
> I mark'd Him in the flowering of His fields,
> But in His ways with men I find Him not.'

God's hand is visible in the physical order, but not in the moral; the history of the stars and of the flowers shows a pattern, but not the history of man. The problem of evil is an urgent one for Arthur. His whole work has been based upon belief in an ultimate moral order, in a system wherein good must finally prevail—and yet, as he looks back upon the history of his Round Table, he sees the Cosmos which he created out of Chaos succeeded merely by a new Chaos. And with the final doubt of the moral order, Arthur doubts himself: 'I know not what I am, Nor whence I am, nor whether I be king.' But as he prepares for death by the surrender of Excalibur, symbol of his kingship, the 'arm, clothed in white samite, mystic, wonderful', which catches the flung sword, by its very appearance and action proclaims again the reality of his kingship, and by its repetition of the beginning affirms the pattern. What the pattern is, Arthur cannot see; but that his life began with a solemn arming and ends with a solemn disarming suggests the completion of a cycle, a cycle whose meaning may not be clear to Arthur, but is clear to those who armed him.

With the reassurance thus established, Arthur is able to affirm a faith in the order of the historical process. The flux of events is not a blind flux; the growth and decay of institutions, of societies, is not a mere mechanical sequence of phenomena. Nor does the fact of change carry implications of moral relativity. Every new order is a mode of actualization of the ideal: 'God fulfils himself in many ways, Lest one good custom should corrupt the world.' The ultimate truth is the paradox of the permanence of the ideal which underlies the transitory shifting phenomena. The history of Arthur 'is not the history of one man or of one generation but of a whole cycle of generations'. The war of Sense and Soul is an 'unending war of humanity in all ages'. The Ideal which Arthur symbolizes has found embodiment in many forms, in many ages, in many places; it has fought its battles and has, in each form, yielded place to new. It passes but never dies. As Bedivere watches the speck of Arthur's barge, it vanishes 'into light, And the new sun rose bringing the new year'.

Tennyson is asserting through the *Idylls* the primacy of the Unseen, the ultimate reality of the Spiritual, which is manifested in a constant succession of phenomena, and gives permanent meaning to them. The phenomena are not merely shadows or illusions; they are 'real' in that they are the temporal actualization of the ideal. Man's task is not to pierce through the evil of appearances and brush it aside; it is to recognize the relationship of appearance to an ideal reality which he cannot fully know, and to work in the realm of phenomena towards more complete actualization of the ideal in so far as he knows it. And Tennyson believes that the activity of working itself brings fuller knowledge. His idealism, in short, serves to guarantee the religious and ethical values (both for the individual and for society), while not permitting a retreat into contemplative passivity; the temporal aspects of individual and social problems are the aspects under which we are bound to see, and bound to attack them. The Creed of Creeds must be worked out by human hands; the watchword is 'Do Well'. The task is not to be fulfilled by a denial of human nature and of human problems; asceticism is a retreat. Nor is it to be fulfilled by the search for personal intellectual certainty of the Unseen; this again is a retreat from the real duty.

Man's proper task is that of securing order and harmony in all phases of human activity: in the individual, the harmony of senses, passions, reason, ordered by conscience; in society, harmony of individuals, and of social groups in their relations to each other, ordered again by conscience operating as a sense of justice, loyalty, duty or responsibility, and love. The threats to order come from within and without. Within there are crimes of sense: lust, pride, anger, gluttony; and crimes of malice: slander, wilful breach of trust, envy of the lost good, and so on. Without there are active powers of malevolence and brutality, symbolized traditionally in the poem by the powers in the North. These have success only against those already weakened internally.

When the real nature of the *Idylls* is properly understood, it is possible to appreciate their quality, which is essentially that of dramatic allegory. The twelve poems fall naturally into three groups of four, corresponding closely to the three acts of modern drama. The first act opens with the highly symbolic 'Coming of Arthur', and closes with 'Geraint and Enid'. Each of the four poems it includes has what can be considered a happy ending, and the general theme of all is the establishing of order and the victory of good over evil. Arthur is characterized by sharp clarity of vision; Gareth shows similar sureness and fixity of purpose. Gareth knows from the first his end in life, and recognizes easily Arthur's kingship. He finds freedom in service, and resolutely overcomes the Star Knights and the Knight of the Castle Perilous. He and Enid provide exemplars of the ideals of Arthur. Geraint and Lynette, in their perverse obstinacy and reluctant recognition of values represent internal obstacles to be overcome, rather than external forces threatening the good. But we are kept aware, during the triumphs, of the threats to Arthur's reign. The knights are few, and include slothful officers, mean-spirited knights like Sir Kay. Outside the court lie the wasteland and the dark powers of the North, violent and brutal, denying Arthur's kingship and doubting his origin. And already there is suggestion of falseness at the very heart of the realm; it is a rumour about Guinevere that leads Geraint to mistrust Enid. All these elements moderate the pattern of success and prepare for the second act.

This opens powerfully with the grim 'Balin and Balan', and ends with the climax of 'The Holy Grail'. The forces of disruption move suddenly into sharp focus: the illicit love of Lancelot and Guinevere, formerly an uncertain and shadowy rumour, becomes a hard certainty; evil emerges, conscious, deliberate, and triumphant, in Vivien and Garlon. The fierce and tragic opening is modulated through the 'Merlin and Vivien' to the pathetic involvement of the innocent Elaine, and finally to the complex pattern of splendid holiness, shameful sin, glorious achievement, and foolish futility of 'The Holy Grail'. Arthur, who in the first act is shown presiding at the Hall of Justice, is left at the end of the second 'gazing at a barren board, And a lean Order—scarce return'd a tithe'.

The last act opens with the bitterly ironic 'Pelleas and Ettarre'. Pelleas is reminiscent of Gareth, particularly in his youthful eagerness and zeal, but he has none of Gareth's clarity, and his conception of knighthood is not, like Gareth's, one of religious service; it is wholly secular. His is the ideal of the courtly lover, seeking fame for a lady. He is abashed by the fleshly beauty of the harlot Ettarre, 'as tho' it were the beauty of her soul'. Ettarre is no Lynette or Enid; she values experienced worldliness, not young enthusiasm. And when Pelleas, betrayed by Ettarre and Gawain, goes half mad with disillusionment, it is significant that he turns against Arthur and the vows. 'The Last Tournament' completes the theme of corruption by presenting the form which the spirit has left. The irony becomes deeper and all-pervading, in the title of the tournament, the prize offered, and the winner. Victory goes merely to the most experienced, who is also the most open repudiator of all that Arthur stands for. The defence of Arthur is given to Dagonet, the fool, the sad and lonely remnant of the king's following. All that remains is for the form to collapse. The last two idylls present the *dénouement*, and in the repentance of Guinevere a final statement, now tragic, of the worth of what has decayed. The choric comment by Arthur in the last poem sets the whole action in cosmic perspective, with a levelling off of emotion, and an affirmation of faith in order. The total dramatic effect seems to me to have considerable power.

That Tennyson sees a particular relevance for his own time in what he is saying is clear enough. The *Idylls* present in allegory the philosophy which pervades the whole of Tennyson's poetry, the philosophy which he felt it necessary to assert throughout his poetic lifetime. Penetrating all his poetry is the strong faith in the eternal world of spirit, expressed particularly in 'The Higher Pantheism', 'De Profundis', 'The Ancient Sage', at the end of 'Locksley Hall Sixty Years After', and in 'Merlin and the Gleam'. The assertion of the validity and necessity of idealism is reinforced by continual warnings of the dangers of materialism: 'The Vision of Sin', *Maud*, 'Aylmer's Field', 'Despair', and 'Lucretius' are the chief vehicles for these warnings. Like most sensitive thinkers of his day, Tennyson was deeply concerned with the growing materialism, with the new hedonism, with the utilitarian ethic with its relativism and naturalism, with the attack on the religious foundation of the Christian ethic not merely by the higher critics but particularly by those who were applying evolutionary principles to show the 'natural' origin of moral ideas. He was concerned with the apparent decay of ethical principles in commercial, political, and social life, and with the growing tendency to defend all sensual gratification as 'natural'. He saw that religious leaders were not always effective in combating these tendencies, since they were on the defensive, and were busy trying to 'demonstrate', to 'prove' Christianity. The expenditure of effort against Huxley over the Gadarene swine is significant and symptomatic. The laity could hardly be blamed for thinking that Christian doctrine ought to be susceptible of the same kind of verification as scientific fact; they either wearied and perplexed themselves in the search for certainty, or sank into agnosticism. Tennyson is asserting in the *Idylls* that Christianity is not so much a set of facts to be argued about as a system of principles to be lived by; that the proof of these principles is to be established not by external empirical evidence, but by the power with which they unify and give stability and meaning to the life of man and of societies. He wants to make the reader understand how these principles become neglected, and what must happen to individuals and societies who neglect them. He is voicing a warning to his own age and nation, and to all ages and nations. He is consistently opposing a revival of the Lucretian philosophy, with its materialism, its naturalism, and its secularism. To him it is the philosophy of pessimism and despair, of defeat and social destruction.

Against the Lucretian spirit Tennyson upholds the Vergilian. The two have been well characterized by the late Professor C. N. Cochrane:

> The one holds up an ideal of repose and refined sensual enjoyment; the other, one of restless effort and activity. Lucretius urges the recognition that men are limited as the dust; that the pursuit of their aspirations is as vain and futile as are the impulses of religion, pride, ambition which ceaselessly urge them on. The purpose of Vergil is to vindicate those obscure forces within the self by which mankind is impelled to material achievement and inhibited from destroying the work of his own hands. . . . The one . . . accepts the intellectual assurance of futility, the other . . ., like all enlightened men, is beset by the problem of finding a reasonable ground for his faith.[1]

The last line of Tennyson's 'Lucretius' presents acutely the implications of the Lucretian philosophy: 'Thy duty? What is duty?' The man or society who can find no answer must perish.

1949

---

[1] 'The Latin Spirit in Literature' (*Univ. of Toronto Quarterly*, ii. pp. 330–1).

INDEX

Poems and topics which form the subject of entire essays are listed in the Contents, pages v and vi, and are accordingly not included in the index, save when they are further alluded to in other essays.